Illegality and the
Production of Affluence

Illegality and the Production of Affluence

UNDOCUMENTED LABOR AND
GENTRIFICATION IN RURAL AMERICA

Lise Nelson

UNIVERSITY OF CALIFORNIA PRESS

University of California Press
Oakland, California

© 2025 by Lise Nelson

Cataloging-in-Publication data is on file at the Library of Congress.

ISBN 978-0-520-41637-6 (cloth)
ISBN 978-0-520-41638-3 (pbk.)
ISBN 978-0-520-41639-0(ebook)

GPSR Authorized Representative: Easy Access System Europe,
Mustamäe tee 50, 10621 Tallinn, Estonia, gpsr.requests@easproject.com

34 33 32 31 30 29 28 27 26 25
10 9 8 7 6 5 4 3 2 1

Contents

Illustrations

Acknowledgments

As with any intellectual endeavor, there is collective labor underlying this project. I must start by expressing gratitude to all those who participated in the research in Rabun County, Georgia, and Routt County, Colorado. I am grateful for their trust and willingness to share their lives, and I hope that this book will do justice to their experiences and aspirations. I also want to express my deep appreciation to Dr. Peter Nelson, my coinvestigator on the research project, funded by the National Science Foundation, that represented the starting place for the analysis developed here. Pete was generous in supporting my desire to draw on the data that my research assistants and I collected in Georgia and Colorado to write a solo-authored book. More recently, he allowed me to quote one of the interviews he conducted in Colorado so that I could represent more effectively the role of H2B visa workers in Steamboat. I want to recognize and articulate my gratitude to two research assistants involved in the NSF fieldwork—(now) Dr. Laurie Trautman of Western Washington University and (now) Dr. Graciela "Meche" Lu of Environmental Legal Alliance Worldwide. Both were invaluable as collaborators and assistants in fieldwork and early data analysis from 2010 to 2012. Two organizations in Steamboat Springs, Colorado, Integrated Community/Comunidad

Integrada and the Visiting Nurses Association, provided critical support and insight during Colorado fieldwork.

Between the time I started data collection and the publication of this book I have been a tenured faculty member at three universities: University of Oregon, the Pennsylvania State University, and the University of Arizona. These three institutions supported me in distinct ways, perhaps most importantly through University of Oregon seed grants and Penn State funding to return to the field to collect additional data in 2015. I received a Penn State Humanities Center Fellowship in 2018, which allowed me to devote a semester to writing and receiving feedback on chapters from valued colleagues. All of this support was vital as I inched the rock up the hill.

Colleagues and friends at these three institutions and beyond provided me with invaluable support along this journey. I must start with my brilliant and beloved PhD adviser, Vicky Lawson, to whom I always owe a great deal. Other colleagues who have provided feedback and support along the way include Alicia Decker, Lorraine Dowler, Verónica Ibarra, Josh Inwood, Jason Jurjevich, Diana Liverman, Brian King, Sallie Marston, Jennifer Bickham Mendez, Ellen Scott, Barbara Ellen Smith, Lynn Stephen, Dan Tichenor, and Melissa Wright. Graduate students whom I advised over the course of this journey also provided important intellectual inspiration: Kelsey Emard, Lauren Fritzsche, Wendy Luna Garcia, Sonia Kaufman, Ignacio Krell, Meche Lu, Lindsay Naylor, Ingrid Nelson, and Laurie Trautman.

It has been rewarding to finish a book on issues that have been at the center of my scholarship for two decades, and ones that I care deeply about. It has been a long process, full of fits and starts, but the richness of the data and the complexity of labor and social geographies explored here could not have been captured in a shorter format. Thank you to University of California Press and my editor Naja Pulliam Collins, as well as external reviewers, for recognizing the unique contributions of this monograph and for helping me make it stronger. After my first set of external reviews I engaged developmental editor Dr. Sara Appel to provide feedback on the manuscript, which helped me improve the clarity of my writing.

I was lucky during the process of designing the research, collecting the data, and writing the book to also be a mother to two remarkable children. They were babies at the beginning and young adults as I write these acknowledgments! Axel and Simon have been there all along, living in Colorado and Georgia during several field trips and providing love and laughter throughout. Thanks always to Mitzi Cline, who has been an incomparable source of affirmation and support in my life.

Finally, my husband Andy Schulz has been an important intellectual and emotional touchstone for me along this journey. He would listen and share his insights while I mused about data, theory, ethics, and analysis. Equally important, he encouraged me to keep going even when it felt like I would not make it. I dedicate this book to Andy, as well as my mother Elfi Smith. My mother, who died shortly before it went into production, was an immigrant who encouraged in me a love of languages and cross-cultural respect and curiosity, setting the stage for who I became as a scholar and as a human being.

Note on Terminology

This book explores the recruitment of people from Mexico and Latin America to work and reside in two "new immigrant destinations" in the United States, places that have undergone rural gentrification over the last twenty-five plus years. The topic creates a number of challenges related to ethnoracial categorization, terminologies that are never innocent and have been changing rapidly. These include labels such as Hispanic, Latino, Latina, Latino/a, Latinx, and Latine (prounced la-teen-eh). The terms Latinx and Latine have been used by activists and scholars to undermine the rigid gender dichotomies implied by Latino or Latina, to be inclusive of nonbinary experiences and identities. I am persuaded by Bentacur's contention that *Latine* is the most inclusive of the two because it can be pronounced in Spanish and is accessible to communities embedded in oral versus written traditions.[1] Throughout this book I use the term *Latine* as the descriptor of population groups, such as "Latine immigrants," in order to be more inclusive and to undermine assumed gender dichotomies implied by other terms. However, in certain instances I use the terminology *Latino* and *Latina* when I am referring to highly gendered processes—such as the recruitment of female-identifying people of Latin American origins into house-cleaning work or the recruitment of cisgender males into construction work. As a gender-specific recruitment strategy, I felt that relying on the gendered terms in these instances was important to the analysis. When sharing direct quotes from interviews I do not change the terminology used by the interviewee, making visible the various ways people deploy ethnoracial categories in daily life. Finally, I have chosen to capitalize *White* when referring to White people or groups in order to avoid treating white racialization as an unmarked category.

Introduction

LANDSCAPES OF AFFLUENCE,
GEOGRAPHIES OF EXCLUSION

Flipping through a 2010 copy of *Steamboat Magazine*, a quarterly publication produced and distributed in the mountain resort community of Steamboat Springs, Colorado since 1979, one finds a sepia-toned photo of an empty, summertime alpine field, emblazoned with these words:

> In this place like no other, there's a genuine feeling of the rich western heritage, of small-town charm, of friendliness and neighborliness everywhere you roam. It's a feeling as real as the people of the town themselves. It's something you can sense in an instant here. This place is different. It's something that, once you've experienced it, you never want to give it up. Maybe that's why so many locals fell in love and never left. For others it's a longing desire to return as often as possible. The desire to own a little piece of this heaven for themselves and feel the exhilaration and relaxation that is Steamboat.[1]

The exact purpose of this copy is unclear until one turns the page, to see that it is the opening of a real estate ad in Routt County, Colorado—for condos priced at the time at $1.3–$1.7 million. The image and text together convey what the developers and their advertising strategists believed potential wealthy buyers were seeking: small town charm, friendliness, authentic community, a return to nature, and a little piece of heaven. For some buyers, that heaven has been found on the slopes; for others, it has involved summertime access to hiking, fishing, mountain biking, or rafting down the Yampa River.

Contemporary Routt County continues to embody a rural landscape of affluence and recreation. If you drive into Steamboat from Denver, you cross Rabbit Ears Pass and descend into a valley, struck by the beautiful vista. You pass clustered housing developments several miles outside of town, interspersed with what one would call "hobby" ranches: properties brandishing new barns, manicured lawns, and newly built homesteads designed in a historic western motif. These ranches may have cattle, but they are not likely to serve as a means of livelihood for the owners. Once in town you can stroll down Lincoln Avenue (main street), bordered by nineteenth-century buildings refurbished into high-end clothing stores and restaurants. From the perspective of self-identifying "locals," who have contended with the rising cost of living in Steamboat, this landscape of affluence may reflect a process of cultural and/or material displacement, even as the in-migration of the affluent has afforded some new economic opportunities.[2] Many self-identified locals have had to move far out of town, have to commute in daily to work, and rarely get to enjoy the high-end dining that surrounds them.

The landscape changes described here inspire the term *rural gentrification*, which like its urban counterpart refers to intersecting economic, cultural, and political processes associated with the colonization of space by wealthy, mostly White newcomers. These wealthier newcomers move to a new location (urban or rural) for its perceived amenity and lifestyle possibilities, often displacing longtime residents.[3] In rural spaces, displacement may be more cultural and political than strictly physical dispossession, which lies at the heart of urban gentrification. Nevertheless, both urban and rural gentrification have been driven by cycles of accumulation that have disproportionately benefited wealthy and overwhelmingly White people, increasing their capacity to buy real estate in urban *or* rural places.

Fifteen hundred miles from Routt County, Colorado, another rural community, Rabun County, Georgia, has undergone parallel processes of gentrification. Although lacking the name recognition of Steamboat Springs, Rabun County has attracted an expanding number of amenity migrants since the late 1990s, largely from Atlanta and Florida. These wealthy newcomers have sought cooler summer temperatures in the mountains of northern Georgia and access to the area's pristine lakes and forests, as well as the beautiful vistas, expansive golf courses, boating opportunities, and other outdoor activities. An article in the 2010 issue of *Newcomers Guide to Rabun County* deployed similar narratives to those found in Routt County's local magazine:

> Standing on a peak, gazing across the layers of mountains dressed in their smokey blue splendor, one could imagine that it looks no different than it has for the past one hundred years. . . . The mountains remain the same but time marches on, bringing with it change. Those fortunate to be born in the mountains know they are blessed. Others, after visiting, know that they, too, want to call the mountains home. And thus, from this phenomenon, the real estate industry in the mountains was born. . . . In an area where the quiet pace of life is welcome, a slowdown in the economy isn't.[4]

Narratives of belonging, timelessness, and "empty" nature available for consumption have also been mobilized in this northern Georgia community to sell property to wealthy outsiders.

Gentrification in Rabun County, Georgia, has produced impacts on longtime locals that parallel those that have transpired in Routt County, Colorado. By the late 1990s and early 2000s, housing prices were rising steadily in Rabun's most sought-after locations on the lakes and within its bucolic valleys. Many longtime residents in this northern Georgia community have felt a sense of displacement, feelings rooted less in physical/ spatial dislocation (most held onto their homes) than in economic and sociocultural loss, as newcomers wielded significant economic, political, and cultural influence.

Dynamics of displacement and loss are topics that have received significant attention in the literature on rural gentrification. Namely, the interdisciplinary scholarship on rural gentrification and amenity migration in the United States takes as a central theme forces of displacement related to class, including class-based stratification and struggles over distinct conservation and environmental imaginaries that often erupt between locals, gentrifying newcomers, and developers.[5] Yet as I will demonstrate over the course of this book, gentrification in both Routt and Rabun Counties has also been a story of *emplacement*, a term that refers to processes that are "set in position" or "set into place." Rooted in the eighteenth-century

French verb *emplacer*, the concept of emplacement is used in geology to mean the process of setting something in place or being set in place (e.g., the intrusion of igneous rock into a particular location).[6] I use it here to capture a dynamic that is distinct from *displacement* and related terms such as *dispossession*—both of which are commonly used to frame how we conceptualize gentrification and capitalist transformation.[7]

A key indicator of gentrification as a force of emplacement was the steady growth of Latine immigrant populations in both Routt and Rabun Counties starting in the mid- to late 1990s, demographic change that reflected a suite of new social relations emplaced in the context of gentrification. During this period immigrant workers, many undocumented, were recruited into rapidly expanding sectors linked to gentrification, such as construction, landscaping, and other service industries. They were recruited by employers who had no prior experience with immigrant labor. Today there continues to be a significant presence of Latine residents in both places. Census data indicate that by 2020, for example, they represented 7.6 percent of the Routt County population and 7.9 percent of Rabun County.[8]

The focus of this book is the period between the mid-1990s and the early 2010s, when recruitment processes emerged, and immigrant labor regimes solidified in ways that made them fundamental to the process of rural gentrification. According to the U.S. Census, in 1990 Routt County's population was 96.7 percent "Non-Hispanic White," and 2.5 percent was of "Hispanic or Latino" origin (these are the labels on the census categories). By 2010 nearly 7 percent of the county was Hispanic/Latine, a growth of 180 percent.[9] In Rabun County these changes were even more dramatic, with a 1990 population that according to the census was 98.4 percent non-Hispanic White and 0.6 percent Hispanic/Latine. By 2010 the Hispanic/Latine population, overwhelmingly foreign born, had increased to 8 percent of the county's population, an increase of more than 1230 percent compared to 1990.[10] While census data do not capture what percentage of foreign-born Latine immigrants lacked documentation, our fieldwork suggests that the vast majority lived and worked without authorization. Thus this crucial period, 1990–2010, witnessed the emplacement of immigrant labor regimes in these rural gentrifying areas, during a time when living and working without papers was changing. Living in a space of "illegality" was shifting as interior border enforcement/mass deportation policies came into effect in the mid-2000s.[11]

I use the term *illegality* to theorize critically a category that is often taken at face value, as a transparent status reflected in a common epithet: "What part of illegal do you not understand?"[12] Anthropologist Nicholas de Genova articulated the concept of illegality to problematize sociopolitical processes of illegalization and the everyday, of the palpable sense of deportability and racialized exclusion this produces.[13] Discourses about "illegals" are overwhelmingly directed toward brown bodies and normalize the treatment of Latine workers and residents as essentially criminal and undeserving—regardless of their actual legal status or nativity. A number of scholars have explored how the figure of "the illegal" produces a compliant, docile, and productive labor force that has benefited a wide range of economic sectors in the United States.[14] Residents who are assumed to be illegal are much less able to assert their belonging apart from their "proper" role as laboring bodies. I return to this concept in more detail in chapter 1.

Illegality and the Production of Affluence examines empirically how rural gentrification recruited low-wage, racialized, and often undocumented workers to two high-amenity rural communities in the United States. As gentrification took off in Rabun and Routt Counties, businesses responded to the growing demand for housing and a range of services. Employers in these sectors who had never hired immigrant employees began to recruit low-wage and mostly Latine immigrant workers, many without legal papers. As elaborated in chapter 3, this recruitment was motivated initially by a shortage of labor, but over time it consolidated into a preference for Latine immigrant workers in certain sectors, forming the basis for the emergence of immigrant-based labor regimes in a gentrifying economy. It is this basic structural linkage—the arrival of wealthy, White amenity migrants generating economic demand that stimulated the recruitment of a distinct migratory stream—that is the starting point for the analysis presented in this book. It sets the stage for introducing one of its core claims: that rural landscapes of affluence have often been intimately connected to broader landscapes of illegality and racial hierarchy in the United States.[15]

To say that the two migration streams into Routt and Rabun Counties have been positioned differently is an understatement: one group is wealthy and racially privileged, the other low-wage, racially marked, and often undocumented. Yet this second stream has been just as integral to the gentrification process as the first. Newly arrived immigrant workers have provided labor essential to constructing and maintaining houses and condos built in the 1990s and beyond, and their labor has been critical to a range of businesses expanding in response to the arrival of privileged in-migrants—from restaurants to cleaning and/or landscaping services. Indeed, the arrival of Latine workers in Rabun and Routt Counties during the late 1990s and the 2000s had profound ripple effects within a broad range of social and cultural terrains. As workers essential to the gentrification boom, they settled and contributed to shifts in the social geography of everyday life: the Latine student population in public schools rose, English as a Second Language (ESL) teachers were hired, and (the shrinking) spaces of affordable housing began to house both the White and Latine working-class residents. Although the most visible and commodified landscapes in Routt and Rabun Counties were and are ones of luxury—ski slopes, pristine lakes, hiking trails, multi-million-dollar homes, and quaint, boutique downtowns—these spaces have been produced in conjunction with less visible and certainly less publicly commodified geographies of marginality and racial hierarchy.

My focus on the emplacement of immigrant labor in Routt and Rabun Counties is not intended to deny that displacement remains relevant to gentrification in these places or within processes of rural gentrification writ large; it is to argue that there is more to the story. A singular focus on displacement (in this case of longtime locals) can obscure dynamics of emplacement and the role and lives of low-wage immigrants within landscapes of rural affluence. By recruiting a transnational and largely undocumented workforce to build and maintain gentrified landscapes, the process of rural gentrification in the United States often emplaces social regimes of life and work stratified across race, class, language, and legal status. This process echoes similar dynamics of emplacement of immigrant labor regimes in globally oriented cities during the 1980s and early 1990s.[16] As such, Routt and Rabun Counties are two pieces of a broader puzzle linking globalization and the production of precarious, undocumented (civically constrained) labor in the United States. Estimates are that the undocumented population in the United States peaked in 2007, when approximately 12.2 million undocumented immigrants lived and worked in the United States, across a wide range of regions and economic sectors.[17]

But globalization, *how*? As places, both Routt and Rabun Counties are experienced as unique, spectacular, and seemingly far away from the pace and flows of the global. Despite their apparent isolation, these communities nevertheless have been intimately connected to structural transformations that are regional, national, and global in scope. First, high-amenity places across the United States and the globe—from Highlands, North Carolina, to Pucón, Chile—have received an influx of wealthy amenity seekers since the late 1990s, a class whose wealth has mushroomed in the context of neoliberal globalization.[18] For the 1 percent, places like Routt and Rabun Counties have been excellent areas to "get away" *and* to fix their surplus capital—by buying property as an investment in relaxation and recreation as well as another source of profit. Second and relatedly, Routt and Rabun Counties found themselves caught in the crosshairs of transnational low-wage labor markets as employers responded to new market opportunities afforded by amenity-migrant purchasing power by recruiting immigrant workers (a transnational low-wage workforce) to settle in their communities. In this way, like places urban and rural across the United States and the world, Routt and Rabun Counties' economic development over those two decades became more deeply connected to patterns of capital accumulation generated by globalization and its associated transnational labor markets.[19]

While other scholars of rural gentrification/amenity migration in the U.S. context have begun to include the *presence* of immigrant workers in their analyses, a literature explored in depth in chapter 1, none explore in empirical detail the recruitment of immigrant workers, evolving labor regimes, or the complex social geographies produced and undergirded by these dynamics—geographies crosscut by hierarchies of class, race, and legal status. Through comparative qualitative analysis, *Illegality and the Production of Affluence* explores two representative communities impacted by such recruitment. It exposes the processes through which low-wage and often undocumented Latine immigrants were invited to work and settle in these high-amenity rural areas, areas that before this time were largely off the map of Latine immigrant settlement in the U.S.[20]

This book also situates *geographies of social reproduction* as a grounding concept, which I will take a moment to explain. As a number of feminist scholars have theorized it, social reproduction refers to activities and labor undergirding paid work and the formal economy.[21] The notion of social reproduction, in the words of Cindi Katz, speaks to "the material social practices that sustain and reproduce a society—its people, its production systems, and its cultural forms and practices."[22] Appending the language of "geographies" to "social reproduction" highlights these activities as spatially uneven and differentiated: from spaces of the home and housing to spaces of education, recreation, religion, and civic engagement.[23] In the context of the research explored here, the term allows me to link labor regimes and the hierarchies upon which they rely with life and spaces outside of work. Such spaces and practices are critical to reproducing the labor force and to the naturalization and racialized experience of illegality. Moreover, the spaces of social reproduction represent entry points for assessing dynamics of belonging and exclusion for immigrant newcomers. I show the interdependence of production and social reproduction, offering insight into the ways a range of local actors navigate and at times contest the profound tension between the economic inclusion of immigrant bodies and their simultaneous social, civic, and racialized exclusion.

Fine-grained, ethnographic exploration of the emergence of immigrant labor regimes and geographies of social reproduction in places where they had not existed before is timely and significant for reasons that are both scholarly and political.[24] For scholars of immigration, the proliferation of new immigrant destinations in the United States over the past twenty-five plus years, primarily although not exclusively driven by the arrival of Latine immigrants, is a topic of significant interest, to the point that it has developed into a recognized literature: new immigrant destinations (NID) scholarship.[25] Chapter 1 discusses how globalization deepened labor migration between the U.S. and Mexico and reviews scholarship on the diversification of settlement patterns. It examines NID literature in more depth to argue that new immigrant destinations research has overlooked rural gentrification as an important pull for immigrants arriving in small-town America. The analysis presented in this book not only expands the *kinds* of cases explored thus far by new destinations scholarship (add rural gentrification and stir), it furthers efforts among a subset of qualitatively oriented new destinations researchers who engage globalization studies, critical race theory, and feminist conceptualizations of social reproduction, to develop nuanced examinations of the social relations of everyday life in new destination communities. This includes the work of

Helen Marrow, Leah Schmalzbauer, and Jamie Winders, who, in different contexts, use the lenses of feminist and critical race theory to examine shifting social geographies of new destination communities, linking political economic change to local and embodied accounts of immigrant arrival, incorporation, and struggles over belonging.[26]

Illegality and the Production of Affluence also contributes new insights into scholarship on rural gentrification (and related terminologies such as *amenity migration, exurbanization,* and *lifestyle migration*) by placing questions of labor, race, and legal status at the center of how we theorize and methodologically explore the social, economic, political, and ecological impacts of rural gentrification. As explored in detail in chapter 1, research on rural gentrification in the U.S. has emphasized class struggle (between locals and wealthy newcomers), clashing environmental imaginaries, and ecological fragmentation in high-amenity rural communities. While a handful of scholars have considered the presence of low-wage immigrant workers in these areas, few have carefully situated the arrival of Latine immigrants in these areas within broader analyses of globalization or of U.S. racial formations, particularly as these dynamics are shaped by immigration policies and politics.[27] Even fewer have closely examined immigrant labor regimes and considered in fine-grained detail their role in the production of affluent rural landscapes in the United States.[28] This book therefore makes a timely intervention in the rural gentrification literature, which has not fully grappled with the presence and role of Latine immigrants in sites of rural gentrification across the United States.

Exploring in empirical detail the history of expanding rural landscapes of affluence and the recruitment of undocumented immigrant labor is also timely due to the highly contested nature of undocumented migration from Latin America to the United States. As a society, we urgently need to understand in more depth and complexity the origins and effects of our reliance on undocumented labor, particularly how this reliance is produced and navigated in place, within the context of daily life. The importance of a place-based perspective is critical even as these local experiences and processes are constituted by pressures and transformations more visible at national and global scales. In highlighting how employers in the context of day-to-day decision-making discovered, recruited, and incorporated undocumented workers into their businesses, we can see origins of unauthorized labor migration across the U.S.-Mexican border—processes that may apply to small-scale businesses in urban and suburban labor markets as well as rural spaces.

Making mundane processes of recruitment and (economic) incorporation visible also counters narratives—pervasive in media and political discourse—that portray Latine immigrants as lawbreakers and criminals.[29] This book contributes to existing scholarship that reframes such discourse by demonstrating how consumer choices, lifestyle desires, and business strategies recruit workers across the border.[30] It points to the problem of the exploitation of immigrants, flipping the script that casts immigrants as exploiters of the U.S. labor market and society. It traces the multiple ways the labor of undocumented brown bodies makes landscapes of affluence possible, a reality ignored in these broader xenophobic and racialized narratives of the undocumented immigrant as inherently criminal and a drain on society.[31]

Local processes of recruitment are tied to deeper historical dynamics, from the history of U.S.-Mexico border policy to the economic displacement of millions in Mexico and other sending regions in the context of globalization. Yet at the end of the day, the undocumented Latine population has grown in Routt County, Colorado, Rabun County, Georgia, and a host of other places in the United States because local political economic change has been predicated on the recruitment of new populations and the emplacement of new social relationships. Examining these processes of emplacement on the ground makes visible how low-wage, racialized, and largely undocumented immigrants came to play a fundamental role in the U.S. economy over the past three decades. They also provide an entry point for critically excavating the racialized disjuncture between geographies of economic recruitment and processes of social and civic exclusion. These disjunctures shape the operation of the labor market and configure social geographies within immigrant-receiving communities.

PLAN OF THE BOOK

Chapter 1 takes up gentrification as a political economic and cultural process that spans urban and rural spaces, a process that has garnered intense scholarly interest over the last four decades. It makes the argument that rural gentrification in the United States is not only about the arrival of wealthy, White newcomers to rural communities, but in many cases also about the arrival of low-wage, racialized, and "illegal" Latine immigrants, whose presence is linked to the economic changes wrought by the gentrifiers. In theorizing rural gentrification as constituted by linked migration (of wealthy amenity migrants and low-wage immigrants), the chapter outlines how scholars can incorporate critical perspectives of race and illegality into their scholarship. Chapter 1 also historicizes the production of these migration streams within broader political economic transformations linked to globalization and to the history of race, immigration, and borders in the United States.

Chapter 2 shares the methodological approach used to assess linked migration in Rabun County, Georgia, and Routt County, Colorado, specifically in terms of the emergence of immigrant labor regimes and new geographies of social reproduction in both places. I sketch out the methodological design and practices that undergird the analysis presented in this book, practices based on feminist methodological tenets and ethics. As elaborated in that methodological discussion, all interviewee names in this book are pseudonyms to protect participants' identities.[32] Chapter 2 also introduces in more detail the two case study communities, Routt County, Colorado, and Rabun County, Georgia, by providing an overview of how gentrification processes arrived in ways specific to each region. It examines the commodification of place critical to gentrification in each community and explores transformations of place identity and belonging between longtime locals and wealthy newcomers.

Chapters 3 and 4 contain the core empirical findings and analysis of the book. Rather than write chapters that address each case individually—a typical move in comparative analyses—I have chosen to organize these two chapters thematically, to explore labor regimes and geographies of social reproduction across both case study sites. Thus, chapter 3 turns to a comparative exploration of immigrant recruitment by employers in gentrification-linked businesses, employers who generally had little experience working with immigrant workers prior to the mid-1990s. It examines in detail the transition from Latine immigrant recruitment as a stopgap measure to the consolidation of efficient and profitable immigrant-based labor regimes, ones revolving around hierarchies of race, class, and illegality. It considers evidence for the widespread emergence of informal labor brokers in gentrification-linked sectors, brokers who served as the linchpins to most employers' ability to appropriate immigrant social networks to create a highly efficient and profitable labor regime.

Chapter 4 analyzes the relationship between rural gentrification and social reproduction, tracing how the hierarchies that make new regimes of work possible are reproduced in the context of spaces and activities outside of work—within and through the messiness of everyday life. It addresses housing conditions and geographies, as well as questions of how immigrant workers navigate daily life without documentation, face language barriers, and access recreation. The conclusion reconnects the core findings of the book to larger debates concerning undocumented labor in the United States, reflecting in particular on the future of rural gentrification in the wake of the COVID pandemic, which dramatically accelerated domestic amenity migration dynamics in the United States.[33]

At its core, *Illegality and the Production of Affluence* explores the tapestry of daily life in two gentrifying rural communities to show that affluence and illegality in the United States are not ontologically distinct processes, despite loud and public narratives to the contrary. In fact, a detailed empirical analysis of the production of luxury and recreation in Routt and Rabun Counties shows the extent to which affluence in the contemporary United States is often deeply intertwined with, and dependent upon, the presence of racialized subjects marked as "illegal." If we can empirically make that connection more visible—one that exists not only in spaces of rural gentrification but in the most global of cities as well as a range of small and medium cities throughout the country—we can start to face head on the ethical question of why, as a nominally democratic society based on principles of human rights, we let this situation continue.

1 Gentrification, Migration, and Race

The idea of coming to the United States was planted in my
brain, about the age of sixteen, because in those days I felt
sad because my brothers were here in the United States and
when my brothers sent money to my mother and father,
they could see that their sons were doing well economically.
That was when I began to tell my parents that I also wanted
a house. I had a girlfriend in those days, and I was young
but I thought that one day I could build her a house. That is
when I left, leaving my girlfriend, and I told her that I would
only go long enough to make money and build her a house.

—Jorge, Rabun County, Georgia (June 24, 2010)

I lived down there in Wash Park [in Denver], a great place
and I . . . I couldn't stand it. For me, the city gets to be too
much. I get too wound up I guess. Too much going on, and
the people just . . . you can't stop and wave or talk to them.
[. . .] Here in Steamboat there's a lot of good people, everywhere you run into them. You have something in common
with people, you walk into a room and everyone has been
hiking, in the circle you know everyone's been either skiing
that day or that week, or . . . you know.

—Paul, Routt County, Colorado (August 24, 2011)

Well, these people have more money than we [locals] do,
and we are aggravated. One thing is that they come in and
they buy these big places and homes and want their home
fixed and made beautiful and have their own little paradise,
and I would too. [. . .] But they establish themselves and
then become part of the local government and they don't

> want to see an old car on the neighbor's land. They pass
> new rules. [. . .] A lot of these new zoning laws also come
> from the board of realtors I believe, 'cause they want this
> place to look attractive for potential customers.

—Suzanne, Rabun County, Georgia (June 29, 2010)

Gentrification is often told as a story about the movement of capital and its transformation of the built environment and, in urban spaces, the displacement of low-income communities.[1] Yet gentrification, urban or rural, is a story of the mobility of capital *and* people, and critical to these mobilities are dreams and imaginaries of place, community, and belonging. The narratives of Paul, Suzanne, and Jorge provide an entry point into the three key demographic groups interacting in many gentrifying rural communities across the United States: gentrifiers, 'locals," and immigrant residents recruited to work in gentrification-linked businesses.[2] The words of Paul, Suzanne, and Jorge gesture toward the extent to which dreams of place and community motivate the behaviors and choices of all three, even as it is important to recognize such dreams are neither static nor innocent. They are imbricated in cycles of capital accumulation and racial formations. Moreover, the effects of these processes vary over time and space; they are not linear.

The issues visible in these quotations—imaginaries of place and belonging crosscut by assumptions about race, class, nationality, and gender— help us ground gentrification and transnational labor markets in the fabric of everyday life. Jorge, who by the time of our interview had spent twelve years in the United States, made a decision at a young age to undertake a perilous journey, a decision shaped not just by need but by a desire to fulfill a gendered role as a son and potential husband, to build a home for a future family that he could otherwise not imagine being able to afford. Paul, like many gentrifiers, moved to Steamboat Springs because he desired a life and lifestyle that was more relaxed and friendly, slower placed, and closer to nature—a place where he could interact with "like-minded" people, presumably White, who hike and ski. Suzanne, in contrast, did not make a decision to move to follow her dreams of place and home; instead her words reflect a sense of place and belonging being *disrupted* by the arrival of others. Her comments focus on the impacts of the White, wealthy gentrifiers who hold more power than Suzanne feels she has. Listening to these subjective experiences is critical even if we must situate these dreams within broader political economic and historical processes. Toward that end, this chapter aims to situate the broader inquiry within scholarly debates about gentrification; new immigrant destinations; and histories of nationalism, race, and immigration in the United States.

CONCEPTUALIZING GENTRIFICATION

> Gentrification—the transformation of a working—class or
> vacant area of the central city into middle-class residential
> and/or commercial use—is without a doubt one of the more
> popular topics of urban inquiry.
> —Lees, Slater, and Wyly (2010, xv)

This quotation, from *The Gentrification Reader*, points to the centrality of the concept of gentrification in urban studies. A term coined by sociologist Ruth Glass in 1964, the concept theorizes the processes through which the "gentry" (professional and managerial residents) reoccupy marginal urban spaces, and in the process usually displace low-income housing and working-class residents. This process often generates resistance on the part of low-income communities, often communities of color, who claim a "right to the city" in their attempts to resist displacement from their homes and community spaces. It represents an incisive concept for scholars concerned with patterns of urban capital accumulation and the intersection of race and class in the production of—and contestation over—urban landscapes.[3]

There are many eddies within the vast river of scholarship on urban gentrification over the last several decades, from Marxist explanations of it being driven largely by capital to demand-side explanations centered on the shifting tastes and behavior of wealthy gentrifiers; from researchers who study urban social movements resisting displacement to urban planners who seek to address housing costs and green space for low-income communities.[4] Although writing on urban gentrification has sought to bridge the gap between the supply versus demand explanations for gentrification, what is clear in these debates is the diffusion of gentrification over time. By the 2000s gentrification dynamics had begun to move down the urban hierarchy, from large to medium and small cities.[5]

The concept of gentrification caught the imagination of urban geographers, sociologists, and others because it is an entry point into a range of issues at the heart of urban political economic and cultural transformation over the last century, particularly as these landscapes have been remade under neoliberal globalization. By the early 1990s gentrification could be "seen to constitute one of the major 'leading edges' of contemporary metropolitan restructuring."[6] Gentrification has allowed scholars to consider the uneven fabric of the built urban environment and its material and symbolic reconfiguration, one rooted in political economic change linked to sociocultural reordering and displacement. From a political economic perspective, urban gentrification is a particular form of what David Harvey theorizes as a "spatial fix," a temporary resolution to a crisis of accumulation.[7] Neil Smith operationalized this idea in terms of a rent gap that can emerge in lower-cost neighborhoods as private individuals and corporate developers see the profit that could be made between the cost of those properties and their worth if refurbished, renovated, and repackaged as a neighborhood for hip, wealthy, and mostly White professionals.[8] It is a return to the inner city for a group that under Fordist urban dynamics had fled to the suburbs, thus generating a historic shift in the urban morphology typical of the mid-twentieth century United States. What it has often meant for working-class, and usually minoritized, urban communities is displacement and the undermining of community life and identity.[9]

Scholars have explored a range of urban issues linked to gentrification. This includes housing policy and urban planning, mortgage lending practices, the dynamics of gender and urban change, the intersection of race and gentrification, and the role of art and artists in the production of gentrification.[10] The question of how marginalized communities resist and reconfigure urban gentrification processes has been an abiding concern over more than two decades, as gentrification became a focus for a wide range of urban social movements as well as less formal modes and manners of resistance.[11]

For many scholars the term *rural gentrification* is an oxymoron, as most assume gentrification is an inherently urban dynamic. Yet reaching back to the 1980s, UK-based geographers began to articulate the idea of *rural* gentrification.[12] They brought the concept to rural spaces because they observed dynamics parallel to those found in cities: the arrival of wealthy in-migrants to a place (often lower cost compared to their place of origin); a remaking of the built environment as gentrifiers moved in; and the displacement—physically or culturally—of long-term residents, usually working-class people.[13] Scholars from a range of disciplines have worked over several decades researching this rural phenomena, not only in the UK and U.S. but in a range of postindustrial and Global South contexts.[14] A range of terminologies is used to examine these dynamics, including *amenity migration, lifestyle migration, exurbanization, counterurbanization,* and *residential tourism*. As I review the literature here, I bring together scholars who use distinct terminologies because they are all studying and theorizing about basically the same phenomenon, even if from somewhat different angles (migration versus its impacts). I come down on the term *rural gentrification* among these terminologies because the concept captures the intertwined movement of people and capital and allows me to consider dynamics of displacement, emplacement, and the cultural politics of belonging. Moreover, by invoking the term *gentrification* I can show the topographical connections between urban and rural gentrification, rejecting a tendency to dichotomize between the urban and the rural.

Tensions between demographic and political economic explanations have marked the literature on rural gentrification from the outset. Population geographers and demographers working prior to the pandemic era tended to view urban to rural amenity migration in the United States, and resulting rural landscape transformations, as driven by the aging of the baby boom. Demographic analysis has shown that the propensity to undertake an amenity-driven migration increases with age.[15] Others saw the political economic changes associated with globalization as the most critical factor driving high-amenity rural transformations. Primary for this group of scholars has been the rapid capital accumulation by urban professional elites (overwhelmingly White) in the context of globalization during the 1980s and beyond, which allowed some urban professionals and investors to live in the city and afford a second home in (or move permanently to) their favorite high-amenity rural areas, whether that be Highlands, North Carolina, or Sun Valley, Idaho. Relatedly, rising urban property values associated with globalization provided the capital for some urban residents—even if not members of the 1 percent—to move to or own a second home in a comparatively lower-cost but high amenity rural area.[16] At the end of the day, geographies of rural gentrification in the United States and other postindustrial contexts are, like their urban counterparts, a result of the movement of capital and people, driven by patterns of wealth accumulation, the profit motive, and deeply held desires for a particular suite of locational amenities. For those heading to rural spaces, it is commonly a desire for proximity to nature and outdoor recreation, as well as the longing for the "rural idyll" (an idealized imaginary of rural space).

The theme of displacement has been central to scholarship on gentrification both urban and rural. However, the nature of displacement wrought by the arrival of gentrifiers is often distinct when comparing urban and rural dynamics. In the constrained space of a city, low-income communities experience pressures of physical displacement as property values and taxes rise and housing becomes unaffordable for working-class people. Given the paucity of affordable housing in large cities, this often leads to the dissolution of historically vibrant low-income communities and communities of color, who have little recourse for staying and surviving in the city. This explains, in part at least, the social movements that have arisen to contest processes of urban gentrification.[17]

In rural places, by contrast, gentrification-driven displacement is not necessarily or primarily physical, but is more often manifested in cultural and political terms. Although in rural communities local residents feel pressure to sell property as prices and taxes rise (like their urban counterparts), this may not signal the dissolution of working-class communities, as the availability of land and space is usually greater in rural places. Working-class, long-standing residents might sell property in prime locations desired by wealthier gentrifiers, but in some circumstances they can continue to live in the area. However, there is nearly always a profound sense of cultural and political displacement on the part of long-term locals in rural communities experiencing gentrification: they witness a shift from landscapes of production (classic rural extractive or agricultural industries) to landscapes of consumption catering to gentrifiers.[18] Wealthy newcomers often exercise significant power in the community economically and may run for local office to reshape the community to reflect their own values and environmental imaginaries—further alienating local working-class and longtime residents.[19]

Much of the interdisciplinary literature on rural gentrification in the U.S. context, whether framed with the terminology of amenity or lifestyle migration, focuses on the sociopolitical effects of gentrification on rural communities, its economic development impacts, or the effects of amenity newcomers on broader land use patterns and ecologies. For example, in the early 2000s geographers Shumway and Otterstrom used cluster analysis to explore transitions in the rural U.S. West in the 1990s, noting that "mineral, cattle and lumber production is diminished by an economy based on a new paradigm of the amenity region, which creates increased demands for amenity space, residential and recreational property, second homes, and environmental protection," all of which change demographic and employment structures.[20] Along similar lines but with emphasis on qualitative data and analysis, geographer Peter Walker worked with sociologist Louise Fortman to explore the impacts of exurban newcomers arriving in large numbers in the Sierra Nevada mountains, analyzing power struggles between locals and newcomers over distinct environmental imaginaries and land-use regulations.[21] Rina Ghose investigated rural gentrification in Montana in the early 2000s, considering how struggles over sprawl, land use, and the commodification of place reflected fundamental class conflict between locals and newcomers.[22]

Questions of class conflict and inequality between newcomers and locals, changing environmental imaginaries and place narratives, as well as land use patterns, remain key foci in more recent contributions to scholarship on rural gentrification in the United States. Sociologist Ryanne Pilgeram, in her 2021 monograph *Pushed Out: Contested Development and Rural Gentrification in the U.S. West*, examines the gentrification of Dover, Idaho. The community, founded by logging companies and with a rich working-class history, struggled after the mill closed in the 1980s and became a site of gentrification by exurbanites over the next decade. By the early 2000s the town voted to turn key public spaces on the lakefront over to a private developer catering to wealthy, White amenity migrants, a process explored by Pilgeram to understand class-based struggles over belonging and development that often occur in high-amenity rural communities of the West.[23]

Jennifer Sherman, in *Dividing Paradise: Rural Inequality and the American Dream*, undertakes a parallel analysis of changes in rural Washington state as she examines the divide between longtime locals, overwhelmingly White, and wealthier White newcomers in Paradise Valley (a place pseudonym). Her work interrogates the economic change these processes generated for longtime locals, whose traditional resource-based jobs declined in relation to an expansion of lower-wage, service sector employment typical in amenity economies. Sherman examines not just an economic transformation, but also the transformation of belonging and place, through in-depth qualitative research.[24] Similar themes of culture clash and class tension can be found in Ulrich-Schad's examination of community identity in a rural Colorado town attracting amenity migrants and in Richelle Winkler's exploration of poverty and inequality in the lake country of Northern Minnesota.[25]

In addition to an abiding concern with class inequalities and tensions between locals and gentrifying newcomers, a number of scholars in recent years have dug into the ecological and environmental impacts of amenity-led rural development. Soren Larsen and colleagues examine environmental learning and identities among exurban newcomers and locals in rural Fremont County, Colorado, showing the ways high-end residential housing for amenity migrants impacted ranching landscapes.[26] Hannah Gosnell, Julia Haggerty, and collaborators undertake sophisticated mixed-method analysis of land use change in the great Yellowstone ecosystem to consider how the expansion of high net worth individuals (amenity migrants) owning ranchlands in the area shaped regional conservation efforts. Sociologist Candace May studies amenity-led development impacts on rural fishing communities of North Carolina, documenting the rising cultural clashes between locals and newcomers, as well as the production of new landscapes of environmental vulnerability.[27]

The preceding review of literature is only a sample of the significant amount of research on rural gentrification/amenity migration/

exurbanization studied by geographers, sociologists, economists, and planners.[28] It is emblematic of the important work that has been done on this topic, scholarship that has provided empirically rich and valuable insights for scholars, local advocates, and elected leaders or planners coping with the social, economic, and environmental impacts of gentrification in high-amenity rural areas. Yet what all the literature reviewed here also shares is that none of these scholars consider the presence and role of low-wage Latine immigrants in rural gentrifying landscapes.

Perhaps immigrants are not mentioned in this literature because in these particular research sites there were few or no immigrants working in gentrification-linked sectors; that is, employers meeting new demands associated with gentrification did not recruit and rely on immigrant workers and instead relied on local White working-class folks. Or it is an oversight, perhaps rooted in the ways immigrant workers are often not highly visible in the community or because their fleeting presence cleaning people's homes or pruning their trees is taken for granted in relation to the seemingly bigger questions of class tensions between White newcomers and White locals, of land use struggles across class.

Looking back at some of the cases explored in the literature, however, it is possible to see census data indicating a growing Latine population in these areas and during the periods under study.[29] In Rhina Ghose's study site in Montana between 1990 and 2005 (she studied the late 1990s/ early 2000s), the Latine population increased by 138 percent. In Dover, Idaho, where Ryanne Pilgeram did her research, the Latine population increased by 40 percent between 2000 and 2010. Richard Stedman, who studied second homeowners' place attachment in Vilas County, Wisconsin, does not consider the presence of immigrants even though census data indicate the Latine population increasing by 48 percent in that county between 2000 and 2010. It is possible that the growing Latine population as indicated in these census numbers was employed in sectors not related to gentrification, but rural *industries* that recruit Latine immigrants, such as meatpacking plants, are often not located in high-amenity areas. Given that the numerous studies suggest that amenity migrants themselves are overwhelmingly White, it is unlikely that growing Latine populations in these sites are, in significant numbers, wealthy amenity migrants.[30]

Perhaps more telling would be to consider those scholars who use place pseudonyms. The use of place pseudonyms makes it impossible to check census data to see if the Latine population is growing in their study sites, but we can consider what populations these scholars choose to center. Sociologist Jessica Ulrich-Schad explores amenity migration in a Colorado town she calls River Town, noting as she describes her methods that according to the census, 90 percent of the population in this town was White. By definition, then, 10 percent of the community was non-White. Nevertheless, her theorization and methodological exploration of how different groups "view and interact with each other" in the context of amenity in-migration avoids exploration of race/ethnicity or racialized dynamics.[31] The non-White population did not enter into her analysis of how groups interacted in the context of rural gentrification, and her interview sample she notes was 98 percent White. Along a similar vein, Jennifer Sherman's study of Paradise Valley in Washington State provides census data only for the non-Hispanic White population in 2010—there is no demographic data provided for non-White populations or any data on changes in the White population over time. Finally, in their exploration of amenity migration in Jackson County, North Carolina, Breen, Hurley, and Taylor make reference to the presence of African Americans in their study site, but the question of how racial dynamics and whiteness shape amenity-migrant driven gentrification is not addressed.[32] Sherman, Ulrich-Schad, Hurley, and others reviewed up to this point overwhelmingly treat the socioeconomic changes associated with rural gentrification as class-based phenomena: class differences underlie environmental struggles, land use change, economic development strategies, and cultural clashes over community and belonging.

This elision of race is problematic not only in those instances where the presence of racialized immigrants laboring to produce landscapes of gentrification may have been overlooked. Drawing on theories of racial capitalism, rural gentrification is always and already a racialized process whether immigrants or other minoritized groups are present or not. Early work by Frey and Liaw argued that domestic amenity migration in the United States could be viewed as "large-scale white flight."[33] This phrase connotes the ways in which rural gentrification is driven by the migration of a particular racialized class that has benefited disproportionately from globalization, which allows them to leave cities for high-amenity areas. Moreover, gentrifiers in high-amenity rural areas often discuss these destination communities as more authentic and closer to nature—deploying the trope of "empty nature" found in White settler imaginaries.[34] Finally, many explicitly deploy racial codes while describing their decision to move to a high-amenity rural area—often discussing their decision in terms of escaping "dangerous" and "unsafe" cities.[35] Whether visible in the motivations articulated by gentrifiers, or within the long dureé of racial formations shaping U.S. history, rural gentrification should be theorized as a profoundly racialized process.

Yet it is still rare to find scholarship that takes race and/or racial formations as central to conceptualizing rural gentrification, or that addresses questions of illegality as a racialized form—this last point a fundamental one in the U.S. context. When Peter Nelson and I developed the broader project upon which this book builds (discussed in more detail in the methodological appendix), we were initially inspired by our own observations of Latine immigrant workers in areas undergoing rural gentrification in the U.S. West. The early stages of our joint project were primarily quantitative in nature and mapped nonmetropolitan counties between 1990 and 2000 that showed critical overlap between White baby boomer in-migration on the one hand (a demographic group that represented the leading edge of amenity migration at the time) and the arrival of Hispanic/Latine populations into gentrifying rural America.[36] While most attention by new immigrant destination scholars had been paid to growing Latine populations in sites of rural industrial restructuring (e.g., meatpacking plants), our analysis showed that Latine workers in these overlap counties were working primarily in construction, services, restaurants, and accommodations—the kinds of sectors most impacted by rural gentrification.

Peter and I were not the only scholars who began attending to the presence and role of Latine immigrant workers in rural landscapes of gentrification in the United States. In 2013 Lisa Sun-Hee Park and David Naguib Pellow published *Slums of Aspen*, a groundbreaking monograph that critiqued environmental privilege in Aspen, Colorado.[37] Park and Pellow tease out the contradictions between the community's dependence on immigrant labor and wealthy residents' enormous lifestyle impact on the environment, a contradiction made more glaring when Aspen voters passed an anti-immigrant ordinance blaming overpopulation and lax border control as the root causes of environmental degradation. Through textual analysis of local media and interviews with city officials, advocacy group members, and immigrant workers living in Aspen's hinterlands, Park and Pellow analyze environmental privilege and its relationship to nativism within environmentalist discourse. By highlighting the often-unrecognized role of Latine workers in the community and their frequently poor housing conditions, Park and Pellow make visible the contradictions of environmental privilege that allows certain groups direct access to nature, organic food, and protection from ecological harm. Park and Pellow situate dynamics in Aspen within globalization, as a driver of transnational low-wage labor migration, and in relation to the fear immigrants experience in relation to U.S. Immigration and Customs Enforcement (ICE) raids and deportation. However, the origins and evolution of immigrant-based labor regimes were not their central concern.

Leah Schmalzbauer, in *Last Best Place*, makes important contributions through her research on the gendered geographies of social reproduction for Latine immigrant families in Big Sky, Montana.[38] Paying particular attention to the intersection of race, class, gender, and illegality for recent Latine immigrants, she paints a rich portrait of regional political economies and household dynamics for immigrants employed in agriculture and construction (the latter often linked to gentrification). Schmalzbauer's experience as a Latin Americanist and someone who speaks Spanish shines through in this important contribution, as these skills allowed her to develop close, trusting relationships with her research participants. These relationships allow her to examine in detail the experience of immigrant men and women negotiating life in Montana as gendered, low-wage, racialized, and often "illegal" residents. In doing so, she bridges new immigrant destinations literature (reviewed later in this chapter) and rural gentrification debates. Although Schmalzbauer situates the arrival of Latine immigrants in rural Montana in terms of labor needs and discusses gentrification as one driver of immigrant labor demand in the area, the dynamic *between* employers and immigrant workers, including recruitment strategies of employers, was not part of her empirical analysis.

The question of Latine immigrant workers in landscapes of gentrification has been taken up by two more recent contributions, *Billionaire's*

Wilderness by Justin Farrell and *Aspen and the American Dream* by Jennifer Stuber.[39] Stuber's book on Aspen centers "the intersecting dynamics of social class and culture in Aspen's place-making process."[40] The book devotes six of its seven core chapters to placemaking and exclusions navigated by mostly White middle-class residents, analyzing how land codes, planning practices, and housing subsidies affect the ability of middle-class residents to live and develop a sense of belonging in Aspen. Engaging Park and Pellow's earlier book on Aspen, and recognizing the economic role of Latine immigrants, Stuber includes one chapter on the experiences of Latine immigrants in Aspen. While Stuber addresses race and legal status in her conceptual framing of that particular chapter, most of the empirical data presented from the interviews conducted with Latine immigrants addresses what motivated them to leave their home country, quotes that revolve around low wages and violence in their home country. While she also discusses their difficult work and housing conditions, the thrust of her narrative is that Latine immigrants are also following the American Dream, like middle-class White residents, and feel grateful for the opportunity. She opens her conclusion of the chapter thus: "'Aspen is my sweet home' (dulce hogar), said Maria a hotel worker from El Salvador. She, like many Latino migrants, spoke about her life in the Roaring Fork Valley with a sense of affection and gratitude."[41] Stuber hired Spanish-speaking assistants to conduct the interviews with immigrant respondents. While she does explore wage differentials between sending regions and Aspen, Stuber does not explore employer recruitment strategies or how illegality shapes work or social reproduction in daily life. Legal status is noted as a challenge for immigrant residents, but it is not examined in depth because she instructed her assistants not to ask questions about legal status.[42]

Farrell's book shares similarities with *Aspen and the American Dream*, and not just because both places are sites of not simply rural gentrification but what some call "super gentrification" driven not by the 1 percent but by the 0.1 percent. *Billionaire's Wilderness* charts the lives and environmental politics of Jackson Hole's *ultra*-wealthy residents, drawing on five years of ethnographic fieldwork with the ultra-wealthy. Farrell pays detailed attention to the cultural practices and identities of (White) billionaires living in fortified "wilderness" enclaves, tracing how environmental philosophies of this group play out in the form of profitable conservation easements, tax write-offs, and Wyoming tax havens. After completing his years-long ethnography of the ultra-wealthy, he realized he was missing a "piece of the puzzle" and returned to study, in his words, the "have-not's" in Jackson Hole, many of whom are Spanish-speaking immigrants from Mexico. "To complete the story I wanted to know how those at the bottom view themselves in relation to such immense wealth."[43] His abiding curiosity in relation to immigrant participants was in assessing how immigrants view the ultra-wealthy, many of whom are their employers. To interview these workers, Farrell solicited help from local immigrant advocacy groups, who recruited the participants and conducted the interviews in Spanish for him. With those interview data in hand, Farrell complemented his detailed exploration of the lives of billionaires—which extends for two hundred pages in the book—with the voices and experiences of immigrants in Jackson Hole.

Farrell develops a forensic account of billionaires' lives, treating them as complex individuals. He reflects closely on his positionality in relation to the ultra-wealthy and the challenges he faced gaining their trust as he conducted participant observation on the ski slopes or during the extravagant parties thrown in private wilderness areas.[44] There is no discussion of his positionality in relation to immigrant respondents and how it might have shaped the data that emerged from those interviews. He does not discuss in any detail strategies of recruitment or how he developed rapport with immigrant respondents; Farrell relies on immigrant advocacy groups to do this work for him (9) and shares that he never even learned the names of immigrants interviewed for the book (317). He frames this as an intentional strategy to protect the anonymity of the immigrant participants, but he did learn the names of the billionaires while protecting their anonymity.

If a researcher lacks the language skills and cultural/historical training (as a Latin Americanist or as a Latine studies scholar) that would position them to interview immigrant respondents and interpret their lives from a position of cultural expertise and cross-cultural dialogue, it is perhaps unsurprising that the interview data from immigrant respondents Farrell chose to share in the book repeatedly reproduce problematic tropes about low-wage immigrants. He opens his first substantive chapter that draws on interviews with immigrants (titled "No Time for Judgment") by describing the life of Carmita, who works full time cooking, cleaning, and providing childcare for an ultra-wealthy family. After working all day:

> The nights provide little respite for Carmita, who with four of her own children to raise as a single mother, juggles a second job in the evenings to cover the costs of their small trailer, where they share a living space with another family. Her experience is typical of how the other half lives here in Teton County, where it is common for people to work two to three jobs and cram multiple families into a two-bedroom trailer.... But Carmita does not wallow in the struggle. There's no time for that. She remains positive. And, from our interviews with her, it is clear that the margins are too thin, and the consequences simply too dire, to be distracted with anything else but survival.... Through all of this, Carmita believes that the struggle is worth it, and views herself as a successful person.... The last part of this book *examines what ultra-wealth looks like and feels like through the eyes of the working poor.*[45]

Farrell interprets Carmita's situation through the lens of long-standing tropes—immigrants as hardworking but grateful—not considering that taking her words only at face value might be misleading. Both her working conditions and a desire to express gratitude must be understood within broader contexts of racism, illegality, and poverty. If Farrell was present at the interview, she might have been aware that he was spending extended time with her employer, a situation that might have shaped her response. In other words, any expressions of gratitude must be understood in relation to structural dynamics of racism and illegality, as well as the concrete embodiment of Farrell himself.

Although Farrell later includes interviews from immigrant respondents who are more critical of the exploitative conditions they face in their daily lives, he neglects to explore how immigrants chose Jackson Hole, the history of labor migration between Mexico and Latin America, or the complex dynamics of immigrant-based labor regimes in landscapes of gentrification. He relies on framing their presence simply as being about how little they made in their home community and how much more they make per hour in Jackson Hole, bypassing the complex political economic dynamics and border politics producing this transnational labor force. Perhaps most troubling, Farrell includes no discussion of how the threat of deportation might be shaping immigrant lives before or during their time in Jackson Hole—from immigrants' relationship to the police to whether they change their behavior and choices due to their legal status. While it is likely that the Jackson Hole police would not be among those police districts that cooperate with ICE, the "deportation regime" writ large has been a defining characteristic of life for undocumented people throughout the United States since the mid-2000s, as explored by a number of scholars.[46] Yet this topic does not appear to be among the list of questions Farrell had advocates ask immigrant respondents, as his overwhelming and stated interest was largely to see how immigrants view the ultra-wealthy, not to understand the complexities of immigrant lives. *Illegality and the Production of Affluence* puts immigrant lives and experiences at the center of our understanding of rural gentrification, plumbing in depth how they were recruited to these places and how their presence transformed businesses and local economies in ways that made them indispensable over time even as they navigated local and national terrains of exclusion.

The central contribution of *Illegality and the Production of Affluence* to scholarship on gentrification/amenity migration/exurbanization is to argue that scholars of this phenomenon need to recognize that, at least in the U.S. context, the recruitment of low-wage immigrants—mostly Latine and many undocumented—into gentrification-linked economic sectors is common if not widespread across high-amenity rural areas nationally.[47] It is this dynamic that led Peter Nelson and I to theorize a process of "linked migration" in the context of rural gentrification, drawing from Saskia Sassen's development of the term *linked migration* to talk about a similar phenomenon in global cities: the structural linkage between urban high-wage professionals and the arrival of low-wage immigrants to global cities in the 1980s.[48] While certainly more research needs to be undertaken to tease out these geographies—exploring the circumstances under which some gentrifying locales might not witness the recruitment of low-wage immigrant workers (whether from Latin America or other places) —this is a widespread phenomenon in the U.S. context and demands a rethinking of how scholars approach rural gentrification.

The presence of low-wage immigrant workers may not be super visible, particularly if scholars are not looking for them, but every researcher of rural gentrification needs to ask the question: Who is providing the labor force for the construction of new built environments linked to gentri-fication, particularly high-end housing, and for the maintenance of the lifestyles of gentrifiers (landscaping, cleaning, restaurant labor, etc.)? Of course, long-standing locals may be a source of that labor, but are they the only source? The presence of Latine or other immigrant groups may not be immediately apparent; it is easy to walk down the streets of Aspen, Jackson Hole, or Highlands, North Carolina, and see only White people, most of whom appear wealthy. Immigrant workers may be living in trailer parks mostly hidden from most public view—as observed by Park and Pel-low, Stuber, and as I explore in chapter 4. They may also be living a com-mute away from the gentrifying spaces, as noted by Farrell when he talks about how Latine immigrants working in Jackson Hole often commute there from nearby counties in Idaho.[49] But wherever they are living, in many high-amenity rural communities undergoing gentrification, they are providing a labor force without which these lifestyles and landscapes could not function.

If linked migration between wealthy White amenity migrants and low-wage, racialized and "illegal" migrants is confirmed to be widespread across landscapes of rural gentrification in the United States, it demands that scholars of rural gentrification (and related terminologies) avoid re-producing the invisibility of immigrants in their scholarship. Whether their interests are in land use transformation, struggles over environmen-tal imaginaries, or changing place identities as gentrification proceeds, these research projects must include Latine voices and experiences. We need to do more, however, than add immigrants to the analysis and stir, as the presence and role of Latine immigrant residents and workers in areas of rural gentrification demand four fundamental changes that are concep-tual and methodological in nature.

First, if immigrants are present as a workforce in these places, we can-not avoid connecting processes of gentrification to multiscale political economic changes in immigrant-sending regions/nations. Many scholars of rural gentrification recognize globalization as the driver of wealth ac-cumulation among those who undertake amenity migration, but we need to push this further to consider globalization-driven processes of dis-placement that mobilize and push a low-wage labor force toward employ-ers, whose recruitment practices emplace a new set of labor and social geographies in gentrifying rural communities. Second, questions of race and illegality must be foregrounded as factors structuring the economy, social relationships, ecological transformation, and politics in the context of rural gentrification. They are not incidental. Third, scholars of rural gentrification should connect studies of the social and economic changes wrought in the context of rural gentrification to histories of racialized nationalism, immigration policies, and border politics that produce these labor flows and "illegality" itself. Fourth, we must embrace methods and ethics appropriate for engaging vulnerable groups marginalized across class, race, legal status, and language difference. Engaging and interviewing immigrant residents, many of whom are undocumented and struggling under poverty, needs to be done by researchers with appropriate linguistic, historical, and cultural expertise. Such expertise is critical to ethically engaging these populations—recruiting them, developing rapport, and asking the right questions—and to interpreting the data effectively and ethically. Holding this expertise does not absolve one from ongoing power relations between researchers and participants, but doing such interviews without the training and language/culture skills is highly problematic. This task cannot be offloaded onto advocacy groups or hired student research assistants who speak Spanish. Of the scholars reviewed immediately above, who have brought Latine immigrants into their studies of rural gentrification, Schmalzbauer is the only one whose conceptual and methodological approach meets all four of these points.

The rest of this chapter begins to enact these principles for approaching linked migration in the context of rural gentrification by situating the flows of in-migrants to high-amenity rural areas—wealthy gentrifiers and low-wage, often undocumented Latine immigrants—in the context of globalization. I then close the chapter by outlining the history of national bordering and immigration policies and politics, all of which are critical to historicizing the production of racial hierarchies and illegality in the United States. The primary data analyzed in chapters 3 and 4—about the emergence and consolidation of immigrant-based labor regimes in the context of rural gentrification and the resulting geographies of social reproduction crosscut by race, illegality, and poverty—are unintelligible without historicizing and exploring in some detail these broader contexts.

GLOBALIZATION, MIGRATION, AND NEW IMMIGRANT DESTINATIONS

The integration of the U.S. and Mexican economies over the last three plus decades is a critical context for understanding the emergence of immigrant labor regimes in the context of rural gentrification in the 1990s and 2000s. Globalization generated new economic dynamics north and south of the border that stimulated cross-border labor flows and changed the geography of immigrant settlement.[50] While Mexico as a source of undocumented labor has declined relative to Central America since the early 2010s, the origins of the labor regimes under discussion here lie primarily in the effects of globalization in the U.S. and Mexico.

During the 1980s both countries underwent an unmistakable shift toward economic globalization, with both enacting a suite of policies instantiating neoliberal, nominally "free market" ideals as a driving framework of economic development.[51] Of course this meant profoundly different things in each country, given their unique histories and vastly different positions in the global economy. Yet neoliberalism in both places led directly to a steady increase in the demand for low-wage, often undocumented, workers in the United States, *and* it expanded the number of Mexicans willing to undertake a risky journey across the border looking for work.[52] A convergence of pull and push, of demand and supply, it was this basic structural phenomenon that led to the steady increase in low-wage and often unauthorized labor migration from Mexico to the United States during the 1980s and beyond.[53] The "unauthorized" legal status of these flows is rooted in the fact that no mechanisms were available for low-wage workers to cross the border legally, despite the persistent demand for their labor. As will be elaborated in the next section, the power of these pull and push factors was exacerbated (rather than slowed) by simultaneous efforts to militarize and fortify the U.S.-Mexican border.

Rabun County, Georgia, and Routt County, Colorado, did not see the effects of these large-scale structural changes immediately, as they were part of a range of "new destinations" that generally did not witness growing immigrant populations until the mid- to late-1990s, but we cannot understand the emergence of new destinations without exploring the longer history of large-scale structural transformations in the U.S. economy. It is estimated that at its peak in 2007, 5.4 percent of the U.S. workforce lacked authorization.[54] While national numbers have declined since that time, with undocumented workers comprising 4.2 percent of the U.S. workforce in 2019, they remain a vital part of the agriculture, construction, and food service labor.[55]

The story of neoliberal globalization in the United States reaches back to the late 1960s and early 1970s, as Germany and Japan began to seriously challenge the global industrial hegemony held by U.S. manufacturers since World War II. Japanese and other companies were able to pressure U.S. industries, ones organized along a Fordist model of mass production characterized by high fixed costs and little flexibility, by creating efficient and geographically flexible production systems.[56] Making use of new communication and transportation technologies to build a global assembly line, these "post-Fordist" manufacturers could respond quickly to market changes, take advantage of geographically uneven labor costs and regulatory environments, and access new markets. From the perspective of places such as the United States, globalization ushered in a process of deindustrialization. By the 1980s these changes accelerated rapidly as neoliberal policies promoting free trade and market deregulation became ascendant under the Reagan, Bush and Clinton presidencies.[57]

Structural changes associated with globalization and neoliberalism transformed the U.S. job market in ways that exacerbated socioeconomic inequality and deepened processes that recruited low-wage labor across the U.S.-Mexico border. The roots of deepening inequality during this period are complex, but a key factor was the loss of high-wage industrial jobs, described previously, in combination with the service sector becoming the driver of new job creation.[58] Service sector employment tends to be highly bifurcated, producing high-wage opportunities and benefits to more highly educated professionals (think software engineer) on the one hand but on the other hand creating low-wage jobs with few benefits for almost everyone else (think of the janitor who cleans the engineer's office or even the engineer's administrative assistant). These low- and lower-wage workers found life more precarious due not only to eroding incomes, but also to simultaneous rollbacks of the social safety net under the aegis of neoliberal and free-market policies. In sum, although by the mid-1990s neoliberal policies had produced economic growth as measured in terms of gross domestic product, corporate profits, and a rising stock market, they also had deepened socioeconomic inequality.[59]

As argued by Saskia Sassen and others, both ends of this bifurcated labor market stimulated the recruitment of low-wage immigrant workers to the U.S., most of whom in this period were undocumented, given the restrictions on the legal entry of low-skilled and low-income migrants.[60] On the high-wage end it became more common in the 1980s for dual-earning, professional families to hire immigrants to take on the work of the social reproduction of home and household—from nannies and housekeepers to yard and property maintenance workers. This phenomenon was particularly visible in the most globally linked cities: Los Angeles, Chicago, and New York. High-wage professionals in the neoliberal era have been well compensated for their work but are also expected to work long hours that have made housework and childcare increasingly difficult without help.[61] In addition low-wage immigrants being directly hired by high-wage professional families, the bifurcated labor market witnessed the expansion of low-wage jobs within the burgeoning service sector and manufacturing industries that did not offshore. From commercial janitorial operations to domestic assembly lines, service and manufacturing employers in the 1980s recruited documented and undocumented immigrant labor to drive down their costs and increase their flexibility in an increasingly competitive environment. Sassen argues that these two sources of labor demand—demand by high-wage professionals themselves and demand from labor-intensive service and manufacturing industries—drove the increasing numbers of low-wage immigrants arriving in globally linked cities during the 1980s and beyond.

Yet the story of expanding low-wage labor flows across the U.S.-Mexico border is not merely one of increased demand north of the border. New labor demands and recruitment strategies in the U.S. in the 1980s converged with newly "liberated" sources of labor in Mexico and other sending regions to create steadily increasing flows of labor across the border. The factors pushing workers out of Mexico during this period are also linked to globalization, and it is worth briefly summarizing what the situation looked like in Mexico.

Global economic integration and restructuring in Mexico not only tied its economy closer to the United States—epitomized by the signing of the North American Free Trade Agreement in 1992—it economically displaced millions of Mexicans both urban and rural, inspiring a growing number to cross the border.[62] This process can be traced most clearly to 1982, the year Mexico declared itself unable to meet its international debt obligations, payments that ballooned due to rising interest rates in the early 1980s.[63] Mexico's declaration of immanent default ushered in what later became known as the debt crisis, as the threat of default swept through other countries of the Global South post-1982. This looming series of defaults not only signaled a crisis for debtor nations, it threatened the worldwide banking system. Moreover, it quickly took on a public character despite the fact that the loans at the time were held mostly by private banks. Viewing this as a looming global financial crisis, the International Monetary Fund (IMF) stepped in, providing emergency loans critical to immediate stabilization for debtor countries on the condition that those debtor nations accept the IMF's new role renegotiating loans on behalf of private banks.[64]

In order to receive emergency loans and renegotiate loan agreements with private lenders, the IMF required debtor countries to sign structural adjustment agreements and transform their economies. Offering a similar formula to governments across the Global South, these agreements required debtor countries to dismantle state-led and protectionist development policies; to promote export production both rural and urban; to deregulate their economies to allow the free flow of goods, services, and investment from abroad; and to slash public spending on education, health care, food subsidies, and more. The logic of these policies, like the deregulation and free-trade promotion policies in the U.S. during the 1980s, was neoliberal: the idea that globally integrated and nominally free and deregulated markets were the best for the economy and society even if they caused "short-term" costs such as increases in poverty and hunger.

As Mexico underwent debt-induced neoliberal globalization, millions of Mexicans saw their livelihoods erode—from peasant farmers who had eked out a living growing food with the support of government price subsidies, to middle-class professionals linked to the public sector, to small business owners who had been protected from global manufacturers prior to debt crisis restructuring.[65] Neoliberal reforms mandated by the IMF produced a period of wage stagnation, underemployment, and rising costs for basic survival items such as food, which in combination rapidly eroded the middle class and deepened poverty during the 1980s and beyond. A growing number of Mexicans turned toward migration and a risky journey across the border to find employment and a better future for their children, many of them following the networks and paths laid down by the Bracero Program during the mid-twentieth century.[66]

Data on the number of undocumented immigrants in the United States reaches back to 1990, when, the Pew Hispanic Center estimates, 3.5 million undocumented immigrants lived in the U.S., a number that grew to 8.6 million in 2000 and peaked in 2007 at 12.2 million.[67] The number has declined since, with estimates indicating there were slightly over 11 million undocumented people in the United States in 2019. Today the majority of undocumented residents in the United States are not from Mexico, as undocumented Mexican nationals as a proportion of the total undocumented population have declined steadily since 2007, with Central American and Asian immigrants taking over a larger proportion since that time.[68] During the period under study here, however, Mexicans represented the vast majority of undocumented immigrants, and the story of globalization in Mexico is a key part of that history. Over 85 percent of our immigrant sample in Routt and Rabun Counties was Mexican.

As large-scale pull and push factors generated more flows across the U.S.-Mexico border in the 1980s, a second characteristic of this flow took shape within a decade: its geographic dispersal. By the late-1990s demographers, sociologists, and population geographers looking at U.S. Census data began to notice these geographic patterns, which for many was unexpected.[69] Routt County, Colorado, and Rabun County, Georgia, like many other places with no recent history of immigrant arrivals, witnessed the arrival and steady growth of a Latine immigrant population in the mid-1990s and beyond.

This dispersal was unexpected because before the 1990s Latine immigrants overwhelmingly had settled in a handful of "gateway" cities—the global cities studied by Saskia Sassen and others. Most scholars of international labor migration theorized that migration processes worked to *reinforce* existing destinations and inhibit the emergence of new sites of settlement. According to this argument, transnational social networks facilitating labor migration and settlement worked to solidify the geography of cross-border labor flows because migrants tend to choose destinations where they know family or friends and can get support to find a job and find temporary housing. This perspective hinges on the concept of "cumulative causation," which Douglas Massey coined to refer to the idea that networks in and of themselves—once established—provided their own momentum (for continuing migration flows) even when the initial conditions that initiated the cross-border movement had ended.[70] The unexpected flourishing of new destinations in the 1990s challenged long-standing theories of network-driven transnational labor migration and inspired a range of scholars in the 1990s and beyond to turn their attention to investigating "new immigrant destinations."[71]

A key set of questions animating new destinations scholarship during this period concerned how and why Latine immigrant settlement patterns underwent such a rapid and unexpected dispersal. Some researchers contended that traditional gateway cities experienced a "saturation" point in the recruitment of immigrant workers, reasoning that job competition in gateway cities within immigrant-based labor markets inspired Latine immigrants to disperse to nontraditional locations. In the words of the main proponent of the saturation thesis, Ivan Light, "[S]elf-correction begins when economic deterioration in the most frequented destinations compels the migration network to reorganize its station list, sending newer migrants to previously low-ranking destinations while reducing the number selecting traditional destinations."[72] Light argues strenuously that cross-border labor migration is largely *supply driven*, and the migration network itself was the key causal factor in the deterioration of wages in traditional destinations, causing "the network" to seek out new areas of settlement.

Other researchers, in contrast, recognized the importance of shifting labor markets in traditional gateway cities, but contended that critical to this dispersal was the Immigration Reform and Control Act (IRCA) of 1986. Passed and signed under President Ronald Reagan with the intention of slowing unauthorized flows across the U.S.-Mexico border, the IRCA legalized 2.7 million undocumented people in the United States, providing them options to move to new places without fear of deportation. From this perspective, undocumented workers are limited in their job choice and seek to maintain safety among coethnics in large cities.

Once legalized through IRCA, Latino immigrants could respond to job market opportunities in new places, leading to dramatically shifting patterns in the 1990s and beyond.[73] The IRCA thesis has been questioned by those who point out that the majority of immigrants arriving at new destinations in the 1990s and 2000s were in fact undocumented, suggesting that mobility provided by legalization under IRCA was not the driving force behind this dispersal.[74]

A final group of new destination researchers argue that new patterns of labor demand represent the central factor inducing the dispersal of Latine immigrants during the 1990s and beyond. Kandel and Parrado point to new geographies of housing construction in the 1990s, an industry that became highly dependent on immigrant labor during that same decade.[75] Cities in the U.S. South, for example, grew rapidly in the 1990s, drawing immigrant construction workers to nontraditional urban destinations.[76] Beyond the construction industry, service sector enterprises in a range of cities across the United States turned toward immigrant labor in the 1990s. From Nashville, Tennessee, to Minneapolis, Minnesota, a range of cities saw their Latine immigrant populations rise steadily during this period as employers recruited them into the workforce. It is not surprising that as globalization and neoliberalism took hold and continued to deepen in the 1990s, low-wage service sector employment expanded across the country. Employers in this sector developed new strategies to expand profits in the context of highly competitive business environments, including the recruitment of a marginalized, pliable, and hardworking labor force produced by illegality, race, and poverty.

A subset of demand-side scholars focused on new patterns of *rural* settlement for low-wage Latine immigrants. A key driver of rural immigrant settlement in new destinations during this period was meat and poultry processing, which shifted en masse from urban to rural locations starting in the late 1980s. Some observers of the meat industry argued that this geographic shift was motivated by an interest in solidifying supply chains, to be more proximate to the animals upon which they rely, while others hypothesized that industrial meat producers sought to escape unionized labor and labor laws typical of larger cities.[77] While the shift was likely caused by multiple factors, the end result was that by the late 1980s meatpacking and poultry processing operations in the U.S. had begun to

move to isolated rural areas that were by and large suffering from population loss and economic decline. In addition to the immediate labor shortage this move often produced (moving to a place of population loss), the
recruitment of immigrant labor by meat processors was tied to the fact
that these new plants were built around a fully industrial and deskilled
mode of meat production that "required" a docile and disciplined yet low-
paid workforce. Immigrant labor tended to fit these needs better than
legal workers likely fluent in English, a reality in meatpacking and a range
of other labor-intensive industries with arduous working conditions.[78]
The end result was that the shifting geography and intensifying industrial
nature of meat production created a host of new immigrant destinations,
transforming demographic patterns throughout the rural Midwest and
South in the 1990s and beyond.

Finally, a number of scholars documented the emergence of new rural
destinations linked to new business strategies of existing industries rather
than the relocation of industry from urban to rural. From horse breeders
in Kentucky and carpet manufacturers in Dalton, Georgia, to tree planters
across the U.S. South and the Pacific Northwest, a range of existing rural
industries that had relied on a nonimmigrant workforce turned to recruiting an immigrant labor pool during this period.[79] Hernández-León and
Zúñiga, for example, examine the transformation of Dalton, Georgia, in
the 1990s as carpet manufacturers, long present in this self-described "Carpet Capital of the World," recruited immigrant workers at levels that rapidly transformed the demographics of the community.[80] The case of rural
gentrification explored in this book fits within this last group. Certainly
contractors, landscapers, and restaurateurs existed in these communities
prior to the 1990s, but a rapid increase in demand stimulated by gentrification in these service industries inspired employers to recruit immigrant
workers previously unfamiliar to them. The research explored here expands our understanding of the range of processes pulling immigrants to
new rural destinations across the United States, as most scholars continue
to assume rural industrial restructuring (e.g., meatpacking, carpet manufacturing, etc.) is the paradigmatic pull factor in rural new destinations.[81]

At the end of the day, the research presented in this book emphasizes
demand-side processes, perhaps given its empirical emphasis on immigrant-
receiving communities and the changes that recruited immigrants to these

locales. Yet it theorizes cross-border migration as produced by multiple factors that represent both demand- and supply-side dynamics, as well as factors that do not fit into this neat simplistic binary, like illegality itself.[82] These factors are simultaneously economic, political, and cultural. Unfortunately, key scholarship framing research on new immigrant destinations in the United States has tended to bracket many of these causal factors in a quest to create a parsimonious model—new flows are either demand or supply driven; IRCA caused the dispersal, or it did not. There is little room for nuanced understanding of the interplay between various actors, institutions, and scaled processes.

One key example of this narrow approach is Ivan Light's monograph *Deflecting Immigration*, which essentially uses the case of Los Angeles to argue that an oversaturated immigrant labor market and deteriorating housing conditions *caused by network-driven migration* "deflected" low-wage Latino immigrants and inspired these networks to seek out more favorable conditions for work and settlement.[83] For Light, demand in the globalizing Los Angeles economy may have initiated this labor flow into LA, but by the late 1980s the arrival of Latine immigrants in Los Angeles was largely supply driven, or in his logic driven by migrant networks themselves. According to his view, even though the demand for workers was declining, the network-driven arrival of low-wage immigrants, documented and undocumented, outstripped demand and drove down wages and housing conditions for Latine immigrants in Los Angeles. These networks then set their sights on more favorable places and conditions. For Light, the role of structural racism in the city is not part of the story of declining housing conditions, and his model does not consider labor demand and employer recruitment strategies in new destination communities. From this perspective, immigrant networks simply invade new labor markets sui generis.

The analysis presented in this book demonstrates that while migrant networks are critical to helping immigrants to journey across a militarized border, they also help employers create a highly disciplined and flexible labor force, expanding recruitment efforts numerically and dispersing them geographically. Rather than following Ivan Light, who sees the migrant network as a quasi-independent and apparently powerful actant determining the geography of labor migration across the U.S.-Mexican border, my analysis shows the power of recruitment, situating these flows squarely within labor market and entrepreneurial strategies rooted in the forces of neoliberal globalization. Neoliberal globalization is fundamental to understanding the demand for Latine immigrant workers over the past three decades in the United States, as well as their displacement from sending communities.

BORDERS: NATIONALISM, RACE, AND ILLEGALITY

While critical, the political economy of globalization examined in the previous section does not provide a complete explanation of changing labor markets or geographies of social reproduction in gentrifying rural places. These dynamics must also be situated in relation to the history and politics of race, illegality, and White nationalism in the United States. As Jodi Melamed argues, "procedures of racialization and capitalism are ultimately never separable from each other."[84] Political economy is always racialized and vice versa, and the very categories of "immigrant" and "undocumented" that underlie these labor market dynamics are produced through border policies and racialized narratives of the nation.

To ground this part of my discussion, I start with a vignette from an interview conducted in Rabun County, Georgia, in 2011. A place introduced in the previous chapter, it has been a site of rural gentrification since the mid- to late 1990s as wealthy people from Atlanta and Florida, in growing numbers, moved or bought second homes in the area to escape the summer heat and access the area's pristine lakes and forests. At the time of our interview Luis had worked in residential landscaping in Rabun County, Georgia, for over two decades, and he asserted that he was one of the first "Mexicans" to settle in the community.[85] Sitting down with him and his U.S.-born, wife Amanda (White, whose family goes back many generations in Rabun County), I asked if Luis experienced racial discrimination living in Rabun County and whether it was worse now or in the past. Without hesitation they responded that it was worse in his contemporary life than when he first arrived:

AMANDA: You didn't have that problem then [with racism] because of Frank. Everybody knows Frank.

LUIS: Ya, everybody know him.

AMANDA: And everybody knew Luis was his Mexican. [. . .] The old timers here, they just looked at him as Ronnie's Mexican. They don't look at him as that dam beaner.

LUIS: No, they're not really bad people here. In that time there was just not that many Mexicans but now I think . . . everybody has a Mexican who does their work, that is why everything has changed. But at *that* time everybody know who that Mexican is. [So they were not afraid.]

AMANDA: They knew where the Mexicans lived, knew where they worked, if there was trouble they were gone.

A subtext to their reply is that a body marked as "Mexican"—brown, perhaps speaking imperfect English—is presumed to be threatening, whether in the late 1980s or the 2010s. The presumed racial hierarchy in which White is the normalized, safe subject fully vested with rights is a taken-for-granted context for Luis's and Amanda's comments that locals were not afraid of Luis back in the early 1990s because everyone in town knew who he "belonged to." The language of slavery resounds, as Mexican bodies are threatening unless the ownership is clear, unless the presumably White observer knows the upstanding White person who is responsible for them. In contrast, by 2011, when Latine people (overwhelmingly foreign born) represented nearly 10 percent of the county's population, lines of "control" were usually unclear, increasing anxiety among many White locals, which was palpable to Luis and Amanda.

What had also changed in the interim was the extent to which the politics of the presumed illegality of brown bodies had shifted nationally. During the 1990s narratives about "illegal aliens" as invading and threatening intensified, and the devolution of immigration enforcement in the 2000s to local police changed the nature of daily life for undocumented residents.[86] When we circled back to the present day in the interview, Luis and Amanda bemoaned how many times—despite now being a legal resident—Luis had been pulled over by police for a broken rearview mirror, expired tags, and other minor infractions, which never happened when Amanda was driving the same car. Luis's actual legal status did not prevent him from being racialized as a threat in public—neither by the police who seemed to be targeting Latine drivers nor by a wider community that did not realize who he "belonged to" and so treated him like any other "Mexican," presumed to be "illegal."

There are many layers to this brief exchange with Amanda and Luis, many of which are addressed in chapters 3 and 4 when I examine in greater detail how hierarchies of race and illegality are woven into labor regimes and spaces of social reproduction in Rabun County, Georgia, and Routt County, Colorado. I use the exchange here to provide a visceral sense of how the demographic, economic, and social changes wrought by globalization and rural gentrification are intimately connected to the long durée of racism and the territorial politics of White nationalism. It is critical to sketch this history briefly.

The United States is a settler colonial nation, meaning that its territorial and ideological consolidation as a nation-state was predicated on systematic violence against and forced removal of indigenous peoples.[87] Ideas of manifest destiny and White superiority that undergirded these violent actions produced a seemingly empty frontier to be settled by White colonial subjects.[88] Although there are different variations of settler colonialism, what distinguishes it from conventional forms of colonialism is that colonizers arrived in larger numbers, in both sexes, for permanent settlement predicated on the erasure of indigenous peoples as well as "de facto or de jure political independence from the metropole."[89] A first pillar of White settler colonialism is thus the discursive production of an "empty territory" through the physical and cultural genocide of indigenous peoples, making way for the widespread settlement and territorial occupation by White colonists who feel they are *the* authentic and rightful occupiers of this territory—the founding of a new racially normalized White/Euro nation located in a non-European territory.

In relation to the arguments presented in this book, it is important to focus on a second pillar of stable colonial settler rule and its legacies. As noted by Daiva Stasiulis and Nira Yuval-Davis, the second pillar "has been to maintain unity within the dominant settler population, a cohesion which is never guaranteed" in light of ethnic, religious, and national differences.[90] In the context of the U.S., White settler colonialism initially directed at the native other was transformed and solidified through the institution of slavery. The plantation and slave-based economy required a firm and unrelenting Black-White binary that placed black bodies in

a category of subhuman in an effort to legitimize the glaring contradictions between democratic ideals and the institution of slavery. This racial
hierarchy was not about justifying removal, as with native peoples, but an
intimate and subordinate incorporation into the space of the economy, nation, and citizenship. Categories of race relegated enslaved peoples to the
realm of the subhuman, creating a "fatal coupling of power and difference"
in the words of Ruth Wilson Gilmore.[91]

The perceived unity and hegemony of the dominant settler population
was maintained not only through the Black-White binary undergirding
slavery, but as the nineteenth century wore on, through policies and narratives regarding immigrants. This was visible in debates over who was
viewed as threatening, dangerous, and uncivilized and thus who must
be kept out, made temporary, or deported.[92] The idea that the United
States is a "nation of immigrants" that welcomes "the tired, poor, huddled
masses" is a narrative that sits uncomfortably alongside the repeated and
multifaceted efforts to keep out or keep in, but in a subordinate position,
racialized groups who were or are considered as essentially, biologically
threatening or impossible to assimilate.[93]

The ideals of White nationalism rooted in settler colonial imaginaries ran up against the insatiable need for labor that only deepened by the
mid-nineteenth century as slavery in the U.S. was heading toward its formal demise and industrialization gained steam. Growing cities and industries in the East demanded labor, filled largely by Irish as well as Eastern
and Southern European immigrants following the Civil War.[94] The so-
called opening of the West, predicated on continuing the violent removal
of indigenous inhabitants as well as the acquisition of vast territories at
the close of the U.S.-Mexican War in 1848, created significant labor needs
in this sparsely populated region. Companies building railroads, running
mines, and expanding agricultural operations in the mid-nineteenth century recruited to California and other places growing numbers of Chinese,
Japanese, and Mexican workers.[95]

The economic drivers of immigration to the U.S. in this period operated
with and through racialized assumptions regarding belonging and citizenship, tensions reflected in cultural productions, news media, and various
legislative initiatives. Throughout much of this period, for example, the
Irish and other non-Protestants from Southern and Eastern Europe were

treated as racialized others who threatened the stability and cohesion of the nation even as they provided a key labor force, from mining to domestic service.[96] In the West Chinese immigrants, who were initially hailed as heroes during the Gold Rush, became racially vilified in media representations by the 1860s.[97] National legislation reflected the tension between economic need and racialized exclusion and anxiety. In 1864 Congress passed the Act to Encourage Immigration, which sought to facilitate contract labor from abroad through regulations regarding assisted passage (brokers paying passage and enforcing a contract for that worker to repay that debt).[98] This act was rescinded in 1868, and by the late 1870s race-based restrictionist efforts began in earnest, leading to the Chinese Exclusion Act of 1882, the country's first law excluding a group of immigrants solely on the basis of race or nationality.

The idea of the American nation, like all nationalisms, casts it as a timeless, primordial community even as this narrative erases complex historical processes that include shifting racialized boundaries of the national community in ways often tied directly to economic needs.[99] Immigrants from Northern, Eastern, and Southern Europe continued to pour into United States in the 1890s and beyond—escaping persecution and rural poverty and arriving as workers in burgeoning industrial cities such as Detroit, Pittsburgh, and Chicago. Despite their economic role, these immigrant groups were treated with alarm by the mainstream press and political leaders in the United States.[100] As argued by Mae Ngai, the country's first comprehensive immigration policy, the Johnson Act of 1924, sought to address this anxiety by using race-based, national quotas to favor Northern European Protestant immigrants and limit the numbers of Southern and Eastern European immigrants. A key goal of the act was to maintain the Protestant, Northern European racial "character" of the United States.[101] The quotas that discriminated between different European immigrants were predicated on excluding non-European immigrants entirely from the history of national origins of the United States, as the calculation of quota allotments in the Johnson Act excluded Mexicans, Asians, and anyone descended from "slave immigrants."[102] Thus, while the act explicitly reflected anxiety about the numbers of Southern and Eastern European immigrants to the United States, it relied on a distinction between White and non-White that functioned to solidify the boundaries of

White nationalism. This set the stage for Irish and other non-Protestant immigrants, initially treated as racialized figures that undermined the stability of "the nation," to be incorporated into the category of White.[103]

The long durée politics of race, immigration, and White nationalism in the United States is critical to understanding the contemporary politics of unauthorized immigration, but it is also important to understand the specific role of the Mexican and Latin American immigrant in this history, the policy and discursive evolution of the U.S.-Mexican border, and the ways Mexican immigrants in particular became conflated over time with the figure of the "illegal alien."

The territory ceded from Mexico at the end of the U.S.-Mexico war in 1848 was home to over one hundred thousand Mexican citizens.[104] The Treaty of Guadalupe, which ended the war, provided legal protections for Mexican citizens living in California, Arizona, and other parts of the ceded territories—including the right to become U.S. citizens. These protections on paper, however, did not stop the widespread usurpation of Mexican American property, de facto disenfranchisement, and violence.[105] A notable case of such violence was the lynching of twelve Mexican American shepherds in November 1873 in Corpus Christi, Texas, an act that purportedly was designed to pressure their employer into selling his land.[106]

Even as Mexican American communities struggled with racialized violence and retaining their property and lives as "alien citizens" in territory now formally belonging to the United States,[107] the same economic and territorial processes that recruited Chinese and Japanese immigrants to the West also pulled in Mexican workers from south of the new border. By the last two decades of the nineteenth century railroads and agricultural operators in the West were sending recruiters (*enganchadoras*—people who "hook" you into a job, often through deceit) deep into Mexico to bring back workers.[108] As Chinese and Japanese immigrants faced legal exclusions in the 1880s and beyond, employers became increasingly dependent on the seasonal migration of Mexican nationals, who were presumed to be inherently temporary (they could return home seasonally) and thus "safer." The view of Mexican migrant workers as "birds of passage" and nothing more permanent was so deeply normalized that the quota for Mexicans under the 1924 Johnson Act was *zero* despite the regular presence of tens of thousands of Mexican nationals laboring in industries across the West.[109] This moment, according to Mae Ngai, set the stage for the creation of the figure of the "illegal immigrant" and its conflation with Mexican bodies.

The Johnson Act also signaled the first efforts to establish a semblance of border control and enforcement on the U.S.-Mexico line. The act established the Border Patrol and authorized those agents to detain suspected "illegal" immigrants without a warrant. Nevertheless, as demonstrated by Joseph Nevins in his cogent history of the U.S.-Mexico border, the actual, substantive enforcement of the border was minimal through the 1980s.[110] This is not to downplay the effects of illegality and deportation in this period on immigrant lives; it is to argue that the border functioned for many decades as a porous gateway that could supply workers flexibly, as needed by a range of industries. Illegality and the threat of deportation functioned to discipline and control the workforce, paradoxically increasing the demand for these workers by making them more vulnerable, rather than fulfilling its nominal purpose of preventing the emergence of a transnational labor market between Mexico and the United States.

For the first third of the twentieth century, Mexican workers crossed the border with relative ease and were recruited into a range of rural economies particularly in California and the Southwest, from cotton picking in Texas to orchards in the Central Valley of California.[111] This labor migration was generally circular, comprised of male migrants, and seen by many of the White elite of these regions as normal and necessary despite being punctuated by violent expulsions, such as those conducted during the Great Depression.[112]

The fluctuating treatment of Mexican migrant workers in the twentieth century is perhaps best embodied by the Bracero Program, undertaken a few short years after the height of the expulsions of the 1930s. The Bracero Program was a guestworker treaty negotiated between the U.S. and Mexican governments, with the aim of alleviating U.S. worker shortages during World War II. Between 1942 and 1964 the program brought 4.5 million contract workers into agricultural and railroad work.[113] While the treaty included protections for Bracero workers demanded by the Mexican government, in terms of wages, working conditions, and prohibitions against using Braceros as strikebreakers, these rules were widely flouted. In many instances Braceros resisted this treatment, even engaging in open protest and strikes, but these efforts were unable to stop a steady decline in the wages paid to agricultural laborers Bracero and non-Bracero during this period.[114]

In terms of the broader history of labor migration between Mexico and the United States, the Bracero Program dramatically expanded the relationship between employers in the United States and workers in Mexico. These worker-employer relationships included the hundreds of thousands of Braceros as well as a parallel flow of undocumented migrants also stimulated by the program. After it formally ended in 1964, many Braceros continued their migration patterns and shifted from documented to undocumented workers.[115] At the end of the day the Bracero Program functioned to expand migrant social networks facilitating border crossings and the employment of migrants.

Broader immigration policy reforms during the 1960s continued to shape transnational labor markets across the Americas. In the same year that it passed the Voting Rights Act, in 1965, Congress passed the Immigration and Nationality Act. Also known as the Hart-Celler Act, this legislation abolished national, race-based quotas—increasingly seen as out of step with liberal democratic ideals—and replaced them with numerically even, formally nondiscriminatory quotas as well as preferential entry on the basis of family reunification and skills.[116] Hart-Celler represents a watershed moment in the history of U.S. immigration policy. Through its family reunification provisions, which operated outside of a country's or region's formal quota, the number of Asian and Latin American immigrants to the United States rose rapidly. Nevertheless, as Mai Ngai argues, it deepened the illegality of Mexican immigrants simply because of the cavernous disjuncture between the de facto level of labor market integration between the two countries and the de jure number of entrants allowed from Mexico as part of the "Western Hemisphere" quota.[117] U.S. employers in a range of sectors had relied on and recruited hundreds of thousands of Mexican workers for decades, but there was little option for these workers to arrive legally despite the gesture toward civil rights and formal equality in the Hart-Celler Act. The result was to solidify the "illegality" of long-standing and economically essential labor flows between Mexico and the United States.[118]

Labor mobility between Mexico and the United States, both authorized and unauthorized, continued to expand in the late 1970s and throughout the 1980s. This was due to the groundwork laid by the Bracero Program (by establishing extensive cross-border social networks between workers and employers), and as described in the previous section, the power of economic recruitment linked to neoliberal globalization. Yet these political economic and social processes were also shaped by the uneven capacity to enforce the border in this period.[119] Workers from Mexico could be recruited by employers with relative ease, and they could migrate for a few months or a few years and return home during this period without facing high risk or expense. For Mexican immigrants during the 1970s and into the mid-1980s, circular migration of mostly men was still the norm, with most transnational migrants crossing the U.S.-Mexico border regularly while maintaining their home base south of the border.

By the late 1980s and into the 1990s, labor flows across the border began to take on new characteristics. In short, more women were undertaking the journey across the border, migration became less circular and instead led to permanent settlement, and by the 1990s more of these migrants were settling beyond gateway cities into a range of new destinations.[120] The previous section touched on some of the economic drivers of these changes, including new kinds of labor demand in old and new destinations that were year-round and less conducive to circular migration. Here, I emphasize how policy changes shaped this phenomenon.

In 1986 President Ronald Reagan advocated for Congress to pass the IRCA. The act sought to slow undocumented migration through a massive legalization program that led to the legalization of 2.7 million people, mostly men, who were much more likely than women to have been in the U.S. long enough and with steady employment records to qualify.[121] The act also expanded funding for the Border Patrol (hardening the border) and instituted new verification requirements for employers, as well as employer sanctions for those knowingly hiring undocumented workers. The verification requirements and sanctions for employers are widely agreed to have failed, as they simply generated a market for false documents that employers were eager to look at and declare adequate.[122] While millions of workers gained access to legal status, the demand for undocumented workers continued to expand as particular sectors of employers, from farm operations in rural communities to janitorial services in large cities, continued to find it very profitable to hire people who due to their undocumented status worked hard and complained little.[123]

While there is widespread agreement that the IRCA failed to slow the number of undocumented immigrants being hired in the United States, there is evidence that it helped slow down *circular* migration of unauthorized immigrants, as greater border militarization increased the expense and risk of crossing the border, inspiring migrants to settle permanently in the U.S. Some of this move toward permanent settlement might be due to the informal family reunification processes that often occurred if a male legalized and gained enough stability to bring his family, even if those family members were undocumented (creating an expansion of mixed-status families). But it was the effort to step up border enforcement with the IRCA, a process that deepened under later initiatives such as Operation Gatekeeper in 1994 and Operation Rio Grande in 1997, that made the border more dangerous and expensive to cross. This encouraged undocumented workers, once successfully inside the United States, to stay long term if not permanently.[124] Billions have been spent on border patrol agents, physical barriers, and military-style surveillance equipment over the ensuing decades (e.g., the Border Patrol budget increased from $1.06 billion in 2000 to $3.8 billion in 2015),[125] but there was nevertheless a steady increase in the unauthorized population through much of the first decade of the twenty-first century, until the economic recession of 2008, when employer demand declined.[126] Increased border patrol and enforcement did have the effect of pushing migrants onto more remote entry points, leading to a dramatic increase in migrant deaths and the expansion of smuggling networks, ones increasingly controlled by sophisticated criminal networks often linked to narcotrafficking and violence along the border and along migration routes.[127]

If the 2000s witnessed border militarization reaching new heights, at great expense and with little demonstrated efficacy, it also was the decade during which *interior* border enforcement and the legal and institutional basis for large-scale deportation took hold. This led to historically unprecedented levels of deportation, with more people being deported between 2000 and 2010 than had been deported in the entire history of the country.[128] Instead of unauthorized migration being policed mostly at or near the physical border, the post-9/11 period saw the emergence of a large-scale deportation regime (gaining particular steam in 2005 and beyond) that relied on local and state police working collaboratively with ICE to reach into communities and longtime settled families living far from the border. This effort relied on new legal and institutional mechanisms to criminalize and more easily deport undocumented immigrants, whether they had committed a crime or not.[129]

Many of the legal mechanisms for deportation in the 2000s were laid down in the 1996 Illegal Immigration Reform and Immigrant Responsibility Act (IIRIRA). Yet it was only after 9/11 that these mechanisms began to be used, efforts wrapped in the language of national security and counterterrorism (making them seem "necessary"). Critical to the deportation regime was the devolution of federal authority to enforce immigration statutes to subfederal policing agencies through programs such as 287G (which was part of IIRIRA but not used as such until 2006) and the Secure Communities Program in 2008. These programs granted new authority to local police officers to check immigration status and send people to ICE for likely deportation. As Mathew Coleman writes, "[T]he criminalization of immigration law, as well as the enrollment of proxy immigration officers at sub-state scales, constitute a new localized or rescaled geopolitics of immigration policing."[130] This convergence of factors led to an unprecedented level of "interior" deportations happening in the 2000s and 2010s, ones less likely to be rooted in large-scale raids but instead catching people through traffic stops and other real or perceived infractions. In this system a great deal is left to the discretion of the police officer and local policing agencies, with some cities and localities resisting this function and others embracing it.[131]

It is this painful history and geography of race, immigration, and nationalism in the United States that informs my use of the term *illegality* in this book. Drawing on the work of Nicholas De Genova, illegality allows me to conceptualize the confluence of geopolitical, racial, and economic processes that construct specific and racially marked bodies as threatening and outside of the law.[132] As a number of scholars have contended, practices and narratives normalizing illegality fundamentally shape the labor market and recruitment processes that generate cross-border labor flows between Mexico and the U.S.[133] Residents who are assumed to be illegal are much less able to assert their belonging apart from their "proper" role as laboring bodies. As articulated by De Genova in his research with Mexican migrants in Chicago: "Migrant 'illegality' proves to be a decisive feature of the distinctive racialization of Mexicans in the United States. . . .

'[I]llegality' provides an apparatus for producing and sustaining the vulnerability and tractability of Mexican migrants as labor. In this way, migrant 'illegality' is a spatialized social condition that becomes inseparable from the particular ways that migrant workers from Mexico are racialized as 'illegal aliens' within the United States, and thus as 'Mexican' in relation to 'American'-ness."[134]

Inspired by De Genova and others, this book examines how racialized narratives of illegality constitute specific, place-based labor markets catering to the affluent in high-amenity rural areas. Looking to feminist theorists, I situate these labor regimes within geographies of social reproduction to demonstrate how employer recruitment and dependence on a racialized and "illegal" workforce is sutured to social, civic, and racialized exclusions in the context of daily life. While understanding the matrix of racialized labor regimes and social reproduction is central, the book also reveals the frictions that emerge as these are enacted, negotiated, and contested on a daily basis.

In 2018 President Trump defended his family separation policy as humane, even as nearly five hundred children remain separated from their parents.[135] That situation, coupled with campaign and presidential speeches unabashedly marking Latine immigrants as a profound national security threat, shows the extent to which virulent anti-immigrant and racially charged rhetoric has taken center stage in U.S. immigration policies and politics. While they have taken alarming turns, Trump's rhetoric and policies are rooted in the long history of White nationalism in the United States, a history saturated in violence and an array of legal, institutional, and cultural mechanisms of exclusion and segregation. Immigrants have occupied a complex and contradictory role in forms of U.S. nationalism— discursively invoked in the narrative of the nation ("we are a nation of immigrants") and critical to the U.S. economy even as immigration policy has been central to the production and reification of racial hierarchy and exclusion. It is these tensions—between economic transformation and social/civic/racialized exclusion—that frame the daily lives of Luis, Amanda, and other residents of Rabun and Routt Counties explored over the course of this book.

2 Methods and Case Studies

> Researchers need to understand the different cultural contexts influencing the diverse range of cultural schemas and norms of their immigrant participants. Indeed, generalization of research without comprehending the international, historical, social, political and cultural context of these communities could be considered a violation of the Belmont principle of respect for persons.
>
> —Hernández et al. (2013, 43)

> Feminists have deepened their reflections on issues of empathy, rapport, and reciprocity in interview situations, with a recent focus on how to navigate differences of social positioning. . . . Ongoing reflections on the complexities of 'otherness' have highlighted the increasing set of challenges that face researchers as they attempt to know others who are different from themselves across multiple axes of identities and experiences.
>
> —Doucet and Mauthner (2008, 334)

These quotations provide an opening to discuss the methodological principles, strategies, and ethics that underlie the analysis and findings explored in this book. The words of Hernández and colleagues are situated within migration studies and critical race scholarship, while Doucet and Mauthner speak primarily to feminist methodologies and theories.[1] Despite their distinct substantive foci, both literatures begin from a similar epistemological position, one that views research as (1) a socially embedded process shaped by histories and geographies of social power and (2) producing situated rather than quantitatively generalizable knowledge.[2] These presumptions have profound implications for methodological design and practice, in that trust, mutual respect, and dialogue between researcher and research participants are paramount for the production of rigorous and ethical knowledge.

The previous chapter outlined four principles that I argue should guide any scholar of rural gentrification in the U.S. context, particularly those who notice the presence of an immigrant labor force in the community or communities where they are working. These principles have key conceptual dimensions, such as rejecting implicit assumptions of whiteness in rural spaces and analyzing closely how racial hierarchy and its intersection with illegality (in the U.S. context) might be woven into the economic and social landscapes of high-amenity rural areas. Yet it is important to signal that these principles also have methodological implications. Understanding the intersections between race and illegality, or labor dynamics and social reproduction, requires fine-grained qualitative data collection across the kinds of hierarchies and social differences that remain an abiding concern for feminist researchers and migration scholars alike.

The first goal of this chapter is to outline the methodological approach and concrete data collection practices underlying the findings explored over the course of this book, practices shaped by the critical epistemologies just introduced. The second objective is to introduce the two case study sites, Rabun County, Georgia, and Routt County, Colorado, examining their unique histories of gentrification. I illustrate how both communities have been transformed by rapid demographic and economic change related to amenity in-migration, focusing in particular on shifting place imaginaries and dynamics of belonging between self-identified locals and amenity migrants, overwhelmingly White in both Colorado and Georgia. The case study introductions provide a place-based grounding of geographical differences between the two sites even as subsequent chapters undertake comparative inquiry that finds commonalities across them.

METHODS AND METHODOLOGY

Much of the data underlying the analysis and claims presented in this book were collected under the aegis of a research project developed with Peter

Nelson of Middlebury College.[3] We developed the hypothesis of linked migration and sought to test that core hypothesis through a mixed-method research project that was eventually funded by the National Science Foundation. Our project used quantitative data analysis and mapping to explore the spatial overlap of domestic amenity migration and the arrival of Latine populations in high-amenity rural areas nationally.[4] From that quantitative mapping we selected the two case study sites in Georgia and Colorado for qualitative fieldwork. We sought to sample regional variation in these dynamics, given that most scholarship on amenity migration and rural gentrification in the United States has often presumed it to be a phenomenon of the West.[5]

Our project used interviews, observations, and the collection of primary textual data in Georgia and Colorado to assess (1) whether employers in gentrification-linked sectors were recruiting Latine workers, (2) how the arrival of Latine immigrant workers impacted the local workforce, and (3) the extent to which race and ethnicity were shaping new divisions of labor locally. The National Science Foundation funding supported me and two University of Oregon research assistants, Laurie Trautman and Graciela "Meche" Lu, to be in the field for fourteen weeks in 2010 and 2011; Peter spent six weeks in the field during these summers, a shorter time related to his focus on more accessible employers and gentrifiers. For more detail on the methodological design and evolution of this joint NSF project, please see the appendix.

Both Peter Nelson and I are economically and racially privileged subjects in relation to most of the participants of this research, perhaps excluding many of the gentrifiers, who were overwhelmingly White and wealthy. These positionalities, combined with our own particular research interests, shaped how we formulated our research questions, the kind of data we collected (by shaping how our participants read and interacted with us during interviews, etc.), and how we interpreted our findings. What feminist and other critical methodological approaches recognize in this context is that there is no space through which to conduct research that is not shaped by these "blinders," and thus the process of collecting and interpreting data is always partial and situated.[6] University of Oregon graduate research assistants were positioned differently, with Laurie Trautman identifying as White and Meche Lu as Latina.

The Oregon research team spent more time in the field because we were recruiting and conducting interviews with immigrant residents, in addition to all other groups sampled in the project. We were aware that these efforts needed additional time due to the more vulnerable social and legal position of immigrant participants. My choice to spend a longer time in the field was also rooted in the epistemological commitments outlined above: I wanted to take more time to develop relationships with participants and immerse myself as much as feasible in these two communities. Toward that end, I returned for additional solo fieldwork in 2012 and 2015 after the original project's timeline had ended.

Spending longer periods of time in the field—and visits over several years—allowed for repeated interactions and conversations, both formal and informal. It allowed me to interview all groups relevant to the project: employers, gentrifiers, local officials, "locals," and immigrant newcomers. Most importantly, the longer time frame provided space to enact more accountable and dialogic research encouraged by feminist methodologies. This is not to claim that power differentials were erased or that those methodological practices provided transparent understandings of immigrant and/or nonimmigrant experiences. Instead, it is to point out that the richness of the data underlying the arguments presented over the course of this book would not have been possible without linguistic and intercultural skills critical to working ethically with immigrant participants. Nor would these findings have been possible without the time to enact dialogic methodologies rooted in decentering the control of the researcher in the production of data. A dialogic and responsive approach allowed me to go beyond the scope of our original research questions. It was in these spaces of dialogue that new ways of thinking about rural gentrification, immigrant labor regimes, and dynamics of social reproduction emerged, ones not anticipated by the original project.

My interview and fieldwork strategies, and those I cultivated with Oregon graduate research assistants Laurie Trautman and Meche Lu, recognize that it is not possible to *erase* the power differentials between the researcher(s) and research participants. Nevertheless, we can mitigate these differences using specific methodological strategies (e.g., dialogic interview techniques, practicing ongoing reflexivity). These strategies were particularly relevant for our interactions with low-wage Latine immigrant residents and working-class White residents. When recruiting and developing rapport with Latine immigrants, my fluency in Spanish was critical, and both Laurie Trautman and Meche Lu speak Spanish, Meche as her native language. Beyond linguistic skills, we all had cultural experience and historical knowledge of Mexico and Latin America that gave us the ability to engage more effectively and ethically in rapport building and developing effective interview strategies. Interviews by the Oregon team in both seasons were mostly conducted by me alone, or by me with the graduate research assistant. Laurie Trautman and Meche Lu conducted a small number of interviews without me (19 out of the 163 completed by the Oregon research team).

Recruiting immigrant participants for this research happened differently in Colorado than in Georgia, but there were similarities. The biggest challenge in Georgia was an absence of any advocacy or support groups for immigrant residents—perhaps a key characteristic of many rural places where immigrants are living and working compared to urban destinations. We could not recruit through advocacy groups, and we felt it was unethical to recruit respondents through employers, as potential participants might feel coerced into agreeing to the interview and might not be forthright if they thought we were allied with their employer.[7] In Georgia, Laurie Trautman and I first reached out to a key informant, a local businessperson, who introduced us to a local White woman who provided weekly English classes for free to immigrants (this was an example of individual volunteerism in support of immigrants but was not part of a formal group, nor was it very stable in organizational terms). She allowed us to attend one of the sessions and introduce ourselves. We also introduced ourselves and the project to the owner of the local Mexican grocery store where tortillas and salsa were sold and money could be sent internationally. Equally important was the fact that even in spaces such as the laundromat, which as explored in chapter 3 functioned as the de facto "day labor site," we could approach folks as strangers and they often responded with interest about what we were doing. At the laundromat people often had time to talk, waiting for laundry or waiting to be hired by someone passing through the site.

I believe the immediate spark of *confianza*/trust with potential immigrant participants lay in the fact that we were speaking Spanish fluently.

In Georgia few White people speak fluent Spanish, not to mention using the colloquial terms typical in rural Latin America. Many immigrant residents whom we approached seemed pleasantly surprised. Typically, they asked me where I learned Spanish, giving me the opportunity to tell them of my time living in Michoacán, Mexico. If they were from Michoacán we would start talking about it lovingly; if they were Mexican but from another state we would launch into talking about the differences between their home community and Michoacán. And if they were Central or South American we would talk about the particularities of their country compared to Mexico. When we described our interest in understanding people's experiences in the United States, promising anonymity and explaining our goal as researchers, potential participants were often interested to share their stories.

In Colorado we did recruit some of our immigrant participants through and with the help of advocacy organizations, particularly the group Comunidad Integrada/Integrated Community, a nongovernmental organization founded in Steamboat to support immigrant residents. We also practiced in Steamboat random introduction in spaces such as parks, laundromats, and social gatherings, which worked quite effectively if people had time to do the interview at some point down the line. We employed snowball sampling from these initial contacts in both places, with people often providing names and contact info of other people they knew in town. We usually interviewed people in their homes, but occasionally in parks or other public spaces where we could nevertheless have a private conversation (in Steamboat the public library was a great spot, with small private rooms we could use).

It turned out that the most difficult group to recruit for this research was White working-class men, particularly in Georgia. They were frequently more reluctant to speak with us than undocumented Latine immigrants. In the first weeks of the project we were able to connect with a number of women who were self-identified "locals" and working class; they were interested in speaking with us, and we gained insight from their stories and experiences. We thought it a good strategy to snowball recruit men through these women, since many had brothers, cousins, and partners who were working class. This strategy was ultimately the most effective one for interviewing White working-class men who identified as local—but it was still harder than we expected. As one of our respondents, Virginia, said when I asked if she thought her cousin would want to talk to me, "Well . . . he won't hardly talk to me [about anything personal], so why would he talk to you?"

Most employers in gentrification-linked sectors, such as construction, landscaping, restaurant work, and home maintenance, were accessed fairly easily given that we could reach out to them through their business contact information. We also reached out to business associations and chambers of commerce, which allowed us to speak to business leaders and snowball through them to others in the industry. The vast majority were interested in speaking with us, and most were surprisingly open about their hiring practices and business challenges/strategies during the gentrification boom and beyond. We did not ask these respondents specifically about whether they hired undocumented people, just about the characteristics of their labor force and challenges over time. Frequently, the status of their workers was implied in how they discussed their labor challenges and their business history—whether they mentioned that they loaned out the company car to one of their workers to prevent them from being deported or they talked about reassuring their workers (that they should not leave town) after anti-immigrant legislation passed in Georgia in 2011. Roughly a third of our interviews with employers included quite open discussions of their efforts to hire undocumented people—they said it up front and without an apparent second thought. Perhaps they decided to trust in our promise of anonymity and/or they might have felt comfortable doing so because it was a normalized practice in their industry. Employers in this last group usually complained about the lack of legal means for their workers to be in the United States.

Between 2011 and 2012 Laurie Trautman, Meche Lu, and I transcribed and organized 163 interviews, fieldnotes, and primary textual documents collected over the first two summers of field research. Primary texts included policy documents and local publications, such as Rabun County's Comprehensive Development Plan, and newspaper articles from 1990 to 2010 published in the *Steamboat Pilot* or the *Clayton Tribune* (local newspapers). We coded these data in Atlas.ti, applying codes to the data based on our research questions as well as developing unanticipated codes "en vivo" that were inspired by patterns that emerged in the data. I checked coding by research assistants, and we maintained a regular dialogue about the evolving nature of the analysis, the meaning and boundaries of specific codes, and our theoretical engagements. After I returned to conduct additional fieldwork in 2012 and 2015, I added 32 interviews to those collected as part of the NSF project, including interviews with business owners in gentrification-linked sectors, immigrant residents, local civic leaders, and gentrifiers. I coded this last group of interviews with the same codes from the original project, extending the analysis. The total of interviews conducted by me or by one of my research assistants between 2010 and 2015 was 195, 82 with Latine immigrant participants and 113 with White participants. As mentioned in the introduction, all names associated with interview data in this book are pseudonyms, and every effort has been made to protect the anonymity of participants.

What emerged from the triangulation of interview, observational, and textual data collected over that time was a fine-grained portrait of how gentrification as an economic, but also a fundamentally social and political process, expanded in both Rabun County, Georgia, and Routt County, Colorado. It was possible to trace how gentrifiers decided to move part- or full-time to places they considered beautiful sites of rest and recreation, how longtime locals experienced the demographic and sociocultural changes associated with gentrification, why and how low-wage immigrant workers were recruited to these areas by employers, and why immigrants chose these places and made them a permanent home. Employers frequently described their recruitment of Latine workers as a process of "stumbling" upon a new workforce initially as a stopgap measure to address labor shortages during the gentrification boom. They shared how these workers became essential over time, and how immigrant workers transformed their business. These narratives demonstrate how the presence of immigrant workers and residents transformed spaces of social reproduction across class, race, and legality in these high-amenity rural communities.

CASE STUDY: ROUTT COUNTY, COLORADO

A 2009 local print real estate ad for Marabou Ranch outside of the town of Steamboat Springs shows a picture of an older, White couple sitting on a log cabin porch, the man with a fishing pole in his hand and the woman offering him a cup of coffee. Next to the image one can find the following text: "It's time to do something different. Ever since Cynthia was a child she wanted to live on a ranch. She did not want the hassles and responsibilities of owning and running a ranch. And that is the magic of Marabou. It is all taken care of for you."[8] At Marabou you do not buy a home, but a "homestead" that is part of a 1,717-acre master planned community, with homes spaced sufficiently so that you do not often see your neighbor's house—providing that sense of being on the frontier. The ranch continues to raise cattle, but homesteaders are assured they are not required to participate in the cattle operation. Prices for these homesteads in 2009 started at $2.9 million.

Steamboat Springs is situated along the Yampa River in northwestern Colorado, at 6,867 feet in elevation, with a large ski resort looming over downtown a short two miles away. The name *Yampa* is said to derive from the yampah flower, whose carrot-like roots have formed part of Native American foodways across the West, including the diet of the Utes, whose summer hunting grounds traversed this territory. The Marabou Ranch ad just quoted was found in the *Yampa Valley Quarterly*, a full-color publication put out by the Yampa Valley Sustainability Council, founded in 2006 to promote sustainable development. The organization's promotion of sustainability was intertwined with justifications for further land parcelization and development catering to a very wealthy clientele, as reflected in the Marabou ad. The same issue, summer/fall of 2009, titled "Green Living," contained articles that reviewed five local "green" builders, touted the importance of using an "eco-broker" to purchase real estate, and guided readers on how to find "eco-furnishing options." Vocabularies of sustainability, ideals of eco-consumption, and the commodification of Old West motifs have been deeply imbricated into the sale of real estate and processes of gentrification in Steamboat.

The transformation of Steamboat and Routt County from a ranching economy and identity in the 1950s to a retreat for the wealthy in recent decades can be traced to the installation of the first ski lift in 1960 and subsequent waves of amenity migrants, distinct in their origins and impacts. Map 1 shows census population data over this period. Note the jump in population between the 1970 and 1980 censuses, and again from 1990 to 2000.

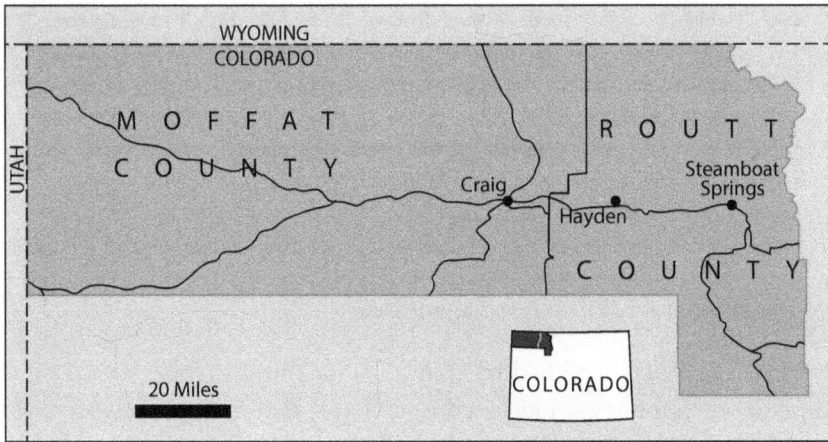

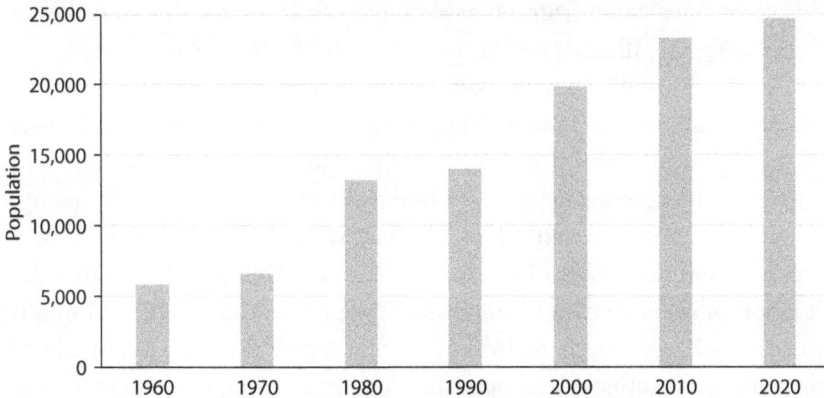

Map 1. (*top*) Map showing Routt County in Colorado. Cartographer: Graciela Lu. (*bottom*) Population data from the U.S. Census, 1960–2020.

The first amenity migrants in the late 1960s–1970s, often described as "ski bums," were overwhelmingly young, White, and usually not particularly wealthy, and most worked seasonal jobs related to skiing in the winter and other outdoor activities in the summer. They left town during the "mud season" (spring and fall) when seasonal jobs dried up. One of our participants from this early wave, Rachel, described her arrival from California as linked to a 1975 visit to a friend from college who lived in Steamboat:

I just decided I needed a new place to live and I LOVED it. I loved it here, I loved the people immediately, everyone was so friendly, everyone was so happy, and there was no airs about, people were just real, genuine people, and I just loved it immediately. [. . .] So I moved and interesting thing back then, things were a lot different, it was much more laid back in Steamboat. I lived in a tree house, a tepee, cabins where you had to bring your own water, but we loved it. I was 24, it didn't matter, we spent the day chopping wood or hauling water or doing whatever, heating the tree house and it was great, it was fun. Very cheap to live here, [my] place was how much? [looks over at her husband]. . . . It was $300/year.

Rachel, like others who had lived in town for thirty to forty years at the time of our interviews, identified as a "local" and differentiated herself emphatically from later and wealthier waves of gentrifiers. Members of this early wave came from an assortment of places, but high on the list were California, Illinois, and various states in the Northeast.

The discourse of "being a local" (quite distinct from one's actual birthplace) was ubiquitous in how White people in Steamboat described themselves and others, and it is a narrative that must be situated in the long dureé of White settler histories. White residents of Steamboat frequently discussed themselves and others in relation to who was a local and who was not, tied not only to time in the area but often in relation to a calculation of one's proximity to nature (I return to that theme below). In any case, whatever one's definition of what makes one an authentic local, claiming this status sidestepped the history of indigenous peoples violently displaced from this landscape so that it could become an "empty frontier" for White settlers. In the frequent debates about place and belonging in this community, the history of the Yampatika Ute and Arapahoe peoples is hardly mentioned, an omission built on the assumption of an empty landscape for which Euro-American belonging is taken for granted. And as I will return to below, Latine residents are also largely missing in discourses of who qualifies as a local.

Ben, an amenity migrant who arrived in 1994 and owned a retail shop downtown, responded in this way when I asked him who was a local:

What is being a local? Maybe the guy who showed up here in 1970 living out in his van and all he wanted to do is ski, you know.

Then he became the contractor who all of the sudden got successful building these custom homes twenty years later. [And his customers came for] the same reason he was attracted to come here: for the outdoors and the skiing and the small town environment and this valley is just gorgeous. So you now got people who can afford to come here at a different level compared to how the local got his foot in the door.

Ben did not identify the remaining ranching families as the true locals, but the first wave of amenity migrants. Ben's framing about who qualifies as a local was reflected in numerous interviews: it is tied not to birthplace but usually to length of time in the area—a marker more available to someone who arrived in 1975 than in 1994. His comments also illustrate what drew most newcomers in either wave to Steamboat: outdoor amenities, connection to nature, and imaginaries of small town life.

If the early wave of amenity-driven newcomers in the 1970s and 1980s often started their lives in Steamboat building alternative lifestyles in cabins without running water, the socioeconomic status and character of amenity in-migrants began to shift by the 1990s. Not only did the numbers of people moving year-round or part time to Steamboat grow rapidly during this decade, but these newcomers were often quite wealthy, moving from globally integrating cities including Denver, Los Angeles, Chicago, Houston, and New York. Unlike the back-to-the-land types of the 1970s, these newcomers were able to pay top dollar for homes and condos in "their" rural paradise. This created new incentives for developers and new opportunities for a range of businesses, even as it generated significant pressure on the cost of living and the existing sense of place and community. Housing prices in Steamboat climbed steadily through the 1990s and beyond, save for a brief period during the Great Recession in 2008.[9] Working and middle-class locals were squeezed out of housing and over time had difficulty making ends meet, even with multiple jobs. Local political struggles erupted over development, affordable housing, and open space, with a coalition coming together in 1995 to defeat the proposal for a second ski area proposed to be built in the valley.[10]

Wealthier gentrifiers in this post-1990 wave were often driven by the same desires as the postcollege ski bums in the 1970s: outdoor amenities, connection to nature, the Old West, and small town life. But it became a lifestyle and place imaginary undergirded by new levels of capital accumulation and commodification compared to the earlier arrivals. Images and desires for "connection to nature" "authenticity," and "small town" life became ubiquitous in advertising in real estate and services catering to the wealthy, such as the Marabou ad cited in the opening of this section.

Through this process, questions of class rather than merely amount of time in the area shaped the idea of who qualified as a local in Steamboat. A conversation with Logan, a thirty-six-year-old male who at the time of our interview in 2011 had lived in Steamboat for thirteen years, illustrates the embodied dimensions of "being a local" and its complex relationship to class. Logan earned his living maintaining irrigation systems and other landscape infrastructure on private homes and residential properties in Steamboat. He was employed in those sectors that had expanded greatly in the context of the gentrification boom, and he worked fifty to sixty hours per week. With his employed spouse he was able to purchase a house in Oak Creek, a small town forty-five minutes from Steamboat—a common strategy for those who could not afford Steamboat proper. Logan identified as a "local" because of the amount of time he had lived in the area, *and* because he considered himself to have a more authentic connection to place than wealthier newcomers who may have arrived around the same time. When I asked him about the relationship between "locals' and wealthy newcomers, Logan said:

> We feel bad for them [the rich people] . . . because they want to come in and buy this place, they want to go on this fishing trip and they are going to pay for it. And someone's going to show 'em a fake experience, walk you down right there and we're going to tie your fly and put you in the right spot, and all you gotta do is plunk it in the water. [. . .] We put up with them because that is where all of our money comes from. [. . .] I separate myself from them because, how do I say it, I don't go to the same places. You will not find me walking on Fish Creek Falls trail on the 4th of July. I know where to go and how to avoid those folks. [. . .]
>
> We pay [for this place] in the way of work and struggle and they pay in the way of money—it is two separate ways to an end I guess. Last week I spent time on the river catching fish all day and saw a bald eagle hunting. You put your time in to have that kind of experience, and you know that not everything is for sale.

Notions of "being a local" are refracted through a sense of connection to nature, both of which carry social currency evident across many interviews with White residents of Steamboat. It is a narrative that is also shaped profoundly by class, as it was common to hear working-class White residents, from maintenance workers like Logan to waitresses and other service workers, frame their identity as a "local" in relation to the sacrifices they made (multiple jobs, long hours, living far out of town) while having a more authentic connection to nature and place. This is reflected in Logan's knowledge of where and how to fly fish on his own, compared to his wealthy clients, and his constant reference to "we" to refer to people who worked for wages. Logan seemed to be in competition with the wealthy White people for this claim to authenticity.

Claiming status as a local invokes a politics of authenticity undergirded by settler colonial imaginaries: local media representations and many day-to-day invocations of "who is a local" presume whiteness as a fundamental marker of "authentic" connection to place. The 2009 "Special Locals Issue" of *Steamboat Magazine* (see figure 1) features short biographies and images of twenty residents who embody the "Steamboat Spirit." These faces are all White and tend to highlight the creative and outdoor spirit associated with the paradise that is Steamboat—from an image of a local artist in her studio to an activist fighting to conserve open space in Routt County. All the people the magazine chose to exemplify as locals embodying the Steamboat spirit are White, show no signs of economic insecurity, and are involved in a range of artistic and upper-class progressive politics.

Discourses regarding who is a "local" tap into a complex and racialized politics of authentic belonging and ownership over place and environment. This is not without its tensions, as this constant striving for a sense of authenticity wrapped up in "being a local" is crosscut by economic inequalities. Like Logan, many of the White working-class people we interviewed claimed to be *real* locals due to their economic struggles. Most arrived before the wave of very wealthy amenity migrants that exploded by the early 2000s. But even if they have developed a foothold in terms of work and housing, they often continue to struggle because gentrification has priced them out of the housing market—akin to urban gentrification. Most middle-class professionals, from teachers to accountants, work multiple jobs, and they often live in nearby communities with slightly lower housing prices, such as Oak Creek or Hayden.

Perhaps most tellingly, Latine residents did not make an appearance in the narratives of who counted a local among our White participants. As

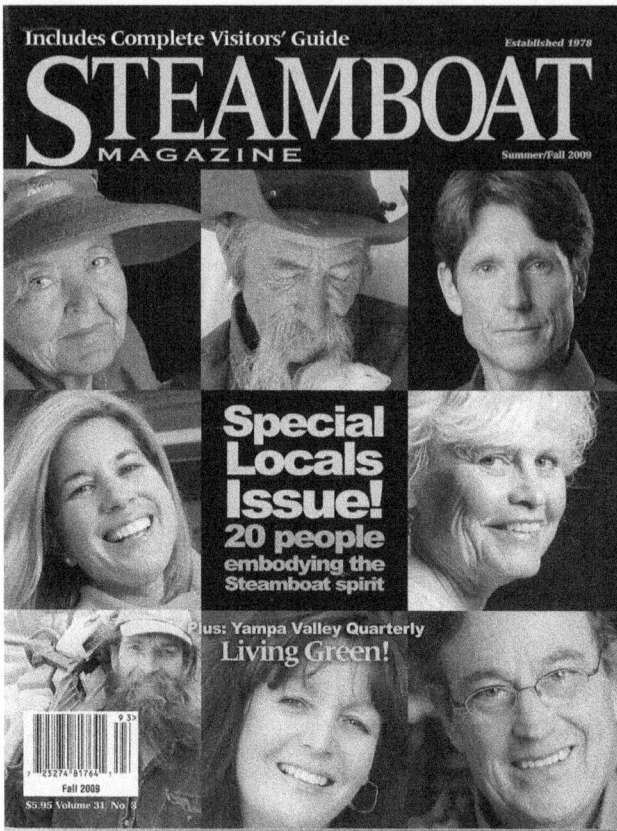

Figure 1. Cover of *Steamboat Magazine*, Summer/Fall 2009.
Reproduced with permission.

I reviewed the coding of the data in Atlas.ti, I pulled up a report for all interview quotes, fieldnotes and primary textual sources (such as real estate
ads) coded "being a local." This code was largely an "en vivo" code, meaning in interviews it was used to indicate when people explicitly brought up
the notion of being a local or if they commented on who qualifies as a local
more generally. In reviewing the data linked to this code I noticed that it
was exclusively connected to White respondents or in the case of media
representations, to images of White people in Steamboat/Routt County,
which tells me that it was not one Latine residents commonly used, no
matter how long they lived in the community.

Interestingly, the physical circulation of *Steamboat Magazine* has relied on the invisible labor of Latina immigrant residents. At the time of our research in 2011, the magazine hosted a monthly breakfast for hundreds of hotel maids—overwhelmingly Latina—to persuade them to take a stack of magazines with them as they left the breakfast and distribute those magazines while cleaning hotel rooms. The magazine gave out prizes and gifts to cement their loyalty and distribution services. Thus, much like the new homes and condos advertised in the magazine—built by immigrant workers—the distribution of these images and narratives of whiteness and place relied on Latina labor as well.

CASE STUDY: RABUN COUNTY, GEORGIA

> Rabun County offers a wonderful mix of residen[ces], from
> multi-million dollar dream homes, affordable family
> residences, and "starte[r] homes," to an assortment of rental
> apartments/properties and superior retirement facilities.
> Here you will discover the best of community living: safe
> neighborhoods, welcoming citizens, immaculate sidewalks,
> mountain views and a wide variety of amenities for every
> lifestyle. Whether you seek a new executive home with ample
> room for entertaining or a log cabin in the woods, you will
> find it in Rabun County.
> —Rabun County Chamber of Commerce (2010, 38)

This text is from an article written by the Rabun County Chamber of Commerce in its 2010 *Newcomers Guide*, a publication aimed primarily at encouraging people to choose Rabun County as a permanent or part-time home. It is filled with real estate and mortgage broker ads, as well as articles marketing Rabun as an ideal place to live, whether you want a "charming lake house" or a "mountain retreat." The guide deploys somewhat similar place marketing strategies as those found in Routt County, Colorado, highlighting natural wonders, amenities, and small-town life for would-be newcomers. Unsurprisingly, narratives circulating in this northern Georgia county are less oriented toward ideas of wilderness and adventure outdoor activities, typical of place imaginaries in the U.S. West like Steamboat. Instead they emphasize living in a place where you can experience rurality from a bygone era, connect with "safe" small town life, play golf, or swim in a lake. In 2010 a regional magazine, *Georgia Mountain Laurel*, advertised Harry Norman real estate listings on Lake Burton, one of the most sought-after locations in Rabun County, ranging from $1.7 to $7.8 million.[11] In the 1970s Rabun's economy was rooted in textile manufacturing and agriculture; today it is amenity properties and consumption lifestyles.

Located at the southern end of Appalachia and the northeast corner of Georgia, Rabun County—like Routt County, Colorado—has experienced distinct waves of amenity in-migration, with the most rapid growth happening during the 1990s and afterward (see map 2 and census data). The origins of these amenity flows can be traced to the early decades of the twentieth century, when Georgia Power Company, seeking to provide electricity to Atlanta, purchased 5.6 percent of the county's land area in order to built hydroelectric dams on the Tallulah River.[12] Residents were compelled to sell their land and/or leave their homes as Georgia Power took over and flooded valleys, obliterating the county's largest town at the time, Burton. Out of this disaster for many in the community came three large reservoirs, which over time attracted vacationers who sought refuge in north Georgia's cooler summer temperatures. As historian Lisa M. Russell writes of the 1910s, "The ten miles of deep valley along the Tallulah River was a perfect setting for this hydropower reservoir [Lake Burton], but something else was created: a private getaway for many Georgians."[13] Within decades of this extensive dam-building project, White Atlantans began to purchase rights to build summer cottages on the shores of the reservoirs: Lake Burton, Lake Rabun, and Seed Lake. These were Rabun County's first amenity migrants, but due to their short summer visits to still isolated lake properties (some reported it took five hours to travel on dirt roads from Atlanta to the cottages), they did not profoundly impact the economy, social structure, or political power in Rabun County for much of the twentieth century.

It was not merely the reservoirs and territory owned by Georgia Power that laid the groundwork for more contemporary gentrification processes. During the 1910s and 1920s, the U.S. Forest Service also began buying land

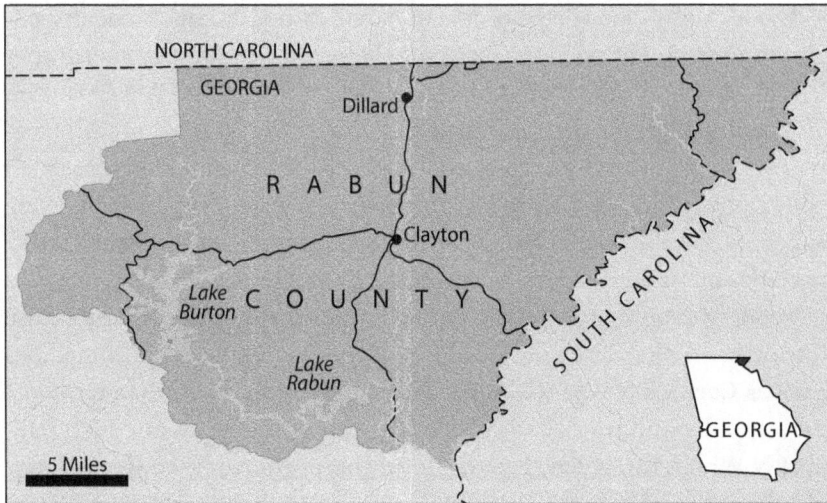

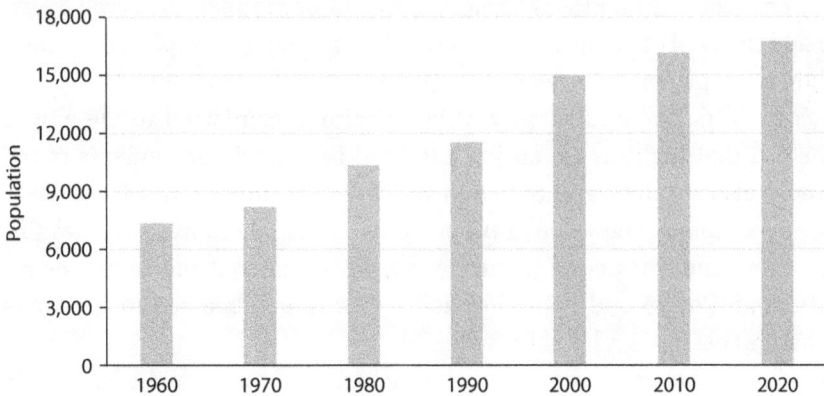

Map 2. (top) Map showing Routt County in Georgia. Cartographer: Meche Lu. *(bottom)* Population data from the U.S. Census, 1960–2020.

across northern Georgia to create the Chattahoochee-Oconee National Forest.[14] By the mid-twentieth century, 65 percent of Rabun County's land area was consolidated, not under private ownership, but controlled by either the Forest Service or Georgia Power.[15] If today real estate brokers can sell pristine mountain views and homes in bucolic valleys, it is because of the intact forests and ecosystems produced by this unusual property regime.

By the late 1990s and into the 2000s the in-migration of amenity migrants grew rapidly and took on a new character, signaling a much deeper transformation in the local economy, society, and politics. The expansion of amenity migrants during this period was driven by the structural factors outlined in chapter 1: geographies of wealth accumulation associated with globalization as well as structural demographic factors such as the aging of the baby boom. Atlanta at that time was one of the fastest growing cities in the United States, expanding from 2.18 million in 1990 to 3.52 in 2000, with annual population growth rates that decade hovering close to 5 percent. As Atlanta exploded, serving as headquarters to companies such as Coca Cola, AT&T Mobile, and Home Depot, the urban economy grew rapidly and unevenly; folks at the top of the economic hierarchy, mostly White, expanded their wealth disproportionately to the majority of Atlanta's residents.[16]

This concentrated and racialized wealth accumulation served to expand the pool of White Atlantans who had the capital to spend on second homes or primary retirement residences, an Atlantan elite who wanted access to nature and rurality while remaining connected to the city. It helped that highway expansion and road network improvements in the 1990s also cut the travel time to reach Rabun County from Atlanta down to 1.5–2 hours. The value of property along the lakeshores rose steadily, and demand for second homes increased throughout the county as retirees and/or second-home buyers became more attracted to the area's "natural beauty" and "quality of life."[17]

The most coveted sites for wealthy gentrifiers have been the lakeshores of Rabun, Burton, and Seed Lakes. Demand for lakeside properties has remained high even though nearly all the land surrounding those lakes is owned by Georgia Power; residential parcels are leased by the company. As a result, few of the wealthy, White newcomers who build or buy lakeside homes own the land on which their home is built. This may be read at first blush as a *disincentive* to purchase those homes, but it is not. Paradoxically, the power company's control over land lies at the heart of why lakeside property is such a valuable commodity: homeowners on the lake benefit from the strict controls exercised by Georgia Power over the territory. The power company requires large buffers between buildings and the lakeshore, limits the size of docks and boathouses, controls the felling of trees to maintain the hydrological function of the forest, and provides very limited public access to the lakeshores. These controls produce a "natural" and pristine looking landscape despite the demand for housing, which otherwise might have increased the density along the lakes and generated deforestation—effects visible along other northern Georgia lakes such as Hiawassee. Other northern Georgia lakes have also attracted amenity development, but not development as exclusive and high end as Rabun County because of this unusual territorial regime.

The demand for construction and other services catering to amenity migrants represented an important change in Rabun's economy, which during the 1990s and 2000s was reeling from the contraction of textile production. A key source of employment for low-skilled workers in Rabun County since the mid-twentieth century, textile production across the United States contracted precipitously in the context of globalization.[18] Rabun County's largest single employer in the early 2000s, Fruit of the Loom, shuttered in 2006 and left 930 workers unemployed.[19]

Thus, during the same period in which many longtime residents experienced changing opportunities and uncertainty in the context of broader structural economic changes also linked to globalization, owning a home on Lake Rabun or Lake Burton became an important "positional good" for the wealthy in Atlanta.[20] A 2001 article in *Atlanta Magazine* illustrates the cachet of lakeshore properties in Rabun County, titled "You Can Buy Your Way onto Rabun, Burton or Seed, but You Cannot Buy Your Way In":

> A red-tailed hawk gazing on the lakes on any given Saturday in the high season could discern, in a few moment[s]' flight, an unparalleled concentration of Atlanta's power elite—some of the richest, most successful, politically connected, creative and influential men and women the state has ever known. Old money, new money; politicians and lobbyists in their eternal embrace; strip-mall developers, dot-com entrepreneurs; Coca-Cola heirs, purveyors of The Home Depot shares. . . .
>
> To a visitor escaping the frenzy of Atlanta, these gilded figures, gracious and genteel, recall . . . a time when Jay Gatsby pursued Daisy, and the American Dream shimmered, not in the distant past or the ephemeral future, but in the here and now. But only to those who seize it. Over the last decade, these pristine North Georgia lakes have become upscale Atlanta's playground of choice.[21]

As these lakes became the "playground of choice" for Atlanta's elite, a construction boom emerged not only along the lakes but in areas throughout the county; hobby farms and vineyards became a popular landscape of choice for White wealthy newcomers eager to own their piece of the rural idyll.

Amenity-oriented in-migrants to Rabun County by the early 2000s included not only Atlanta's wealthiest elites but a range of middle- and upper-middle-class White newcomers, who usually came from either Atlanta or Florida. One participant, Max, worked as a home inspector in Rabun County after moving from Florida. His story illustrates a typical trajectory: "I came from Jacksonsville Florida and the reason I came up here was for vacation for a weekend. And we fell in love with the area, we just loved it because, coming from Jacksonville to here was such a contrast environmentally, socially, the whole thing. But it was kind of like an escape from the city at that point. We came for the weekend and found a house and decided to buy the home." This "escape" from the city, a theme across many interviews with gentrifiers in both Rabun and Routt Counties, often contained explicit coding of rural space as Whiter and safer than the city. As Marilyn, a real estate agent, described her family's motivation for moving from Atlanta in the mid-2000s: "We just enjoy the small-town lifestyle as well as the safety that this town has. It's very insulated from a lot of the demographic issues or any of those things." Her language "demographic issues" (in the city) represents a racialized coding of space, echoing Frey and Liaw's description of domestic amenity migration flows as large-scale White flight.[22]

As in the case of Steamboat Springs, Colorado, identifying as a local and who was a "real" local took on additional social and political meaning as gentrification proceeded in Rabun County. Unlike in Colorado, "older" amenity migrants in this northern Georgia community could not claim the identity of a local no matter how long they had lived there. One self-identified local, Delia, told me that being a local means that your family goes back eight or nine generations, often to settlers who arrived in the wake of the American Revolution. This definition was repeated by many of our respondents. Delia continued the discussion by giving me an example: "Someone can say 'I've lived in Rabun county for 15 years and I'm a local.' And your like, no your not, your not a local. It doesn't matter, if you

were born here, and your family is not from here, then your not a local."
I interviewed one business owner born and raised in Rabun County who
said he is seen in the community as a "transplant" because his parents
moved up from Atlanta in the 1970s. In short, in Rabun County there has
been a bright line between who is a local and who is a newcomer, with
the status of authentic local applying only to those who go back multiple
generations.

The narrative that being an authentic local can only be claimed by those
who trace their ancestry to original White settlers must be situated historically. A community history, *Sketches of Rabun County History*, written
by Rabun County resident Andrew Jackson Ritchie in 1948, illustrates the
power of White settler imaginaries. He describes the founders of Rabun
County thus: "The bravest and hardiest of the English and Scotch-Irish
were the first White men to occupy this mountain region. Thus there were
shown in the people from whom we are descended those fundamental
traits of character which have been demonstrated in each generation from
their coming to America until our day."[23]

White settlers being described as heroic in his account stands alongside the construction of the area's original inhabitants and stewards, the
Cherokee, as savage: "None of us living have spent any time among the
Indians in their savage state or known the mode of life by which they managed to exist and rear their children. For human beings to live and thrive
under the conditions by which they were surrounded must have required
a great deal of the natural instinct that wild animals have. How many of
these people lived in the valleys of our county, we do not know. We have
the names that they gave to our rivers. Tallulah, Chattooga, Tennessee,
are examples."[24] Ritchie briefly laments the tragic history of the "Trail of
Tears," but it remains a small aside disconnected to the otherwise trium-
phant story of White pioneers conquering nature and "rightfully" claiming
territory in northeast Georgia.[25]

Ritchie, who grew up in the post–Civil War era, continues his history
by discussing the rise of agriculture and the arrival of enslaved people
in this north Georgia community, describing slavery as a benevolent institution: "I have personally known some of the men who had the most
slaves and also some of the slaves themselves. I have never got the idea
that slaves were cruelly treated or that slavery was a brutal institution in

this county. On the contrary, all of the information that I have on the subject indicates that the slaves were as a rule kindly treated and well cared for. It was simply a matter of good business management."[26] As Ritchie turns his account to the present (the 1940s), he describes the only remaining Black people in the county as forming a "small colony" in Clayton (the county seat), with no explanation of why the descendants of the formerly enslaved left or why they were found in only one neighborhood. The departure of Black residents continued beyond the brief and bemused mention by Ritchie: by 1990 the U.S. Census found only .004 percent of the population of the county identified as Black.

The physical and discursive erasure of Black people from Rabun's history, like that of its original Cherokee inhabitants and stewards, usually remains unacknowledged in how self-identified locals narrate their history and connection to this place—which frequently starts with pride in how many generations back their family settled in the area, often eight or nine generations back. It is a history that forms the substrate of twenty-first-century debates about who is a local in the context of rural gentrification, not only between "locals" and wealthy gentrifiers, but in relation to the recruitment and settlement of Latine immigrant populations as part of the gentrification process.

As in Steamboat, Latine residents of Rabun County are nowhere to be found in these narratives of who is or is not a "real local"—neither within the commodified representations of place sold to potential amenity migrants nor in the contested politics enacted in daily life that signal who is an "authentic" local. The politics of "being a local" and who can occupy that subject position is reserved for White residents, with the fault line being drawn between wealthy newcomers and multigenerational local families.

Self-identified locals expressed mixed feelings about the arrival of folks from Atlanta and Florida. When asked how the community has been impacted by the arrival of wealthy outsiders, Rose, a fifty-three-year-old resident born and raised in Rabun County, had this to say:

> How I feel about it depends on the persona of the people that come up, if they're Atlanta and they're stuck up and they're acting like they are better than everybody and they wanna run the locals over and everything . . . then that is different. You know you got your Floridians that'll come up and just

blend right in, yeah they may have a couple of homes here and then and the locals may be jealous of the money they don't have, but either way they bring in money to the economy of this area, while they are here. The problem is that . . . well say they live on the lake and the neighbor's got a couple of junk cars in the yard, something like that, they say "I don't wanna see that!" So they make a new rule and change it all and everybody's got to put their stuff away. But people have [old cars in their yard] usually because they don't have the money to get it hauled off, or its something they're working on that they need fixed. It is a different culture.

Many locals interviewed for this research centered their identity and their constructed difference from wealthy White gentrifiers on their working-class ethics and "true" connection to the region's founding as a White settler community.

The dividing line between locals and transplants erupted into a political battle in 2006–2007 when the county commissioners, some of whom were relative newcomers to Rabun County, developed and tried to pass a new Unified Development Code. The UDC draft in 2006 would have integrated land use planning, as well as infrastructure and building regulations, with the aim of protecting viewsheds and ecological integrity (e.g., rules about roadbuilding to reduce erosion). However, once details of the code became more visible to the public, there was a backlash against governmental intervention in private property rights and any effort that would be seen as slowing down real estate development.[27] The county commissioners who were newcomers/transplants were voted out of office based on a narrative of being outsiders, and as one ex-commissioner described it, "after the commission changed, you had . . . because all the locals got involved and everyone went and voted. And then a non-local did not have a chance [to be elected]. And once those folks got in, it was like, years of progress [toward creating systematic land use planning rules] stopped and we all stepped back a decade." This tension between self-identified locals and wealthier amenity migrants with distinct environmental imaginaries and values is witnessed in many rural areas undergoing gentrification.[28]

In short, since the 1990s gentrification has transformed the economy, place identity, and politics of belonging in Rabun County, Georgia. The most publicly discussed and visible debates over belonging have been rooted in differences—and at times tensions—between "locals" and wealthy outsiders. Yet as I show in the next chapter, these debates of belonging and authentic connection to place must be understood in relation to the recruitment of Latine immigrant residents as part and parcel of the gentrification process, a group marginalized across race, illegality and poverty and largely excluded from public debates over belonging in the context of rapid demographic and economic change.

CONCLUSION

Routt County, Colorado, and Rabun County, Georgia, are two rural communities in profoundly distinct geographical settings—ecologically and culturally—but they nevertheless share White settler histories and the rapid in-migration of amenity migrants in the 1990s and beyond. Both places have become commodified as sites for the wealthy to not only live proximate to nature and recreational amenities, but also connect to small town values and culture. Gentrifiers repeatedly invoked racially-coded language of being attracted to "safe" rural communities and highlighting the possibility of connection to "pristine" nature.

The transformed social and economic landscapes in Routt and Rabun Counties exemplify broader processes of gentrification that are both urban and rural in nature. White newcomers, whose wealth as a class grew tremendously in the context of neoliberal globalization, have brought urban capital to rural spaces, a process that is written into the landscape in the form of high-end housing and an expansion of retail and other service sectors catering to privileged newcomers' lifestyles and consumption practices. The same racialized class involved in urban gentrification is stimulating processes of rural gentrification, fixing their surplus capital in rural spaces in order to access nature, recreation, and the rural idyll, as well as achieve long-term gains on that investment.

Scholarship on urban gentrification has rightly been focused on processes of displacement, but in rural settings it is a more complex story, as some working-class residents are able to remain physically in the community but often feel more acutely an erosion of political power and their historic connection to place. Narratives of who is a real "local" represent a linchpin of identity and political struggles in both Colorado and Georgia, even as these narratives reproduce the erasure of Native American histories and territorial claims as well as the contemporary presence and role of immigrants. Heated discussions over who is a local in both areas represent competitions waged on terrains of whiteness.

A qualitative, feminist methodological approach was essential to teasing out the shifts in identity and belonging explored in this chapter, as it was for eliciting the data underlying the analysis developed in chapters 3 and 4. Reflecting on my own positionality and that of my research assistants was critical in order to effectively and ethically recruit participants and conduct interviews. It was a reflective approach that helped us to meet people with the respect and openness essential to building trust across social differences. By conducting our interviews in a dialogic manner, we sought to decenter our own assumptions and listen closely to how people narrate their lives. Interviews with White working-class participants in Rabun County were among the most challenging in terms of generating trust, but compassion and curiosity led to important insights that form the basis of the analysis presented over the course of this book. While recruiting Latine participants was more straightforward at the end of the day, conducting interviews and interpreting their lives and experiences had to consider their structural vulnerabilities across race and legal status as well as how they perceived me and the research assistants in terms of our relevant social locations.

The remainder of this book focuses on processes of *emplacement* wrought by gentrification, specifically the recruitment of Latine immigrant workers critical to the construction and maintenance of gentrifying rural landscapes. The commodified images of rural amenity landscapes as sites of leisure and luxury make no mention of the Latine workers critical to their production. Nor do the dueling narratives of who is a "local"—who can claim an authentic connection to place—entertain the possibility that a racialized, 'illegal' body could count as a local. The paradox of economic dependence (laboring bodies critical to the production of gentrified landscapes) and social marginalization are the focus of the following chapters.

3 Immigrant Labor Regimes

> I think about, if I had to get rid of the nine Hispanics that
> I've got tomorrow and replace them with locals, to get the
> same amount of output, I would have to hire fifteen instead
> of nine and I'd probably have to pay them $1 an hour more
> each, and that figures up quick. And there's some times that
> you just can't find people to do the work.
>
> —Adam, contractor, Rabun County (July 1, 2010)

> This is how it went with every Hispano that came into the
> company: the boss said what he needed, and I told my
> people. [. . .] And more or less I knew all of the jobs [in the
> company] and so I went around supervising everyone.
> I would tell them [the workers], "you should do this and
> this." Because they understood me, they would do it. The
> boss would arrive and he liked the work. "This is good."
> They did it quickly and so little by little he began to trust
> me more. Soon he was leaving me alone, in charge.
>
> —Roberto, construction worker, Rabun County (June 25, 2011)

This chapter traces the emergence of immigrant-based labor regimes
in Routt and Rabun Counties, drawing largely on the voices and stories
of employers as well as employees—immigrant and nonimmigrant. The
quotes from Adam and Roberto provide a snapshot of the immigrant-
based labor regimes at the center of the analysis. In short, employers like
Adam realized over time that immigrant workers had become essential to
their business due to their seemingly essential "work ethic" and employers' perceptions of their willingness to accept a lower hourly wage. But it

was much more than these two factors that made undocumented immigrant workers extremely attractive and ultimately essential to employers, which we can see in Roberto's words. Roberto is telling the story of how he became the informal "labor broker" for his employer: supervising and managing other Latine immigrant workers in the company. During interviews with employers and employees in Routt County, Colorado, and Rabun County, Georgia, we heard over and over how most relied on an in-house labor broker, without whom employers could not effectively extract the most value from the immigrant labor regime. The labor broker took over recruitment, hiring, firing, and supervising workers in ways that took most advantage of subjects navigating life at the intersection of race, illegality, and poverty. The labor brokers did not escape the effects legal status and racism, as most were also undocumented, but they functioned as linchpins for the low-wage labor market in Routt and Rabun Counties.

At the heart of immigrant labor regimes explored in this chapter lie the social networks within which most immigrants, particularly undocumented ones, are embedded during the migration process and after settlement. Social networks are critical to crossing international borders, particularly without authorization. Significant research has demonstrated immigrant social networks function to facilitate transnational migration by providing information and support for border crossing.[1] These same networks shape urban immigrant labor regimes after international borders have been crossed.[2] Yet much of this second literature on immigrant labor markets is framed in terms of how networks facilitate immigrant workers' job search, rather than on how these networks transform the workplace in ways that increase the profitability and decrease the stress of employers.

This chapter demonstrates how immigrant social networks, which facilitate cross-border migration, are a resource for employers once they learn how to use them. And I show that the benefits of using these networks to transform one's business model goes far beyond paying workers less (which is often assumed when we use vocabulary of "cheap labor" when referring to immigrant workers). Over and over employers describe their "discovery" of immigrant workers as critical to the growth of their businesses during the gentrification boom—providing them with a highly productive, flexible, and trustworthy workforce that led to further recruitment and incorporation of immigrant labor. For most employers, achieving the highest level of productivity and flexibility required developing an in-house, informal labor broker. The analysis in this chapter presents the voices of nonimmigrant workers in these same sectors, to assess how their engagement with work also shifted, and in ways often linked to hierarchies of race and legality.

This chapter is organized around different economic sectors linked to gentrification and with distinct gendered labor market dynamics: construction and landscaping, home property maintenance and housecleaning, and finally the restaurant industry. I explore commonalities and differences in these sectors across the two case study sites. I take this approach because each sector has a slightly distinct story in the context of the gentrification boom, particularly in terms of recruitment strategies and the ways Latine immigrants were incorporated into specific industries. Each section includes how employers in that sector recruited and incorporated Latine immigrant workers, how immigrants found these jobs and their motivations for settling in Rabun or Routt Counties, and how the presence of immigrants over time changed the fundamental business model and productivity in these sectors.

CONSTRUCTION

The construction industry in both Rabun County, Georgia, and Routt County, Colorado, represents the leading edge of economic and landscape change produced by wealthy amenity migrants purchasing primary or secondary residences in these areas. As demand for homes increased in the late 1990s in Rabun County, and during the early 2000s in Steamboat, it was the construction industry that felt it immediately. This growth is reflected in the number of single-family housing permits issued in each county during this period, with Rabun reaching its highest number of annual housing permits in the period under study in 2004, a growth of 187 percent over the number issued annually in 1992. Similarly, Routt County reached its peak number of single-family housing permits in 2006, a growth of 138 percent over the total issued in 1992.[3]

In both Colorado and Georgia local contractors already in business prior to the gentrification boom described the difficulties of expanding quickly enough to meet the demand for new build construction—demand that was not only numerically greater but accompanied by expectations about a higher level of productivity and efficiency of construction. In other words, exurban amenity migrants desired a pace of construction that had not been the norm in either community prior to that time—they wanted increasingly larger homes built on a tighter schedule. These two factors necessitated not only more workers in the sector but new modes of organizing and managing construction businesses. As shown in more detail below, immigrant workers, largely undocumented, became the solution to both of these challenges.

There were many parallels in the emergence of immigrant labor regimes in the construction industry between Rabun and Routt Counties— perhaps more than in any other sector across these two regions. Employers in both places describe confronting a profound labor shortage—which occurred in Rabun County by the late 1990s and in Steamboat in the early 2000s—in which they would hire any "warm body" that they could find. When asked how they found and recruited Latino immigrant men, many repeated a similar scenario: in order to meet the level and pace of demand, contractors subcontracted out specific jobs, such as drywalling, to companies located in distant, larger cities (Atlanta in Rabun County and Denver for Routt County). In both Colorado and Georgia employers described renting out hotel rooms to house these crews for three to eight weeks during busy times, allowing them to make progress on multiple houses under construction. These crews were comprised largely of Latino immigrant workers, as construction labor markets in large cities had already transitioned to relying extensively on an immigrant workforce.[4]

For many of our contractor respondents, using these out-of-town crews was the first time they had worked closely with immigrant workers, and most reported being impressed by the productivity and efficiency of these crews even though most workers could speak little English. In both Colorado and Georgia more than one contractor described that the first time they recruited a Latino immigrant as their own employee was when they sought to convince a member or two of one of these out-of-town crews to come work for them, to move permanently to Rabun County, Geogia, and/ or Routt County, Colorado. Employers incentivized the move by offering them higher wages than the subcontracted business and by helping them access housing to aid in their transition (sometimes putting them up on their own properties). Alan (age 56), a contractor in Steamboat, in business since the mid-1980s, described the situation this way:

ALAN: The boom would have been way more disastrous than it was and challenging than it was without the immigrant labor. Even though you often see that immigrant workers are doing more manual labor or less skilled, the best carpentry craftsmen I have ever had come from that source. [. . .] These guys, they wanted to work and they worked hard and they would work from sun up to sun down.

LISE: How did you find them?

ALAN: I found them through a subcontractor who is from Silverthorne but he did work throughout the state and so he had developed a crew over a period of time and there again, because he was working throughout the state he probably had a more consistent level of work and was able to keep that group together. That was actually the group I was subbing to, and I met Jaime [pseud.] and offered him an opportunity to stay here.

Alan went on to say that Jaime seemed to him motivated to stay in Steamboat Springs less by the wage than by an opportunity to avoid being on a crew constantly on the move around the state—he described Jaime as wanting to put down roots, and Alan remarked that Jaime eventually brought his family to the Steamboat area. Alan recruited Jaime to create an "in-house" drywall crew that would liberate him from having to sub out that work, which during very busy periods was not only expensive but unreliable. Paying Jaime and helping him find housing was well worth it in terms of the productivity and efficiency of his business as it expanded rapidly in the early 2000s.

A very similar story emerged among contractors and construction workers in Rabun County. Thirty-four-year-old Diego arrived in the United States in 1998, first working in Texas and then Louisiana doing various jobs, from roofing to cement and rock walls. He was deported from Louisiana but returned to the U.S. within three months, this time to Atlanta, where his brother was living. He began working for a roofer in Atlanta. When I asked him how he arrived in Clayton, he answered:

One day this Americano [who owned the roofing company] had a job here in Rabun County, at a time when many people began to arrive here to build houses and all of that. So he took his company from Atlanta and brought [his crews] here to work, and my brother came with him. That is how it started, this is how we arrived here to this part of Georgia, this is how it started. One arrives, two arrive, and I spoke to my compadre and my compadre brought his family and his family brought a brother, and the brothers brought their cousins and . . . that is how we arrived . . . that is how it continues to be.

After moving to Rabun County, Diego was on a roofing job when a private homeowner with a fairly large piece of property/hobby orchard recruited him to work for her exclusively. At the time of the interview Diego's primary work centered on providing maintenance and landscape care for this wealthy landowner, originally from Atlanta, on ten acres of land. Despite shifting to this new employer, Diego nevertheless regularly helped his brother recruit and manage labor for the roofing business on an as-needed basis.

While many contractors reported their initial recruitment of immigrant labor as a stopgap measure, most said that over time immigrant workers became more fundamental to their business growth than they originally had anticipated. They hired more immigrants, and most developed a *preference* for immigrant workers over the years because immigrants commonly demonstrated qualities (as described by the employer) such as diligence, productivity, flexibility, and loyalty. These qualities cannot, however, be read in essentialist terms: they are produced at the intersection of illegality, racism, and poverty—structural underpinnings that Jill Harrison and Sarah Lloyd, in their research on dairy farm labor regimes in Wisconsin, describe as the structural production of "compliant workaholics."[5] I illustrate the production of these labor force characteristics over the course of this chapter.

Recruiting and retaining immigrant workers was a fundamental component of a shift in the organizational culture and pace of the local construction industry. As Mark, a contractor in Rabun County described:

Everybody was at such a slow pace here. I remember hearing stories from the 1990s that contractors would just shut down a job and wait a month for the local drywall guy to show up, because he was good and someone had worked with him for so many years, they were friends. But during the boom you saw a lot more subcontractors from Gainesville, Athens, Atlanta come here, and the homeowners could see that it didn't have to take two years to build a 4000 square foot house, it could be done in nine to ten months. Then you got pressure. People had to be a little more open to outside subs and people they weren't used to. [. . .] I still try to use local plumbers, the majority of my subs are local, but just barely probably 40% are coming from out of town. And that got the price a little more in line but more importantly it got the scheduling.

The pressure of urban clients moving to Routt and Rabun Counties changed assumptions about the pace of construction, putting pressure on contractors to increase the speed and efficiency of their operations, which previously had been more laid back.

To achieve that pace of construction Mark turned to a workforce that was productive and disciplined, yet flexible according to ever-changing needs and schedules. Latino immigrant workers provided these qualities, in ways most business owners did not anticipate at the outset. Mark continued:

I cannot fathom now hiring a local laborer for anything but finish carpentry, which the Mexicans do not usually know how to do. I have been working with a Mexican rock mason for eleven years. I keep him employed full time, he usually keeps at least two guys with him, but when we get on a big job I tell 'em to pick up three more guys, he brings in the remaining.

Mark's story about his relationship with the rock mason reflects a pattern that emerged in my interviews with contractors in both Routt and Rabun Counties: the development of an in-house, informal "immigrant labor broker" who became a linchpin for the management of a highly productive and flexible workforce. This workforce allowed contractors (and other businesses) to take full advantage of the qualities of immigrant labor produced at the intersection of class, race, and illegality.

These changes affected White construction workers, many of whom had grown up in the slower-paced business before the boom. For many of the White workers interviewed, the growing presence of immigrants in their workplace was marked by ambivalence: some doubt and hostility but eventually, in some cases, friendship. John, a construction worker in Rabun County who was in his fifties at the time of the interview and had worked construction since high school, described the arrival of immigrant coworkers in this way:

JOHN: Up until maybe fifteen years ago, we didn't really have any migrant help-ers that worked in that. But the work became so overwhelming we went from crews of three people to crews of fifteen people to carry the work-load. And the work became so overwhelming that the migrant workers were a necessity. And it's tons of work not only in the construction part of it but every part of it. Even in the restaurants and everything.

LISE: Was it an adjustment to have immigrants working with you?

JOHN: The language was always kind of a barrier because . . . well, it was more of an irritant than it was anything, because they would be talking amongst themselves and you're not really in the conversation and you don't know what's being said. There was a little tension there but over the years I think we've become more tolerant of that. I don't think they're mad at us or we're mad at them anymore. [. . .]

We have had some workers for a long time. Let's see . . . Juan has been here for nineteen years, and Alejandro for fifteen years, and the other guys over twelve years. These are the ones that come and don't have the sense to slow down at all. They are the high-end people who want to learn. So we couldn't do our job if we didn't have them, we couldn't find people to replace them.

LISE: Do you feel that you have gotten to know these guys? Would you call them friends?

JOHN: I have become real good friends with all of those guys, they. . . . I had some health issues. I had to have open heart surgery. [. . .] They all sent me cards and checked on me all the time. Still, some normal friends have asked me why they did that. . . . There is still a little bit of separation there.

John recognized that his employer (who is a friend from high school) needed to hire immigrant workers, but he admitted to feeling uncom-fortable about it at first, and perhaps a little resentful that they had "no sense to slow down." He describes feeling the pressure working alongside people who were highly productive, but over time he saw how indispens-able they were. These work relationships evolved into care networks—it was Juan and Alejandro who brought him food when he was recovering from surgery—even though he differentiated them from his "normal" friends. Most White workers spoke positively about immigrants working alongside them, but frequently maintained broad sentiments that were anti-immigrant in the same conversation.

Before diving into the qualitative data that helps us see the emergence and nature of informal labor brokers as linchpins within immigrant labor regimes in the context of gentrification—from construction to housecleaning—it is important to explain the use of the qualifier *informal*. I use the term *informal labor broker* to distinguish this role from *formal* labor contractors, who are also ubiquitous within unauthorized immigrant labor markets, particularly as they relate to agriculture and agro-industries (such as poultry and other meat processing), which draw on an undocumented immigrant workforce on a large scale.[6] Formal, regulated businesses (governed by state laws) exist to contract out crews to farms and other rural enterprises, a history that reaches back to the mid-twentieth century.[7] These labor contractors provide a mechanism for large employers to hire undocumented workers but not take responsibility for their status, because the hiring is done by the labor contractor (a separate business).[8] The regimes described here and the role of the *informal* labor broker differ from these systems visible among large-scale employers. It is informal, in that said labor broker is an employee of the business (e.g., contractor/construction company in the case), and his role as labor recruiter and manager is part of the job. (I use the pronoun "his" because in construction workers are all male, but similar female brokers exist in work coded as female, as I explore below.) My use of the term *labor broker* throughout the rest of this book refers exclusively to these informal relationships, and most often to the one person running the recruitment and management of the immigrant labor in a construction or other type of business explored in the rest of this chapter.

As noted, locally owned construction contractors in both Rabun and Routt Counties often recruited what they described as their first immigrant employee from a subcontracted crew coming in from larger cities. Usually, among early recruits—which the employer hired out of desperation during boom times—one recruit began to stand out as particularly adept at getting the job done, taking responsibility for managing others, and having wide networks. The qualities that led to the transformation of someone from being only a worker to becoming an informal labor broker/manager included an ability to be conversant in English (serve as a liaison between monolingual Latine workers and the boss), to have significant contacts and trust in the immigrant community to recruit workers on short notice, and a willingness and capacity to take responsibility for those workers.

The employers gave me the sense that most of them had stumbled into the relationship with the worker who became their immigrant labor broker—they certainly did not start out hiring someone off a subbed crew because they envisioned such a change in their organizational structure and culture. One contractor in Routt County, Tom, told the story of "his guy" Adrián, whom he initially hired simply for his ability to lay drywall. One day Tom mentioned to Adrián that he needed more drywallers. Adrián said he would take care of it. The next Monday three more guys showed up, whom the employer trusted because he trusted Adrián. Adrián managed these workers, because they spoke only Spanish, and so those workers interacted very little with Tom. Adrián transitioned over time from being a drywaller to supervising all the immigrant workers in the company. His evolution paralleled that of Roberto, the Rabun County labor broker for a contractor quoted at the opening of the chapter, who very soon was bringing in "every Hispano" who came to work for his boss and eventually was left alone to supervise jobs.

The relationship between the owner and the person who evolved into their labor broker- manager was often very personal and cemented by the employer using a language of family and familial trust, a form of paternalism as labor control. Several business owners who embraced fully the transformation of their business in relation to this new, highly flexible, and profitable immigrant labor regime described the worker who functioned as a labor broker as being "like a son." One contractor in Rabun County, Brian, felt so close to Miguel, a man from Guanajuato who had worked with him over twelve years at the time of our interview that Brian took his own family to Mexico to visit Miguel's hometown and family there. Miguel could not make the journey himself because of the risk, given his undocumented status.

The immigrant labor regime discussed in this chapter would not be possible without the emergence of this informal labor broker-manager. This labor broker–facilitated immigrant labor regime, visible in all of the interviews with contractors in both Routt and Rabun Counties, also emerged in other gentrification-linked economic sectors, discussed below. While certainly the role of formal labor contractors in hiring undocumented workers has been studied extensively, particularly in agribusiness contexts such as industrial farming and meatpacking, little has been written about the informal labor brokers explored here.[9]

LANDSCAPE DESIGN AND INSTALLATION

If rural gentrification is driven by the accumulated wealth of urban elites whose desires are shaped by racialized constructions of the rural idyll (nature, open spaces)—which they often explicitly talked about as a reaction to the "danger" and "dirtiness" of the city—it is unsurprising that this desire also dramatically affected landscaping businesses in gentrifying rural areas. Arnold, a fifty-two-year-old owner of a landscaping business in Steamboat, described the scope of his work with mostly high-end, residential clients since he began his business in the late 1990s:

> Our business is solely, from a construction standpoint, we started building the best design, the most interesting design of outdoor living spaces. [...] We look at it as rooms that are outside. Rather than just a yard. You pass from room to room, and you have different experiences. Just like inside a house. Here is a fire pit and a water feature. Boom. Then over here you have a different setting. So we got into this whole concept of creating outdoor rooms and transition spaces. So our designs are very . . . complicated might not be the best word, but complicated. [...]
>
> We put together a very comprehensive maintenance plan [for our clients] . . . we are going to take your yard from this finished state where everything is done but it is immature and we are going to bring it through to maturity. As we do that we are going to have carte blanche to do what we need to do to make sure that your property is the way that we both see that it should be developing.

Landscapers such as Arnold, working with high-end clientele, and those providing plants, design, and installation for middle-class clients building retirement or second homes in Rabun County, Georgia, and Routt County, Colorado, all reported an increase in demand for their products and services during the gentrification boom in the late 1990s through mid-2000s. And like contractors, the landscapers in Routt and Rabun Counties found the recruitment, retention, and effective management of immigrant workers to be key to their ability to respond and profit from the new level of demand.

An aspect of the recruitment story for landscapers echoes the emergence of immigrant labor regimes in construction: most people involved in the landscape industry began to rely on a Latine immigrant workforce, largely undocumented, as gentrification took off. They also frequently told stories of how they managed labor in ways that reflected the emergence of immigrant-based labor regimes similar to those described in the construction industry, in which informal labor brokers/managers were the linchpins to running, and profiting from, a highly productive and flexible workforce. Landscapers, however, seldom reported that their first exposure to/ability to recruit immigrant workers came from subcontracted crews, simply because subcontracting is not as ubiquitous in landscaping as it is in construction. However, many did make contact and recruit immigrant workers through business networks that connected to larger urban areas—Denver and Atlanta being the primary markets.

One landscape business owner in Rabun County, Rick, had run a plant nursery and offered the installation of plants and hardscape since the late 1990s. He first recruited an immigrant worker when he was visiting a wholesale operation in Atlanta in the early 2000s. He simply was walking down the aisle of the wholesaler, started chatting with a Latino worker there, and on the spot asked him if he wanted to move to Rabun County to work for him, giving him his number. When Gonzalo called him a week later, Rick offered to provide him housing and higher wages if he moved to Rabun County. Still other landscapers in Rabun, because they often owned land for their nursery and knew adjacent farmers, recruited their first Latino immigrant workers from farm labor crews who had been seasonally present in Rabun County since the mid-1980s.

Another family-owned nursery and landscape installation business in Rabun County was owned by Jack, who started out making some extra cash by digging up boxwoods in the forest and selling them to nurseries in Athens and Atlanta. By the 1990s, however, Jack had expanded into owning a nursery (land inherited from his family), including designing and installing residential landscapes: "I was known for precision work, walks and dry creeks and the whole thing looked like it's been there a long time and old." When I asked him about his workforce needs and the arrival of immigrants as wealthier newcomers built vacation homes, he responded:

JACK: The Mexicans. Yeah. Yeah. That was super, I borrowed them. One day I borrowed some from [a farmer], two or three of those guys to help me. Boy, just got so much done so quick, you know, they worked like five times as hard. I said to my wife, "I gotta get one of them." I could see right now that's gotta be done as quick as I can do it. I just wish I'd known in order to have 'em you gotta build your own separate little bunk out there. Yeah. House to keep them. So when you want to go get 'em you have 'em, they'd be there. I built a block house. 'Cause they, they pretty rough, you know, a bunch of men stuff you need to cement, cement, house walls and floors, you know.

LISE: How did you find workers over time, always farm labor or?

JACK: Oh, you just stop on the side of the road, stop, give one ride or something. Ask them once you get one, you tend to say, d'you know somebody else needing to work? Yeah. How many you want to be there? I can make a phone call right now and have yard full of them this afternoon.

Jack's experiences show the efficiency (from an employer's standpoint) of network recruitment, which provides a high degree of flexibility in addition to highly productive workers. Jack viewed the need to "get one of them" as essential to his business, a model predicated on access to and control of workers through employer-provided housing. The history of Jack's business, as told to me, did not include the development of a labor broker with whom he developed a close personal relationship, as was very common in a range of gentrification-linked economic sectors. That does not mean he did not develop such a relationship or have such "broker" roles in his business over the years. He may have simply not mentioned them when I asked about his labor needs, or they were transient relationships (not the typical decades-long and deeply personal relationships that emerged for many business owners). Nevertheless, he had relied significantly on immigrant workers since the 1990s, except in the retail section of the business, men he housed in a similar fashion as most farmers in the area—in isolated bunkhouses. The provision of housing was critical to the control of labor and to have access to workers "so when you want to go get 'em they are there," and echoes the infrastructures of racialized exclusion and control found within farm labor camps.[10]

For either source (urban contacts in the industry or farm labor crews), it was common in Georgia for landscapers to provide housing for their workers, particularly their "labor broker" as a mechanism to inspire them to move and as a means to control and supervise the workforce. Contractors and landscaping employers in Rabun County often describe putting a mobile home in their "backyard" to house an immigrant they had recruited for their business. (Sometimes it was their own backyard, sometimes it was behind the nursery, and one time it was rooms added on to the back of a contractor's workshop.) Workers often described that when they used employer-provided housing, they were at the employer's beck and call seven days a week.

In 2010 I interviewed Carlos, an immigrant resident in Rabun County who had worked in landscaping for over fifteen years. His migration story and job history help illustrate immigrant workers' experiences of this labor regime. Carlos arrived in Texas in 1988 but moved to Gainesville, Georgia, a year later to work in a poultry processing plant—drawn he said by friends he knew who told him they made 35 percent higher wages per hour than he was getting in his job in Texas. From poultry processing, which he described as very hard work, he took a job planting and pruning trees for the U.S. Forest Service in Northern Georgia, after which he worked for a cut flower operation near Gainesville in the early 1990s, packing lilies into crates to be shipped to flower stores.

CARLOS: I worked in a packing plant for day lilies, they sent them off in crates. It was not hard, but it paid very little. One day I went with the owner to help him buy trees at a nursery up here, and the owner of the nursery took me aside and he said he wanted me to work for him. I changed jobs, he treated me well. I worked for him for twelve years, until 2004. He raised trees, he created gardens. At the beginning I was the only one working there. But then later the work became too much for one person, and the boss told me "look for others." [. . .] I lived in an apartment downtown [Clayton], and there were other Mexican people. When I met my wife in 2000 the boss let me live in a trailer behind his house.

LISE: What happened in 2004?

CARLOS: I worked for him for twelve years. One day I didn't want to go down into a river to haul out rocks. He told me "you will get down there and bring up those rocks." But it was early in the morning, it was very cold water. I didn't want to get sick, and I told him I didn't want to go into the river. He told me "you get down there and get those rocks or your fired!" I left. He didn't believe that I would leave, because I lived in his trailer.

Carlos explained that although he had worked with the nursey owner for so long, the morning when he was ordered down into the river, he decided that enough was enough. He packed his things and moved out of the trailer, began working in a local factory, and continued to engage in yard maintenance on the side. He bought his own piece of land and a trailer, where the interview was conducted. He agreed that he would never have done the interview with me if he still lived in his old boss's backyard.

A unique dimension of the sociospatial architecture of immigrant labor regimes in rural Georgia, as compared to Colorado, was the widespread phenomenon of employers providing housing to "their" immigrant workers, particularly if someone served as a labor broker. We found no evidence of a similar relationship between employers and undocumented workers in Colorado. Even though some employers there did help workers find housing, in no cases did we find them housing workers on their own property. I continue to discuss the impacts of this spatial configuration throughout this chapter, and return to it in the next chapter, on social reproduction.

To close out this section on the landscaping industry in the context of rural gentrification, I return to the landscaping company owned by Arnold quoted in the opening paragraph of this section, a company that since the mid-1990s has catered to high-end residential landscape design, installation, and maintenance in Steamboat Springs (Routt County), Colorado. I share his business history because Arnold began using H2B visa workers (guestworkers) from Guerrero in the late 1990s, providing a window into how guestworker programs can figure into processes of rural gentrification. The nonagricultural H2B visa is a category of temporary worker visa that has grown steadily since the late 1990s, save for a steep but short-lived decline in 2008–2010.[11] In 2000 the United States brought in 45,037 H2B workers, a number that rose to nearly 130,716 in 2022.[12] To provide a full picture of evolving labor regimes in the context of rural gentrification, it is important to consider the role of H2B visa workers in landscaping and other sectors in Colorado.

For large-scale employers who needed significant labor for only a few months annually, it made sense to invest time and money to apply for and bring in guestworkers, as I explore in relation to Arnold's use of H2B guestworkers, discussed below. But one key finding, not only in relation to Arnold's company but to a handful of other Colorado business owners we interviewed that used H2B workers, is that we never found H2B workers *replaced* the use of undocumented immigrant workers—it was not either or, but "yes and." While policymakers often frame guestworkers as a path to reduce demand for and presence of workers labeled as illegal, we found most businesses needed undocumented labor to work alongside temporary workers, and that these temporary workers were not as temporary as they might seem on paper.

Overall the use of H2B workers was evident in gentrification-linked sectors in Colorado but not in Georgia.[13] In Colorado the ski resort and large hotel chains engaged in the recruitment of guestworkers, as did some large landscaping and maintenance companies such as Arnold's, discussed below. In Georgia the only case of a local business using H2B visa holders was an agro-processing facility—not a gentrification-linked business. While H2B visa holders were by definition temporary, we spoke to employers who relied annually on the same group of H2B visa holders and who maintained a long-term relationship with these individuals. Talking about the labor pool when he started his business, Arnold said:

> One of the things that I realized right away was that the labor pool here, I have to watch what I say, all the transient ski kids. At that point in time and still today, this is a very laid-back town. Hippies, Birkenstocks, everybody is getting stoned. You have a labor pool of kids who show up on Monday, on Tuesday they say "man we want to go kayaking. We'll be back on Wednesday." Then on Wednesday they don't show up, and then they show up on Monday and expect to work.
>
> So my first season when I stepped in midseason and started running things, I quickly figured out [that] because I had a big organization, I quickly figured out that this wasn't going to work. I saw that there was a tsunami coming of work in Steamboat. This was going to be a window and I had to catch the wave. But, if I couldn't build a labor force capable of dealing with what was coming and creating a level of professionalism, a brand that we were building the most creative projects and our nursery. I could not do it with the labor pool that was here. At that time, there was no Latino labor [in the area]. [. . .] I had to figure out how to run this business because the labor pool that was here, you couldn't run shit.

Arnold's distain for local White labor was a common refrain among employers in both Georgia and Colorado. In Colorado employers described White workers not showing up if twelve inches of snow had fallen the night before (a fresh powder day), while employers in Georgia said they had a hard time keeping White workers when the hunting season opened.

Arnold was unaware of the H2B nonagricultural temporary worker program until he attended a tradeshow in the late 1990s and came into contact with a private company that assists with H2B labor rules, paperwork, and recruitment. He signed up with them, and as he described it, "the next season, April 15 I had twelve guys show up from Guerrero. They showed up with their suitcases at the Greyhound bus terminal . . . and that was our labor force for the next year." After describing the initial challenges with language, he explained how his use of H2B workers grew from twelve to sixteen to over twenty within three years. It was generally the "same guys" from Guerrero he knew from the first time plus their friends or relatives. The advantage of this long-term relationship with individual workers using H2B visas is that when they arrive in April each year "they start working like they never left. They just go to the job sites. There was no training, there was no nothing. You know, 'build this walkway,' 'build this water feature,' 'now go do this.'" As a researcher I was surprised to see H2B visa workers being incorporated into the immigrant labor regime in much the same way and to a similar effect as undocumented workers—and that these relationships were long term and personal.

This system worked well until Arnold ran into trouble when his request could not be processed because the national cap for H2B workers had been exceeded for that year, a moment that was generally difficult for employers to predict. That experience, plus what he described as "shifting political winds," inspired him to make plans to find a local labor force, by which he meant Latino workers living permanently in Steamboat. That was easier than he expected because "by that time the construction industry was growing so rapidly, that everybody had Latinos working for them. They all lived in Craig (Colorado) basically." He achieved an equilibrium in his labor force by having a mix of H2B and local immigrant workers, whom he implied were undocumented ("as long as they provided us what the law asked us to provide. We were not in the job of verifying whether or not a social security card was correct. We were like most companies"). Moreover, within these crews of mixed H2B and undocumented "local" Latino labor, over time he found it best not to have White foremen on the crews, but decided to train the best H2B workers whom he knew well to be foremen:

And another thing that we did several years ago was that we had the H2B workers but we also had White guys who were the crew foreman. They were [White] guys that had worked in landscape companies in college. Who knew how to do something right. They knew how to build a water feature. And we have those people applying every year, but it was the same problem with those people. They wanted too much money. They were looking at $25 or $30 per hour. [. . .] [T]hey would not show up on Fridays. They would get drunk and not come to work.

So five years ago we just decided that we were going to train the best of the H2B guys to be supervisors. So they could supervise themselves. So then we just went to one [non-Hispanic] person, "Rob," who is my general manager, five Latino foremen and then their whole workforce.

So now we have a blend of about 60–40 or 70–30 of H2B to local [Latino] guys. What we are doing is we are hedging and we are trying to build [local] foremen. That is what most of the local guys are trying to do so that in case our H2B guys cannot come we at least have a certain expertise in our pocket and then we can use these guys to go down and get more of our labor force.

In listening to Arnold's business and labor history, what is surprising is that the H2B workers were the ones who generally had a longer-term, closer relationship to the employer than the "local" Latino labor force, who from Arnold's perspective were more transient and less trustworthy. That may have to do with the fact that H2B visa workers, eager to keep their legal documentation, were compelled to maintain a positive relationship to that one employer in a way that undocumented immigrants in the community were not—they comparatively had more freedom, which made them less useful and reliable for the employer. Yet within these H2B networks we saw a parallel emergence of the immigrant labor manager—someone whom the employer trusted well and who would oversee not only other H2B workers but "local" Latino workers.

Gabriel, an H2B worker from Michoacán employed as a landscape worker in Steamboat for eight years prior to our interview (staying for four to five months each year), joined the H2B program after his brother worked for a landscaper in Steamboat and recommended him to the boss. His brother is also an H2B visa worker for the same employer, a relationship initiated when he responded to an ad in his home community. It has worked well for Gabriel to spend part of the year in Steamboat, always working in landscape installation and maintenance. He can renew his visa as long as his employer continues to put his name into the system, and he returns home for several months at a time annually. His employer arranges for him to live in an apartment complex that is used in the winter to house guestworkers for the Ski Corporation. Gabriel pays the rent, but it is arranged by the landscaping company, so he does not have to find housing on his own (other H2B visa workers suggested that most do not get any help from their employer finding housing). Gabriel described his time in Steamboat as being only about work: he did not go out much socially, and when he returned home to Michoacán he spent three weeks resting before taking odd jobs such as driving a taxi. He described this annual job as essential to maintaining his family at home.

Gabriel did not raise any complaints about his work in Steamboat, but in general he seemed hesitant to say much about his work there—it was more difficult for me to gain trust with Gabriel. This reflected an overall sense that H2B workers felt even more vulnerable than many undocumented residents, as their access to a visa to cross the border with ease depended on pleasing one particular employer. Although this research did not centrally explore the dynamics of employers using H2B visa holders/ guestworkers in the context of rural gentrification, we found the vast majority relying instead on undocumented labor. In Colorado guestworkers were more common among large-scale employers, but they were exceptions in rural gentrifying landscapes built and maintained largely by undocumented labor. While H2B visa holders did not face the deportation regime, they had many other constraints that made life challenging and were also expected to always be available, highly productive, and flexible.

HOUSEKEEPING AND HOME AND YARD MAINTENANCE

The third sector of the gentrification economy examined in this chapter represents a range of activities from formal businesses involved in yard or home maintenance to informal employer-employee relationships typified by a homeowner directly hiring workers to clean or maintain their houses and/or yards. It is also a sector that includes women workers as well as men: women predominantly were hired as housecleaners, while men were engaged in yard work or home maintenance. At the end of the day, when we spoke to business owners who ran home and property maintenance services—whether in Georgia or Colorado—we saw the critical role immigrant workers played in providing affordable and flexible labor in support of the lifestyle of gentrifiers. Homeowners who wanted to skip hiring a formal maintenance service frequently hired Latine immigrant workers directly, often developing a highly personalized relationship with them, to fix a range of household and property needs on a highly flexible basis.

As a stream of wealthy amenity migrants settled permanently or built vacation homes in Routt and Rabun Counties, they not only generated immediate demand for new home construction and the installation of outdoor space as explored in the previous section, they also created a long-term and steady demand for home and property maintenance and cleaning. The buying power most wealthy gentrifiers possess includes not only a capacity to purchase a large home and property in "their" rural paradise, but also an ability to purchase labor for social reproduction—from cleaning toilets, to mowing lawns, to food preparation.

In both Routt and Rabun Counties businesses emerged in the context of gentrification that catered to the wealthiest of the newcomers, offering them not merely home maintenance but "concierge" services that included fresh flowers and a stocked fridge on the day of a family's arrival at their vacation home. Roger, who owned such a company in Steamboat, described how he established a concierge property management company in 2000:

ROGER: I sort of grew up around this wealthy aspect . . . of what people expect and of a certain level that they expect. And this town really wasn't offering that. You sort of had your mountain resorts, you had your smaller management company, they're just a little more casual, they sort of look over the place but they didn't take personal care of the place. And I would have it prepped for them the way that they would expect it to be prepped.

LISE: And did you offer even to stock their fridge?

ROGER: We do everything. I do everything from liquor, flowers at every house, before they come, grocery shopping, we come in and fold their towels the next day, every day that they're here we come in and fold their towels. Its a concierge, not even a concierge service, its like having a butler. It's literally what it's like. And then eventually and so when I saw this need for high end management, not just watching the house but really catering to every need and specializing. [. . .] They know they can count on us for anything. So if they call me on a Sunday and say my husband is out playing golf and has the car and I'm having a dinner party tonight do you mind running some errands for me and getting me this this and this, boom, we go do it. We do anything, anything our clients ask. And so that's where it started snowballing. [. . .] Then maybe a realtor hears that I focus on high end management and so then they sell a $10 million place and the next thing you know I'm getting a call.

When asked about his labor challenges, Roger described starting out his business without in-house repair capacity. At first if there was a plumbing problem in one of his houses he was managing he would call a plumber, then "it got to a point where I realized that me making a phone call is not making me any money. So I created a team that does, so we can do the windows, the housekeeping, the mechanical work, the electrical, basically every aspect that you would have to do. The landscape, the maintenance outside, the decks, everything." He sought to hire people who knew multiple areas, such as someone who would wash windows or mow lawns "I have people who are crafty in multiple areas so that it lowers the number of employees I have."

As we continued our conversation about his workforce, I asked if he hired immigrant workers, and he responded:

ROGER: I use a ton of Hispanics, I love 'em. I love 'em. They all show me papers but I know they're not all legal. And I don't mind, and I don't care, I'm very vocal about it. [Then] my best guy got a knock on the door a month and a half ago. Because his roommate was wanted for something and it was immigration and boom they shipped him off as well, he's gone.

LISE: What did he do for you?

ROGER: Everything. He was the best employee I've ever had, out of every business I've had [over eighteen years], every White guy, every American guy, he's by far the best, most polite and responsible employee I've ever had. It was terrible because literally for all the years he worked for me, he knew my family, he knew my kids, I trusted him more than I trusted anybody working for me. Spoke terrific English, hiked seven days with no water over the border. Best guy, I lost him. [. . .] He was my translator, he was my guy, and that's sort of why the guy who took his place is working for me because he's sort of my translator because I have three other guys that, they understand some English, but some English is like five words. So his replacement is sort of my translator cause he speaks perfect English, he went to high school here and is Hispanic. Born in the U.S. so I guess he's legal through that route. But he's not nearly as responsible, he's a lot younger, he's not as responsible. [. . .] I'm not against hiring local White Americans. I've had too many ski bums. I've had too many guys that are here that are lazy, have different priorities in life, as far as where they want to get to. They are here to ski. [. . .]

The Hispanics work, they save a lot of money, they send a lot of money home, they work their tails off, they don't care if its Saturday, Sunday, Monday, they don't care if they work seven days a week, twelve hours a day, they don't complain, if I treat them well. [. . .] I pay all my guys $25/hour flat out across the board. If they don't do good work, they don't work anymore, but if they do good work, they get $25/hour and I bill out at $65/hour so I'm still making great money and they're making great money and if they're making great money they're happy. If I'm treating them well their happy and if I get a ton of work for them their really happy.

While my interview with Roger was unique in terms of his openness and enthusiasm for hiring Latine immigrant workers, many of whom he presumed were undocumented, his story encapsulates how the immigrant labor regime emerged and became consolidated in gentrification-linked sectors. Roger was willing to pay a premium for loyal, highly dependable and flexible workers—using the immigrant labor force was less about paying low wages than it was about gaining access to "compliant workaholics" who were flexible and dependable through the intersection of illegality, race, and class. Fernando paid a high price for the ever-present deportation regime—a tragedy for his wife and children, who according to Roger moved back to Mexico as a result (Fernando risked jail time if he tried to cross the border again, according to Roger). Although employers such as Roger tended to essentialize and racialize the "quality" of immigrant labor, many of these characteristics were created through the vulnerabilities produced by the threat of deportation, poverty, and racial hierarchy.

Although similar high-end concierge companies also existed in Rabun County, ones that also relied on immigrant workers, much of the residential maintenance and cleaning labor in Georgia was hired directly by homeowners, individual immigrants who cleaned, repaired, or maintained their property. Interestingly, immigrant social networks served as a key recruitment tool and mechanism for creating flexibility here as well. In both Colorado and Georgia cases, by the mid-2000s homeowners had become accustomed to hiring Latine workers for home and yard maintenance. Some turned to day labor sites for these projects, which is not surprising considering the expansion of day laborer sites throughout the United States from the mid-1990s.[14]

In Rabun County the "day labor" site was a laundromat not far from the center of town but not visible from any main roads. As Sarah, a White woman born and raised in Rabun County (going back six generations), described it: "So if you ever need something done at your house, if you want the yard cut and you don't feel like doing it, you've got a bunch of poison ivy you want yanked out or whatever, you know, they'll say "lets' just go down to the laundromat and pick us up a Mexican for the day." While the use of day laborers in Rabun was common, most wealthy newcomers (gentrifiers) we interviewed in Georgia tended to *not* use anonymous day laborers if they hired home or yard maintenance workers. Instead, they commonly developed long-term, personal relationships with Latine immigrants who operated in ways that were not profoundly different from the informal labor broker working in the construction company discussed previously.

The story of Leopoldo Peña (age 35) exemplifies these dynamics. Leopoldo had worked for over a decade in Rabun County supervising other Latine workers in a small-scale food-processing factory. That job, which comes with an apartment, offers him forty-five hours per week reliably, and up to eighty or ninety hours when things are busy. In a slower workweek of forty-five hours, he supplemented his income with small home and yard maintenance work that exclusively came through personal contacts with homeowners. He described one such relationship with a homeowner:

LEOPOLDO: I got to know him through my brother. He [my brother] told me once "this man needs you to work in his garden" and so that is how I met this man [in 1995]. From that point on every time he needs anyone, to work in his flower bed, put in grass, cut grass, wash his cars, fix his deck, I go and help him.

LISE: And what if you are too busy when he calls?

LEOPOLDO: I find someone else if I cannot [go], I send other friends of mine. But always, he [the homeowner] says to me . . . you see he has a

great deal of trust (confianza) in me, and I always tell him that
when I cannot do it I will send a friend of mine. He says that is okay
as long as it is a friend of yours and you know them.

Leopoldo had five homeowners in his network, helping them find (often
on short notice) someone "trustworthy" to accomplish yard or home projects. He described feeling responsible for the workers he sends, that if
they do not do the job right, the homeowners see him as responsible—a
mechanism of labor discipline that individual employers appreciated.
Thus, labor brokers also operated within informal economic activities, in
ways that facilitated the use and engagement of non-English-speaking immigrant workers by individual homeowners.

While men were involved in yard work and home maintenance, housecleaning, unsurprisingly, was coded as a female job. Latina immigrant participants in both Colorado and Georgia were most likely to report working
in residential or commercial cleaning (or restaurant work, which we turn
to in the next section). As discussed in chapter 2, migration decisions and
job market opportunities for men were usually the leading factor shaping
settlement decisions, and women searched for employment after arriving in Georgia or Colorado. In both places most Latina respondents who
cleaned in private homes did not do so for a cleaning company but were
recruited by private homeowners. In Colorado, an equal number worked
for hotels rather than in homes, giving them a formal, corporate employer.
While we spoke to one person in Georgia who worked as a housekeeper
in a hotel, it was much less common largely because as an amenity site
Georgia is more impacted by second-home owners than tourists, whereas
Steamboat has a large tourist sector and a number of large hotel chains
located near the ski area.

We interviewed Diana, a 25-year-old who had lived in Craig, Colorado,
for five years (Craig is about fifty minutes from Steamboat, serving as a
bedroom community for the resort town). She arrived from Honduras as
a documented immigrant because she was sponsored by her grandmother,
who had become legalized in the United States. Despite having legal status, Diana's situation did not differ dramatically from those of undocumented participants. Diana related that she had not intended to migrate
to the United States, she was in her first year of college in Honduras, but

she was pressured by her mother to migrate when, after years of waiting, their papers came through. Her life changed for the worse as she went from being a psychology major with professional aspirations to being a housekeeper:

LISE: What type of work did you do when you arrived here?

DIANA: My grandmother worked in housekeeping, and that is what we were led to as well. My mother and I. I still am doing it.

Diana described how she worked in the same large hotel with her mother and grandmother for several years until the hotel announced they would be paying "by the piece"/by the room. This made her afraid of eroding wages, so she started looking for other work. The owner of a small hotel offered to hire her as a "housekeeping manager," but after she arrived, she realized she was the only worker in housekeeping:

They were supposed to hire other people. Because the hotel is small, because the owner wants to economize to the maximum, therefore there is no housekeeping manager, I am a housekeeper. [. . .] The picture they painted me, it wasn't like that. The only thing is that no one is paying attention to what I do, no one supervises me like before [in the big hotel]. My salary is the same as it was before, but I lost my benefits. I lost everything, including vacation time.

Diana described the difficulty she has had, giving up her aspirations for a college degree and instead working as a housekeeper in Colorado:

The first year was horrible. It was . . . I don't know, the change to living here was not a nice experience. This, because you leave your people, all that is yours. [. . .] I did not see myself in what I am doing right now, I did not see it as a future for me. [. . .] The weather, because I came in wintertime, it comes in September here. [. . .] I felt my feet were icy and it added to my desperation to be in my country.

Her experience differed profoundly from that of her little sister, who was eleven when they both migrated from Honduras. Her sister enrolled in school in Colorado and was on her way to graduating with hopes of attending college—she learned English in school, while Diana struggles with English, because Diana had no access to language instruction.

Elisa is a 28-year-old undocumented resident who arrived in Rabun County seven years before our interview and is mother to two U.S.-born children. She initially worked with her husband in a small manufacturing business in Rabun County (recruited there by her cousin), but after having children she needed more flexibility. First she took a job at a fast-food restaurant, but she soon left that to clean houses, which allowed her to care for her children while working (they joined her at the homes and played while she cleaned): "So I don't have to pay a babysitter. I also try to get those jobs because I can go when I can, and if I hurry and finish a house more quickly it is possible since they pay me a fixed amount. I do not have to be there all day. [. . .] I also do not have to drive through town, down the highway."

Not only are cleaning jobs coded as female, and thus one of the top job categories for Latina immigrants in these rural gentrifying spaces, but residential housecleaning offered many an opportunity to balance care work and paid work. In Elisa's case, the homeowners trusted her and referred her to other homeowners in the area. If they were seasonal residents in the summer, Elisa would accept being employed for a few months at a time, always available when they needed it—the structural flexibility valued by formal and informal employers across all of these sectors. It is also worth highlighting Elisa's last sentence above, that her job choice was also shaped by her everyday geography of fear of deportation and the fact that she was mostly likely to be picked up while driving. The location of the properties she cleans allowed her to avoid driving through town or on the highway, a dynamic I return to in the next chapter.

The cleaning and property maintenance sector in both Routt and Rabun Counties has relied extensively on Latine immigrant labor, largely undocumented, since the late 1990s/early 2000s. The availability of a low-wage, highly flexible, and trustworthy group of workers to maintain and clean residential and hotel properties was essential to the functioning of gentrifying rural landscapes.

RESTAURANT SECTOR

In the context of urban landscapes, scholars have conceptualized key indicators of gentrification to include rising housing prices; conversion and remodeling of existing housing stock; and the expansion of restaurants, coffee shops, and other retail businesses catering to wealthier clientele.[15] Similar changes are visible in high-amenity rural areas witnessing the in-migration of wealthy urbanites seeking a connection to the rural idyll. The expansion of restaurants and retail stores in Rabun and Routt Counties between 1990 and 2010, capturing the period under exploration here, tells a clear story of expansion that is linked to gentrification and the arrival of newcomers with greater disposable income and a desire for dining out. Between 1990 and 2010 the number of restaurants increased in Routt County by 140 percent (overall population growth during that period was 67 percent), and in Rabun County they increased by 125 percent (overall population growth 40 percent).[16]

When fieldwork was conducted in Colorado and Georgia, restaurants in both places were already drawing overwhelmingly on Latine labor for "back-of-the-house" jobs (e.g., dishwashers, cooks, and assistants). In Colorado some front-of-the-house workers (e.g., waiters) were Latine as well, particularly in Mexican and Latin American restaurants. As in the other sectors explored above, restaurants could not function at the level and capacity demanded during the gentrification boom without recruiting immigrant workers, many of whom were undocumented. How workers were recruited by restaurants differed somewhat between Colorado and Georgia. In Georgia, immigrant workers in restaurants were often recruited from farm labor crews—initially in relation to the farms where restaurants would buy produce locally. Immigrant workers in restaurants in Steamboat did not come from farmwork but arrived in ways that paralleled the landscaping sector: they were recruited by Steamboat restaurants through urban-linked business networks (i.e., Denver). I return to elaborate those recruiting practices below, but in a parallel fashion to the history of construction and landscaping, immigrant workers were the "perfect" labor force for an industry with significant labor needs, variable scheduling practices, and tight profit margins. Latine workers gave restaurant owners a workforce that could ramp up or be let go on short notice, disciplined by the intersection of illegality and hierarchies of race and class.

Pedro is a 57-year-old who first came to the United States to work in the tomato fields in Florida, followed by several years traveling the Northeast picking crops. In the late 1980s he came to Rabun County to pick cabbage, one of the biggest commercial crops in the county and that since the mid-1980s had relied extensively on Latine farmworkers during the harvest. He was working the cabbage field when he was "lent" to a business that included a restaurant and hotel during a busy weekend:

PEDRO: We were working in cabbage when the boss with whom we came to work loaned us (nos prestó) to a restaurant so that we could help them one weekend. Saturdays and Sundays were when they needed a lot of people at the restaurant and we would cut vegetables, shuck corn. We were going there regularly when they asked us if we would like to stay. They said they would give us work for the entire year. There were six of us and we said "okay."

LISE: What did you do in the restaurant, you were a cook?

PEDRO: No, I work in everything. I am a cook, I do what is needed there, I am in charge of a group. I have a group of workers for the outside, who take care of the garden, cut the grass. I do not do anything more than go around telling everyone what to do, what is needed over here and over there. But if they need me to be a cook, I am a cook too, or a busboy. . . . I do anything in any part of the restaurant. Now that I have been there 19 years I can do everything, and the boss values me. [. . .] He gives me housing for free, when other workers have to pay to stay in his apartments.

Pedro described an employer who expected him to be available whenever he called, noting that the only time he carved out outside of work was to play soccer every Sunday morning—a topic we return to in the next chapter on geographies of social reproduction.

In Rabun County the restaurant sector not only expanded rapidly under gentrification, it attracted outside entrepreneurs, more so than construction or landscaping businesses—the nicer restaurants in town were most often owned by newcomers, not longtime locals. They came to Rabun County for many of the same reasons as other gentrifiers, but they opened a business when they relocated (not all gentrifiers were retired or independently wealthy). These "newcomer" owners usually had previous experience running restaurants in cities—restaurants that had been fully reliant on Latine immigrant back-of-the-house workers for a decade or longer. It is unsurprising that these exurban restaurateurs recreated labor regimes similar to those they had used in urban spaces—at times recruiting the same people whom they had worked with in Atlanta or Florida. And even if they did not recruit someone they knew from the city, they had a comfort level with and understanding of how to recruit and incorporate immigrant workers into their business—something that local restaurants, which had existed prior to the gentrification boom, generally lacked.

The tendency of higher-end restaurants in Rabun County to be owned by newcomers coming from afar makes sense in another way—they had the knowledge to cater to the tastes of wealthy gentrifiers who were coming from cities, more so than local cooks and restaurants that predated the gentrification boom. In Rabun, longtime restaurants usually cooked classic southern and Appalachian cuisine, while high-end, newer restaurants were cooking Asian fusion or California cuisine—catering to the distinct range of tastes that would attract wealthier newcomers.

It was also the restaurant sector in which entrepreneurial immigrants would open businesses, in both Rabun and Routt Counties. This is not surprising, as the growth of Mexican restaurants tends to follow migratory settlement patterns. One such entrepreneur in Rabun County was Mateo, a 28-year-old who arrived in Rabun in 1999, following his father, who was already working in the area. Mateo's story provides insight into restaurant labor regimes in the context of the gentrification boom; he started in restaurants at age 16 and by 2012 owned his own, successful restaurant.

Mateo's father first arrived in Rabun as a tree planter in the national forest, but he settled down when he shifted to working in a restaurant as a dishwasher and a peeler of shrimp and potatoes. The owner needed more help (there was only one other Latine worker in the restaurant at the time), and Mateo's father called him in Mexico and urged him to come. Mateo was a teen in 1999, and his plan was to enroll in high school in Rabun County and work on the weekends. He arrived and enrolled, relating that there were only about a dozen Latine students in the high school at the time. He graduated high school after four years (starting "back" in the ninth grade) while working weekends at the restaurant. He started washing dishes and working his way up to making salads, then hamburgers, saying, "This is how I began to move up." After graduating he continued to work in restaurants, shifting to some larger resorts outside of town and working as a sous chef; some chefs took him under their wing and taught him additional cooking techniques.

Working under various chefs over several years at the resort, Mateo felt that some were very kind to him (e.g., one took Mateo to visit his family), while others just wanted to "utilize the Hispanos as slaves" in his words. Overall, it was very stressful, even as he received accolades from customers for his cooking. Mateo then moved to a job working as a chef in a high-end restaurant in town, a privately owned restaurant rather than part of a corporate-owned resort. He thought it would be better, but things became more difficult:

MATEO: [B]ecause they were leaving all the responsibility for the restaurant to me, the owner was. I began to feel very pressured. And anything that happened, I had to deal with it by myself. I had to solve the problem, whatever happened, while the owner went on vacation.

LISE: Were you being paid as a manager?

MATEO: No, I was being paid at a normal wage, even less. I told her I wanted a raise, because you see at the beginning during training I only asked for $14/hour, which she said was too much because, "I do not know you. I am not going to pay a chef a high wage that I do not know already." I told her to just let me into the kitchen and I would show her what I can do. In this way little by little I learned her menu. She told me, "I have never said this to anyone, but you are the best." [. . .] People from Atlanta. Actors. They loved my food. So she took a hold of me to do everything. "Do this, do that" but she only paid me $12/hour. I told her I have demonstrated my abilities and all she gave me was 50 cents more.

I told myself that I cannot take it anymore. I started to drink as an escape. In the night to let off steam, to reduce my stress. A year went by and she started to leave and to leave me in charge. It was terrible. She gave me a raise to $13/hour.

Mateo finally quit and then worked in restaurants in Highlands, North Carolina (a thirty-minute drive from Clayton in Rabun County). He eventually opened his own restaurant; most of the employees are members of Mateo's extended family.

In Steamboat the gentrification boom of the late 1990s brought additional year-round residents with the disposable income to eat out regularly—a dynamic similar to what happened in Rabun County. However, because of its longer history as a resort (and its size as a ski resort),

Steamboat had more restaurants before the gentrification boom, causing the evolution of the restaurant sector to be distinct. Based on interviews with restaurant owners, one key difference before and after the gentrification boom was that while there were many restaurants prior to the mid-1990s, owned frequently by members of the earlier wave of White amenity migrants who by that time claimed the title "local," they were often only open seasonally. Moreover, they relied on a workforce comprised of White, college-age kids who needed to earn a living while maximizing their time on the slopes. The expansion of full-time residents rather than tourists—gentrification as we have identified it here—created year-round demand for restaurants and increasingly high-end establishments. This all combined to increase the number of restaurants and the scale of their operations, which like restaurants in Rabun County made the recruitment of immigrant workers attractive and essential.

As in Rabun County, our interviews with restaurant owners and managers indicated that the establishment of *new* restaurants in the mid- to late 1990s, as the year-round population of Steamboat grew, was largely undertaken by later waves of amenity migrants. These newcomer entrepreneurs bought existing restaurants or established new ones, but in either case they brought with them knowledge of and comfort with the recruitment and incorporation of immigrant workers, many of whom were Latine and often were also undocumented. This pattern is most evident among the workers hired for back-of-the-house roles—from dishwashers to bus boys, cooks, and/or the cleaning crew.

One of our research participants, Gloria, described arriving in Steamboat from Juarez, Mexico, in 2002 because her husband took a job in construction. She said that at that time there were few Latine families living in Steamboat, and her kids were among a handful of non-White kids in the public school. When asked about her work, she replied:

> In Mexico I was sitting in a very tidy office with painted fingernails, makeup and everything. When I came here to the U.S. the change was tremendous. All the studies I had there, all the education I brought ... here my degree didn't serve me. As one says vulgarly, it [the degree] didn't help more than to wipe in the bathroom. It didn't help me at all.
>
> I first began to work here (in Steamboat) in a fast-food restaurant, that was the first job. They made me wash dishes. . . . [T]he last one hired is the

one who has to do everything: wash dishes, take out the trash, get things out of the freezer. You have to wash dishes with hot water and then suddenly they need something from the freezer and I am the one who had to go. To go into the freezer, wet. [. . .]

I began to work in the kitchen of another restaurant. For me it was frustrating. After so many years in school, good jobs (in Mexico), to be working in a kitchen of a restaurant . . . one time I burnt myself. One night after the restaurant was closed, we were cleaning and I had to clean the deep fryer with the boiling oil. . . . [T]he machine I was using to clean fell into the oil and splashed hot oil over my arm. I ran and put my arm in the ice machine. It hurt very badly, but when I took it out it was bright red. I thought I would be seeing bone. I am not sure what would have happened if I hadn't put my arm in ice quickly.

Gloria did not ask for workers' compensation for the injury, and shortly after she quit and tried other strategies to get by economically, including cooking tamales and going to construction sites to sell to the workers at lunchtime, which earned enough money during the height of the construction boom in 2005–2007. When the construction industry contracted in the Great Recession, her husband began working as a mechanic, and she began cleaning cars for a car rental agency. While some of the people they knew left during the recession, they were able to make it through and remain in Steamboat.

The restaurant owners and managers in both Routt and Rabun Counties relied less on the "labor broker" figure visible in most construction, landscaping, and/or maintenance operations in part because managing labor in restaurants is less complicated, as everything happens inside the restaurant. Managers, most of the time White, knew enough to communicate and manage immigrant labor essential to the business without turning over significant responsibility to an immigrant labor broker/manager. They did use immigrant social networks to fill positions when needed, but generally White owners and managers maintained control and oversite at a higher level than contractors or landscapers. The story of Mateo shared above is an exception. The owner of the restaurant where he was the chef tried to basically have him run the whole restaurant and work as chef for $13 an hour, but he quit. Restaurant workers worked long hours and were paid low wages, but labor needs did not fluctuate as dramatically as they did in construction or landscaping.

A willingness to do all jobs and respond to employers' needs was fundamental to developing a strong, personalistic relationship with their employers, which for many workers meant a stable—even if profoundly subordinated—place at work. The characteristics of flexibility inspired employers to hire Latine workers in times of labor shortage and economic expansion. They tended also to retain those same workers even as the economy contracted after 2008. The primary work of Rabun County, Georgia, resident Rosa Ortiz (age 42) is in fast food, although she also works as a hotel maid on the side when needed by one local hotel. At the fast-food restaurant, she describes her work since the economic downturn in 2008:

ROSA: I am not the manager, I am an assistant to them, the managers. And I think I am one of the few workers at this place that has not had my hours cut back this year.

LISE: Why do you think that is the case?

ROSA: Well, you see I know all of the jobs in the restaurant. Right now I work forty-two to forty-five hours per week, but when things are bad they only give me thirty-five hours. But there are other employees that get even less, they are down to twenty to twenty-five hours a week. There is little work.

For her job in the hotel, Rosa simply receives a call from the owner explaining how many rooms he needs cleaned on a particular day. If she is able, given her restaurant schedule, to clean the rooms, she does it for $6.50 per room. If Rosa cannot clean the room she calls a friend to clean it, and she pays her $5.00 per room, keeping the difference. The restaurant is able to keep an employee (Rosa) who knows "all the jobs" in the restaurant even as her hours fluctuate, because she balances that work with cleaning hotel rooms that can be subcontracted out when needed. The hotel owner benefits because he only pays for the rooms that need cleaning on a particular day, rather than keeping a maid on a regular salary. This situation is aided by his knowledge that if Rosa cannot clean the rooms she will be responsible for sending another worker. This account demonstrates the complexity of chains of vulnerability and flexibility, and how immigrant networks are fundamental to shifting rural capitalism in the context of gentrification.

CONCLUSION

As wealthy, White exurbanites settled in Routt County, Colorado, and Rabun County, Georgia (full or part-time) during the late 1990s and beyond, they created demand for housing and services that transformed the economies and social landscapes of these amenity areas. As wealthy newcomers grew in number, the relationships of class and belonging shifted among longtime locals, mostly White, and these wealthy newcomers, also mostly White.[17] Less visible were the ways in which increasing demand for construction, landscaping, cleaning, restaurants, and other services put pressure on the local labor market. For contractors and landscapers, the demand far outpaced their existing workforce, inspiring some to hire crews from cities such as Denver or Atlanta to work for short stints, putting them up in hotels for weeks at a time. For many business owners, these out-of-town crews were their first exposure to an immigrant workforce and provided them a means to recruit immigrant workers—often with the promise of higher wages and assistance with housing.

Few employers, particularly contractors and landscapers, truly anticipated how these early stopgap recruitment strategies might change the way they do business, their stress level, their vacation time, and the profitability of the enterprise—their whole business model. In hiring racialized workers who were also often legally and linguistically marginalized, they were accessing, in the words of Jill Harrison and Sarah Lloyd, "compliant workaholics."[18] Employers often discovered that the value of structurally marginalized workers included much more than cheaper wages, although employers generally pay immigrant workers less per hour; it meant having access to workers who seemed to organize their lives around work and who would "accept" being hired and then let go in response to ever-changing business needs. Our interview team heard repeatedly from employers the ease with which they could bring in immigrant workers, and on the flipside as one employer described it, when he did not need them anymore "they disappear." Of course they do not disappear; they have lives, as explored in the next chapter.

At the center of these new regimes, and the profitability associated with them, is vulnerability—vulnerability created by intersecting structural processes. First, undocumented immigrant workers live in fear of deportation and have little recourse for demanding basic rights. Second, even if documented, immigrant workers face racialized assumptions about their right to belong and to a home life. They are often assumed to be "illegal," which feeds expectations about how hard they will work and how little they will complain.[19] (Not to mention that even if documented, many low-wage Latine immigrants have family members who are undocumented.) Third, most of the newly arriving immigrant workers involved in low-wage work struggle under poverty exacerbated by the debt usually taken on to cross the border. The intersection of race, class, and illegality produced a highly flexible, dependable, and productive workforce for the benefit of entrepreneurs wanting to profit from the gentrification boom. These new regimes allowed rural businesses to improve the speed and efficiency of their operations, outcompeting those that continued with the traditional, "local" source of labor and set of labor practices.

The flexibility inherent in immigrant labor regimes consolidated in many sectors around the use of the informal labor broker, the worker who over time took over the recruitment and management of immigrant workers for the White owner or boss. Whether because he or she could speak English and act as a translator of the owner's instructions or because he or she had the networks of family and friends to quickly recruit people based on ever-changing labor demands, almost all long-term immigrant-reliant businesses cultivated a worker to serve as labor broker and manager. Labor brokers, as frequently undocumented as documented, often got paid more than the average immigrant worker, but perhaps most importantly that person gained power. They decided who was hired and fired among the immigrant workers, they acted as overseer and disciplinarian, and they were sometimes vested with significant autonomy over key aspects of the business. Over and over both owner/managers and labor brokers themselves described the owner leaving town for periods of time without worrying about how the business was running—they felt so confident in "their guy." Profound trust and loyalty were cultivated, and the owners sometimes went to lengths to hire lawyers to legalize their labor brokers and to shield them from the deportation regime, as explored further in the next chapter.

The development of labor regimes predicated on accessing workers marginalized by race, language, class, and illegality proved very attractive to employers. Yet as reflected in many of the workers' narratives shared over the course of this chapter, it was a labor regime that produced a highly precarious and consuming work life for immigrant newcomers living in these gentrifying locales. Most immigrants in the sectors explored here worked long and unpredictable hours, were paid minimally (without attention to overtime laws and pay), and were expected to be at the disposal of their employers or managers whenever they called, usually seven days a week. Workers who made the deep commitment to being available also increased their security by learning every job in the restaurant/construction business/landscaping company. They made themselves indispensable.

While the labor brokers themselves might have steady and secure employment—some employers went to great lengths to cultivate trust and loyalty with their labor brokers—most of the "nonbroker" workers had to organize their lives not only to be at the disposal of their key employer, but to hold multiple jobs to hedge against losing a job in the short or long term. We could see this in the story and quote shared earlier by Leopoldo, who worked mainly for a food-processing company in Rabun County but supplemented that work by doing property maintenance for a handful of individual homeowners. He fit in the homeowners' needs if he could in relation to the demands of his primary employer. These relationships provided him with a buffer when the main employer let him go for several months. This was a similar situation to Diego's; he balanced working for a private homeowner with occasional roofing jobs. Latine immigrant participants in both Georgia and Colorado rarely just held one job, particularly men (women's "other job" was usually taking care of children).

I close this chapter by sharing one final story of a worker not yet introduced, to illustrate the intensity of work and juggling multiple jobs for most Latine immigrant workers in the context of gentrification: the story of Jorge, a 24-year-old Mexican national working without papers in Steamboat for three years at the time of our interview. An excerpt from my fieldnotes reads:

> In the summers Jorge works with a crew of other Mexican nationals, including three cousins. His crew moves between ranches on the outskirts of Steamboat to undertake summer-time maintenance tasks. They work on a ranch anywhere from ten to twenty-one days while they repair fences, barns, build retaining walls, and dig ditches, before moving onto the next ranch. In

the winter Jorge shovels snow for a property maintenance company serving wealthy homeowners. He recounted how hard this is when it gets really cold and remarked that his boss only allows them stop working if it reaches 40 below or colder.

In addition to these seasonal jobs, Jorge is on the nighttime cleaning crew for a local grocery store from 9 p.m.–2:00 a.m., six nights a week. After [he] describ[ed] his multiple jobs, I asked him when he sleeps. He laughed, "I only sleep three or so hours a night." He has one day off a week, the only day he could schedule an interview with me.

The structural forces producing these labor regimes, ones creating precarity for workers and significant profit for employers, were not highly visible, and the conditions they produced became normalized over time. Most employers saw Latine immigrants' work ethic, endless availability, and loyalty as an essential characteristic of "the Mexicans" (as many were called no matter their national origin) rather than a condition produced by border policies and practices, the dispossessions and displacements of neoliberal globalization, and racial hierarchies that continue to shape the fabric of U.S. society.

4 Social Reproduction, Race, and "Illegality"

> Without papers, without a license, there is nothing else
> besides work and home, it is our life all of the time. We
> imprison ourselves here at home, nothing more. [...] We
> only go to work, enclose ourselves at work, try to take care
> of ourselves with the police ... this is our life. We are scared
> to go out. We think about going back to Mexico because
> this is not a life, but then we think of our children and we
> know that their lives can be normal, they have rights and
> better schools. We suffer this for them.
>
> —Elisa, housekeeper, Rabun County (June 26, 2010)

During our interviews a few employers described with enthusiasm their experience of "Mexican" workers "disappearing" when they were not needed by the employer. However, they did not disappear. Instead, Latine immigrant residents navigated space and activities outside of work without which their labor power could not be reproduced—from meeting tangible needs such as food and housing to fulfilling less tangible but deeply psychological needs for community, care, and belonging. Elisa's words illustrate one key dimension of life outside of work for many immigrant workers and their families in Routt and Rabun Counties: the ever-present fear of deportation. It is a fear that saturates the daily lives and movements of many immigrant newcomers in gentrifying rural spaces, even as it is refracted through additional challenges marked by race, language, and poverty.

This chapter explores the geographies of life, of social reproduction, for immigrant residents critical to the production of gentrifying landscapes.

Feminist theories of social reproduction offer a broad conceptual umbrella to explore life spaces and pathways outside of, but intimately connected to, work and labor regimes.[1] To develop a multidimensional understanding of geographies of social reproduction, I examine spaces of housing for Latine immigrants, experiences of illegality in everyday life, and spaces of recreation.

While most immigrants interviewed for this research crossed the border to build a better life than was possible in their home communities—a dream that was economic and social-political in nature—most of them navigated significant challenges and profound, ongoing stress trying to build a life in Rabun County, Georgia, or Routt County, Colorado, whether or not they were documented. This is not to claim that people who did not have legal papers did not face unique challenges compared to those with legal status. Instead, it is to recognize that the daily, embodied experience of these apparently distinct categories (documented and undocumented) was not necessarily profoundly different given the ways racism often operated in practice to construct all people of Latine descent as "illegal."

Immigrant residents were critical to the production and functioning of landscapes of rural gentrification, but most faced profound precarity in economic, social, and civic terms. As was explored in detail in the previous chapter, most immigrants—men and women—linked themselves into multiple job networks (roofing and home maintenance, housekeeping and restaurant work, home maintenance and landscaping). Employers commonly assumed that workers were available at any time and that they would prioritize the employers' needs over everything else. To maintain standing in these networks, to be "hirable," meant avoiding saying no—saying no too often could mean you go down on the list of people who are called when jobs open up. The hours of work were long (often across multiple employers), they were constantly in flux, and the wages were low. Most reported working more than forty hours a week for an employer but never being offered overtime and not feeling like they could ask for it (they usually didn't; some employers did pay overtime regardless of legal status).

Thus, the labor regime itself profoundly structured people's lives: for immigrants working without children or partners in the community (these were usually men who left families based in Mexico or Central America), this meant working very long hours/week and living in overcrowded trailers or an apartment with several other adult immigrants. In households with children living in Rabun or Routt Counties, parents struggled to provide appropriate housing (privacy and room for children to play) and care for their children. Throughout the sections of this chapter I weave together and contrast the dynamics in Rabun and Routt Counties, while also attending to the differences between solo workers (mostly male) and households with children.

HOUSING

An article published in Steamboat's local paper shares a core conundrum of housing and rural gentrification:

> One of the study's main findings was that a strong second-home market increases the cost of housing and the demand for low-income jobs. So, while the second-home market creates more jobs, the people working those jobs will have a harder time affording to live in the community where they work. . . . The more second homes there are, the more need there is for jobs, especially those in the service sector such as lawn maintenance, cleaning companies, massage therapists and caterers. The catch-22 for communities is that as the demand for second homes goes up, so do home prices, especially in areas where land is limited. And as prices go up, it is harder for the workforce to live in the community where they work.[2]

The initial project developed by Peter Nelson and I, exploring rural geographies of gentrification, hypothesized that most low-wage immigrant workers would not be living inside the town limits, simply due to the cost of living (part of the definition of rural gentrification is rising housing costs). This turned out not to be the case empirically, at least not in a straightforward manner, as we found a significant number of low-wage, undocumented immigrant workers living inside the city limits of Steamboat and Clayton (the county seat and largest town in Rabun County). We explore these patterns further below.

Whether Latine immigrant residents and families were living "in town" or in a more distant or dispersed low-cost location (commuting in for work), they experienced precarious housing conditions because of the convergence of several factors: their low wages and precarious jobs, the high cost of living, the profitability of overcrowding rental units for land-lords, and the ways that housing choices were shaped by fears of depor-tation and a desire to remain less visible. Housing options and strategies were also influenced in both areas by whether one was a solo worker (usu-ally male), without family living in the same place, or not. The solo work-ers tended to accept sharing an apartment with a number of other people to maximize their savings. While some couples with children described choosing such housing temporarily, they worked hard to find their own space with some room for kids to play and feel safer.

In Steamboat Springs, Colorado, there were several trailer parks near the Yampa River, which housed Latine immigrants (of various legal sta-tuses) and non-Hispanic White working-class people, as they were among the most affordable type of housing in the town (see figure 2). These trailer parks remained in Steamboat despite skyrocketing land values in the area because they were located in a floodplain and could not easily be redevel-oped into condos or other high-end developments. In addition to trailer parks in town, a handful of apartment buildings on the outskirts were used for immigrant housing, particularly the housing of H2B temporary workers hired by the ski resort in the winter (the ski resort tended to re-cruit Australian, Jamaican, and South American H2B visa holders). In the summer these buildings housed summer H2B workers, overwhelm-ingly Mexican and Central American, who usually worked in landscaping or construction. There were small pockets of "low-end" condos near to town that might house immigrant or nonimmigrant low-wage workers, but they were not always visible in an otherwise homogeneous landscape of luxury.

Aside from these spaces in town, a significant portion of immigrant workers in gentrification-linked sectors lived far outside of Steamboat in lower-cost locations, typically in Craig (a fifty-minute drive from Steam-boat), Hayden (thirty-five minutes), or Oak Creek (thirty minutes), al-though the latter two communities were also fairly expensive because they were the location of choice for White professionals who worked in Steamboat but were unable to afford housing there. The need to drive and commute from these communities, an especially risky proposition for undocumented residents, provided more incentives for workers to find something in town.

Figure 2. Mobile home park located in a low-lying area near the Yampa River, Steamboat Springs. Photo by author.

In Rabun County, Georgia, the cost and availability of housing were more variable than in Routt County, Colorado, and the highest property values were far outside of town. Properties on the lakes (Rabun Lake, Lake Burton, and Seed Lake) were astronomically expensive: older lakeside cottages were systematically being torn down to build homes over five thousand square feet in size and $5 to $7 million in value, even when homeowners did not own the land under the house (recall that Georgia Power leases the land to homeowners for most of the lots around the lakes). Gentrifying properties farther from the lakes, houses located in the bucolic and forested valleys, were often large and expensive (from hobby wineries to horse properties) but were often very close to homes and properties still held by longtime locals, often containing lower-valued housing stock. The housing architecture of "locals" in the valleys included traditional Appalachian cabins, mobile homes, and older, modest nonmobile homes. These all had a distinct aesthetic compared to the places built or purchased by wealthy gentrifiers (see figure 3). Unlike Steamboat, where there was little affordable housing for low-wage workers broadly, in Rabun County there were a range of spaces for low-cost housing, even if such spaces were dispersed and often not highly visible, as discussed below.

The population in Rabun County is less dense than in Steamboat, but equally important to housing patterns was the legacy of local families owning a significant amount of land—some tracing that ownership to the eighteenth century, as discussed in chapter 2. As some locals described it, they were land rich but often cash poor. A number of these families had sold off plots, particularly those pieces of land with the best views, but most White, multigenerational locals reported still having a few acres in their name that gave them a toehold for affordable housing—even if in the form of a trailer on that land.

Delia and Virginia were two local women in their forties whom I interviewed together (their choice) for this research; both traced their families back over eight generations. They each worked in administrative jobs with modest pay and no health insurance. When I asked them about local people's access to land and housing, they replied:

DELIA: I think a lot of locals struggle.

VIRGINIA: I do too. And [in my family] we haven't had that problem yet. My grandpa gave each of his kids twelve acres so my mom kept two and will give each of us five. . . . [T]hey haven't been given to us yet, they will be given to us, so I haven't had to deal with land taxes yet. Then my husband, we lived on his parents land which will become ours when his parents die so we haven't had to deal with that yet. And I haven't seen anybody in my family, I've seen a lot of people sell it just because they need the money.

DELIA: And when people come in with money and the locals are desperate to sell land they can get a lot of money for land that is really valuable, that has been in their family for years. Like I know on Betty's Creek, there's like not a lot, it's not real populated but a lot of the land that you see has been carried down over generations. [. . .]

VIRGINIA: And you feel like you have something if you have land. You have something that nobody's gonna take, that you're always gonna have it.

Figure 3. Visual examples of the range of housing quality in Rabun County. Photos by author.

The perspectives shared by Virginia and Delia help explain why there is a microscale of unevenness in housing quality and aesthetic in Rabun County—a significant portion of long-term locals hold onto land even as they sometimes give in to the economic pressure of rising land values and sell some of it off. This creates a particular housing geography in which class inequalities are written into the landscape more visibly in comparison to Steamboat. In Rabun County one can drive down a valley road and see a multi-million-dollar hobby farm, then turn a corner and see trailers, dilapidated housing, and/or rusted cars in a field. It was this patchwork of housing styles and values across class that in the end provided more options for housing for low-wage Latine workers compared to Steamboat.

For Latine immigrants in Rabun County, housing usually consisted of living in a trailer or an apartment, although a handful of respondents rented a small single-family home within a short drive from town. One apartment complex in particular was known as the place where "Mexicans" lived, and according to the manager, White people had not tried to rent there in years (it was fully segregated from other apartment complexes). I call it Black Rock Apartments; it was a large complex but not very visible from any major road in town. While living in Black Rock usually meant sharing one apartment with several roommates, it was conveniently located within walking distance of services, including the "day labor" site by a laundromat, and a fifteen-minute walk to the center of the town. One White long-term local, Betty, who interacted with many Latino families over fifteen years as part of her job, described the segregation of housing in Clayton this way:

BETTY: [Black Rock] Apartments will rent to Mexicans, yes. But there are other apartment owners, right over there, they only rent to couples and teachers and retirees. I am not sure if it is the landlord who decides that, or . . . there are just so many White families they don't wanna live with Mexicans next door. So he just keeps it the same, with White people.

But Black Rock, you know, they rent to Mexicans. It is almost half empty now because so many Mexicans have had to move away [due to the Great Recession]. I knew one man who lived with five other people in an apartment there, they split the rent. The owners don't care how many people live in the apartment, they don't care as long as the rent gets paid. . . . [switching topics] My Mom just had to get rid of a White guy. It probably took four months to get him out, he destroyed the apartment. They've had Mexicans renting before and always left it in pristine condition and they were sorry to see them go. Mexicans are good renters, and the landlords prefer Mexicans as to Whites.

LISE: Why is that?

BETTY: They will pay rent, they won't skip out on the rent, they will pay it.

There is a sense from Betty's story that landlords may prefer immigrant renters because they perceive them to be more diligent in paying rent or as less trouble, or that they will leave when asked without formal eviction procedures. Those claims are hard to verify in a systematic way, although an interview with a trailer park manager in Steamboat indicated a similar perspective. This is how Maggie described the arrival of Latine immigrants in the early 2000s: "They always pay the rent, they always respected me, but not being able to communicate was tough. Telling them you cannot have twenty people living in these trailers, sometimes was hard because they did not understand why since they were quiet and paying rent on time." While neighbors complained about overcrowding, landlords did not always see it as a problem.

In the same way that "illegal" and racialized immigrants feel pressure to accept lower pay, difficult work conditions, or fluctuating schedules, they also at times prove to be the ideal renters for those landlords with low-end housing—they are compliant and flexible tenants. Black Rock Apartments in Rabun County, Georgia, became a key site of social reproduction for immigrant workers and residents during Rabun's gentrification boom, but by the time we were conducting fieldwork only about half the apartments were occupied. As more itinerant and single workers left Rabun County during the Great Recession, a greater proportion of our immigrant worker participants lived on their own in a mobile home or rented a house, whether in town or in isolated spaces down a forest road.

Diego, a roofer and maintenance worker residing in Rabun County, Georgia (who was introduced in chapter 3) lived for several years in Black Rock Apartments, although at the time of the interview he was sharing a trailer outside of town. When asked about his living situation when he arrived in Rabun County, he said:

> We shared an apartment, but we were . . . my brother, a friend whose name was Miguel—who now is back in Mexico—and two other people. One thing that I have never liked is that I do not like living in tight quarters (apretados). I do not like to live with so many people, do you understand what

I mean? I like a little bit of privacy. Now, there are many people here who do not give a damn about how many people they live with because they pay less rent. If the rent is $550, you do not have to pay much if you put eleven people in there. It is just $50 a month! But, with eleven people, you can imagine an apartment of two bedrooms, a small kitchen and a small living room, a bedroom is 12x16. [A]ll those people cannot fit there. There is no privacy. I worked to share an apartment with two to three people, that is it.

The turn toward concentrated and overcrowded housing as a corollary to the rise of immigrant-based labor regimes emerged in Steamboat Springs, Colorado as well. Eric, a 43-year-old White Steamboat resident who considered himself a "local" after having lived there for seventeen years, worked for a number of years as a property manager of condos. He spoke about the overcrowded conditions found in some of the "lower-end" condos:

It would be a four-unit complex with thirty-two cars out in front of it. . . . [I]t gets ridiculous when doing property management, which I did for two years. We had two condos at Whistler, low-end condos. The kind of situation with bed bugs. [. . .] It was too much to handle, you go over there and you couldn't get in the door because there were fifteen pairs of shoes and its just a two-bedroom condo. It was a Mexican family, and no one spoke English, that is the only people we got in there. Like we advertise forever. They take the place over and it's, I mean the music is playing, the cars being worked on, and the dogs are around and kids everywhere. It's insane! I would not want to live there. I mean it's not just the peace and quiet I want, you know. And the guy that bought there, you know their property values are going down all the time.

Eric's perspective on immigrant housing employs a common racialized trope regarding housing for low-income workers, which places the blame for the conditions on the residents themselves rather than on a situation produced at the intersection of low-paid work and the profitability for landlords of overcrowding degraded and unhealthy housing (it is hard for landlords to rent a place infested with bed bugs). When I asked Eric why the owner he worked for was renting to multiple families a single-family apartment, he paused and seemed at a loss for words, eventually saying that he thought it was one family, just with many kids. He sidestepped speaking directly to the role that the landlords had played in the production of overcrowded and dilapidated housing.

There was a close relationship between job precarity and housing precarity for the workers building and maintaining the landscape of gentrification and the lifestyle of gentrifiers. Aitana, the restaurant worker who worked seven days a week for years after she arrived in Steamboat Springs, described her living situation:

AITANA: There is a place that I first moved, I was paying $650, which was a condominium. But when you walk inside the place there is something in the carpet that gets in your nose, irritates your nose and you start sneezing and sneezing, "Whats wrong with this place?" and then I have to leave the house, outside I am fine, but the minute I get in the house something gets in my nose. I was sharing it with another person, but something was bothering me there. [. . .]
          It was cheap but I had to move because it was making me sick. I moved into a place with roommates, there was eight of them in a house. So I stayed there to save, that's the reason. I went there to save money, save save save. But after a while I got tired because there's drunk people slamming the doors.

LISE: Were they also Latino/Hispano?

AITANA: Mostly Latinos. They also want just a room because, so they can work, save money and send money to Mexico. A lot of them. I stayed there for a year. I was paying $350, everything included, you don't have to pay for cable, water, trash, electric, gas, nothing. So that was pretty good.

LISE: But when you had eight people did you have to share rooms?

AITANA: Well at one time I was sharing it until there was an empty one and I could go in there. But if you really really want to move in you have to share with somebody [at the beginning.] And then as soon as one leaves, and then you are the number one, you have the option to move into your own room. When you're sharing a room they only charge you like $200. And when you move out of the shared room you pay between $300 and $400 depending on the size of the bedroom. So I did that and after I saved and saved I moved out with a friend and I said lets go find something else, which is right on 8th street and it was a place for $850, but it was two bedrooms, nice kitchen, nice living room. But every year when the owner comes to town, because she goes to Arizona, every year she comes she asks for $50 more, $75 . . . so I'm like this is not going to work if every year it is increasing. And she says, well "Aitana, help me with the laundry, you can clean and collect the quarters and when I come give me all that." [. . .] She was only paying me $100 to water the grass, to do the laundry, cleaning and do everything and collect the rent from the other six people. I have to make sure everybody pays me and everything so I can deposit the money. And so shes paying me $100 and I'm like, maybe she'll deduct something from my rent . . . nope. I still paid the full amount and she would just send me a check for $100 a month. I did that for two years.

In Aitana's story and those preceding it, we see the emergence of a flexible tenant regime that mirrors in some ways the flexible, immigrant-based labor regimes explored in chapter 3, but in terms of social reproduction rather than production. Aitana was resourced as a property manager by the owner of the complex and paid very little for that work—perhaps the owner thought that Aitana valued being able to rent there so much she would take it all on for little money.

One way to navigate low-wages and fluctuating employment is to lower one's expenses as much as possible, a pressure that is particularly present if one is a single earner trying to send money to distant families. These were usually men who felt that any "extra" expense was taking away from their family and so tried to "put up with" (aguantar) a lack of privacy, unclean housing, and the tensions these living environments usually produced. Immigrant workers with families in either Georgia or Colorado had a distinct calculus and tried to avoid the overcrowded apartments, opting more frequently for mobile homes. In Rabun County, those mobile homes were not infrequently down unmarked dirt roads in the forest, deeply hidden.

In Steamboat Springs, mobile homes usually were only available in mobile home parks, a couple of which remained in the floodplain, or if not in a park they were located at a distance from town. These decisions and trade-offs made by documented and undocumented low-wage workers in the context of rural gentrification are reflected in comments made by Pablo, a documented immigrant working as a cook for over twelve years in Rabun County:

But many people that come from Mexico and do not have papers, who are not legal, they come to make money. They come and live, many of them, in one house. Ten. God knows they come to make money, and this is why there are here, true? So they live many in a house, but we (my wife and I) do not like to do this. Because we are going to live here our whole lives.

So, okay, there are many points of view. If I come here, and I have my family in Mexico, and I come to make money, I am going to share housing with more people to save as much as I can and go back. Now, if I have legal status and I see that I want to have a family here and a life with my family then what am I going to think about? In buying a house, in living more privately and to give my children a more comfortable space.

Pablo is in a strong position to comment on housing dynamics for Latine immigrants in Rabun County, not only because of the length of time he has spent there, but because he has wide social networks not only in the Latine but in the nonimmigrant community (I cannot share more details of why due to confidentiality concerns). He himself is documented but started out in the United States as undocumented. The only qualifying statement I would make about what he said is that there are a significant number of undocumented people raising families and staying permanently in Rabun County, such as Elisa and her husband.

I will close this section by discussing another housing strategy among Latine immigrant residents in Rabun County (mentioned in the previous chapter): employer-provided housing. While we ran across contractors in both Rabun and Routt Counties who rented hotel rooms for three to five weeks at a time to house out-of-town subcontracted crews, it was only in Rabun County that employers and/or workers routinely reported employers providing housing for workers, often on their own personal or business property and for the long term. These situations were usually created for a worker who occupied the "labor broker" position discussed at length in chapter 3 and were clearly in the interest of the employer, as noted by Arturo, who lived in employer-provided housing when he first arrived in Rabun County in the early 1990s:

ARTURO: In that time, there were two brothers of mine that worked there with me, and we lived there as well. There were some apartments right behind the restaurant.

LISE: Did they charge you rent?

ARTURO: No, they did not charge us rent but we were available at any hour that they wanted us. [. . .] There were five to six people in a room that he had for us.

LISE: In *one* room?

ARTURO: Yes, in each room, it was only for sleeping. We ate in the kitchen of the restaurant. He had all the people there that washed the floors at night, the people who worked in the back.

The previous chapter discussed this employer-provided housing as a key mechanism of control of workers' labor; I bring it up here as part of the array of immigrant housing arrangements found in our case studies of rural gentrification, and one with particularly constraining implications for a worker's life and social reproduction.

In the case of Arturo, the restaurant was located several miles from any services such as a grocery store, so once a week the employer gave the workers a ride into town to get groceries, do laundry, go to a clinic, and so forth. Such arrangements made it very difficult for workers to connect to community and have any life outside of work, and this story was usually only told by solo male workers (no immigrant families lived in employer-provided housing in our sample). Arturo worked for two years at the restaurant under these conditions, before he was let go because he raised a complaint about the boss sexually harassing a female colleague. Over his seventeen years living in Rabun County, he learned English at an exceptional level, which allowed him to work in a stable and in a higher-paying retail job linked to the construction industry. At work he interacted with clients in both English and Spanish. Although undocumented, he shares a house with his brothers that is within walking distance of work and allows him to avoid driving most days—his older sibling is documented (owns a business) and purchased the house.

The local, circulating meanings ascribed to spaces of social reproduction for Latine immigrants, particularly in terms of housing, differed between Routt and Rabun Counties. In Rabun County, as mentioned previously, Black Rock Apartments were publicly coded as where "Mexicans" lived, and the complex was adjacent to the day laborer site in Rabun County (a laundromat) and very close to a Mexican tienda that provided international money transfers, tortillas, and other items of interest to Latine residents. For nonimmigrant longtime locals, the condition and "fullness" of Black Rock Apartments was a marker of the presence of immigrants in the community—even if Latine immigrants in reality lived across many dispersed spaces in the area. The normalized racial coding of those apartments was often redeployed by immigrant residents as well, such as Nelly, a cook with two children (her entire family is undocumented): "I am a little arrogant in this way. I see that many people that do bad things live in the Black Rock apartments down there—drugs, drinking, prostitutes—people I do not want my kids to be around. So my husband and I, we decided that it would be more work to pay a higher rent but our children were going to have a better space. We have always lived on our own. When we first arrived we lived on this street in a very small house, but a single-family house." White long-term locals generally avoided the area except to pick up day laborers and reflexively framed it as a space of danger.

Local racialized narratives regarding spaces of social reproduction for immigrants were distinct in Colorado, in part because immigrants were not as clearly segregated *within* Steamboat into one identifiable spot to the same degree as Black Rock Apartments. While many Latine immigrants lived in trailer parks if they lived in the city limits, these trailer parks contained many White working-class families as well, undermining explicit racialization of mobile home parks. Moreover, Steamboat had an "easier" time erasing the presence of Latine immigrant residents because a significant percentage of Steamboat's immigrant workforce lived in Craig, Colorado, a fifty-minute drive that displaced the spaces of social reproduction such as housing, schools, and churches to a distinct county (Hayden and Oak Creek, two other key bedroom communities for Steamboat, are also in Routt County and share the school district). While a larger percentage of Latine immigrant workers in Steamboat lived in town than we originally anticipated, these housing spaces were not highly visible—the trailer parks in the flood plain were surrounded by trees and brush that made them less visible when driving down most major roads. It is perhaps this invisibility that led to surprise and outcry when the local paper reported a fire in August 2010, which decimated an apartment housing eighteen Latine immigrant residents.[3] That immigrant residents were housed in this space was framed as a surprise by the paper, and subsequent letters to the editor commenting on the article focused on the presence of immigrants and "illegals" in town rather than on fire risk or housing.

While we expected to find few immigrants living close to town in either Rabun or Routt Counties, the story emerging from our interviews revealed more complicated housing dynamics shaped by not only income but race and illegality. Some Latine immigrant workers in the Steamboat area lived in Craig, Colorado, and drove nearly an hour each way to work (more in the winter if the weather was bad). However, a significant percentage of Latine immigrant workers in Routt County lived within the city limits or relatively close to Steamboat Springs in less visible "pockets" of lower-cost housing stock—typically mobile parks located in floodplains, in spaces difficult to redevelop. In Rabun County, Georgia, there was a discursively produced and deeply racialized assumption that all "Mexicans" lived in Black Rock Apartments (centrally located), when in fact they were dispersed throughout the county, given the uneven cost of housing in many spaces beyond the lakes themselves. The key commonalities between these two case studies include the production of the "flexible tenants" who proved very attractive to landlords—folks who earn low wages but might be willing to live in overcrowded, unhealthy conditions; who are unlikely to complain or demand any semblance of tenant rights. The precarity of labor conditions was intimately linked to the precarity of housing and represent a key dimension of social reproduction for immigrant residents of these two communities.

ILLEGALITY IN EVERYDAY LIFE: DRIVING AND DEPORTATION

> It is very difficult, the fact that one has to drive and how you
> do not know if you will come back or not come back . . .
> because the police stop you and next thing they call
> immigration. This is a very, very frustrating life despite the
> work one does, the family that needs you. It is very hard.
> —Liliana, house cleaner, Routt County, Colorado (August 16, 2010)

Processes of racialization and illegality have suffused the theoretical framing and the empirical analysis explored in this book. That is because race and illegality are intimately intertwined with how immigrant labor markets function in the context of gentrification in Rabun and Routt Counties, and they are constituitive of broader narratives and practices related to borders and the political economy of migration discussed in chapter 1.

They are also deeply embedded in the geographies of social reproduction examined in this chapter, from housing to recreation. This section focuses on the anxieties and coping strategies shared by immigrant respondents facing the possibility of being deported, an anxiety that usually centers on the fear of driving and getting pulled over by police and subsequently swept into the deportation process—a life-altering event for themselves and their families. Nicholas de Genova grounds his theorization of illegality in terms of deportability—including the discursive maneuvers that normalize unauthorized residents as "outside the law" and criminal in their racialized essence. It is a narrative that produces a normalized "solution": expulsion, deportation. I draw inspiration from De Genova, who as an anthropologist seeks to analyze "deportability" in everyday life.[4]

The fear of deportation permeates the lives of low-wage Latine immigrants of Rabun County, Georgia, and Routt County, Colorado, shaping a range of day-to-day decisions and behavior. As explored in detail in chapter 1, since the mid-2000s deportation has occurred less commonly in the context of *workplace* raids and much more frequently when people are driving and pulled over for a traffic violation. When local police work closely with ICE (some jurisdictions have resisted this role, while others have embraced it), drivers who are pulled over can be placed on "immigration holds" and end up in deportation proceedings.[5] This capability for local police can be traced to the 287G Program, which starting in 2006 allowed local jurisdictions to apply for training and authorization with Homeland Security to identify and process "immigration offenders" during their regular duties.[6] The risks deepened, however, with 287G's successor program, Secure Communities, which was piloted in 2008 and had enrolled 1,595 jurisdictions by 2011.[7] While the discretion of local police still mattered in the scope of its implementation, Secure Communities *required* that all fingerprints sent to the Federal Bureau of Investigation database (a routine step in most jurisdictions) also pass through Homeland Security. This resulted in immigration detainers being issued for routine engagements with police and narrowed the options for local jurisdictions to resist.[8] Together, 287G and Secure Communities led to the massive expansion of interior border enforcement and deportation mechanisms, with an estimated 3.4 million people being deported under the Obama administration.[9]

Immigrant residents were aware of these dynamics at a visceral level, with folks in Georgia sharing that at the time they felt the Clayton police were not actively linking into ICE (they wanted money for the ticket, but would not call ICE for minor traffic violations), whereas the Mountain City police (a few miles north) were much more likely to pull over a "brown" driver under minor pretexts and more willing to call ICE in the process. Comments from Sergio, a roofer in Rabun County who had lived there without documents for eleven years, reflected these shifting perceptions:

SERGIO: A majority of people left here for Franklin [North Carolina] because a law came into effect here that also was one in which those that they caught without a license or they brought them in and they ended up in jail, that those people would be deported. As a result many people began to move to Franklin but in Franklin it turned out to be worse, because there you get into jail they will deport you. . . . [I]t is worse than here actually. Here you end up in jail but they only want money from you. You go and you pay your money and they let you go.

In Colorado, the Steamboat police department was not actively calling ICE for traffic stops during this period, but in Moffat County (where many immigrants working in Steamboat lived, and where Craig is located) immigrant residents felt at greater risk of deportation in any contact with police. While these evaluations are based on perceptions rather than hard data, immigrant residents' perceptions are critical to their coping strategies and to how they navigate spaces of social reproduction.

As many scholars have shown, the anxiety about deportation weighs heavily on people's minds and bodies.[10] But *how* the fear of deportation shapes people's lives depends somewhat on their situation. The classic solo male worker typically expressed the least concern about the possibility of being deported (although they did not welcome it, either). Anxious narratives about deportation figured more prominently in the life stories of immigrants with families in the U.S.—the vast majority of whom were mixed status, meaning that some members were documented and some were undocumented. Sometimes partners would be mixed status (one documented, one undocumented, with men more likely being documented), but we found a significant number of households with children in which both parents were undocumented, and the children were citizens or mixed status (older kids undocumented, younger ones U.S. born).

Parents raising children in the U.S. frequently expressed worry about the safety and well-being of their children. This held particular resonance when sacrifices for children were also at the center of immigrants' narratives concerning why they endured the risks, humiliation, and poverty associated with living as an undocumented person in the United States. Those with U.S.-born children found themselves planning for the loss of a parent or both parents with little warning—how to prepare their children, who would take care of them, how they would survive.[11] They knew this would most likely happen while they were driving in their cars, and if it happened they would have little recourse. They would likely not see their family members again for months if not years, no matter how minor or "real" the suspected infraction. At the time, broader narratives deployed by federal officials under the Obama administration claimed that "criminals" were the target of deportation, but for the majority of people deported under the ever-expanding deportation regime of the 2000s, either they were noncriminal in nature or the crime was rooted in a driving infraction.[12]

While many immigrant residents of Routt and Rabun Counties were not deeply familiar with the intricacies of the laws and how/why immigration enforcement was devolved to local police departments through the 287G and Secure Communities programs discussed in chapter 1, they have had enough people in their lives disappear through deportation to have it shape their everyday decisions and dreams. A restaurant worker, Lola (age 31), shared her understanding of the deportation regime and how it had affected her:

> They grab you even if you have not made a mistake, you have to pay with jail. When you arrive in jail they find out that you do not have [immigration] papers. They are in communication with ICE in that same moment, and now you are not going to leave, if you are illegal. Many people are afraid to drive because whatever small problem, they will stop you.
>
> This has been something that has been very hard, now I drive but only what is absolutely necessary. If not, I do not go. For example, in all of this time I have not gone to Grand Junction. In this town (Craig) there is nothing to do. It is a small town. In order to get out and go shopping for clothes for the children, it is best to go to Silverton or Grand Junction, or all the way to Denver. But now I do not go to these places because even if I drive to

Walmart from my home, I am driving afraid. I am always afraid they will stop me. But sometimes you have to go on an errand, and so one always has to drive with caution. [pause] There are people that truly need a license, we do not want it to do bad things, it is because we need [to drive] to get any small thing. [. . .] Therefore we go around driving knowing that the moment they grab us, we are off to Mexico.

Immigrant residents work to constrain their movements to lessen the chance of being swept into deportation detention and proceedings.

Aitana, the restaurant worker in Steamboat who shared her housing challenges also discussed her strategies for dealing with the deportation regime:

AITANA: [My dad] can just come and go to Mexico anytime because he is a permanent resident, but he never applied for us I don't know why. We don't have documents, I just have to find a way to pay taxes, which I always do, which is so in the future I can apply for a green card. You need to pay taxes.

LISE: So you don't have permanent residency or documentation?

AITANA: No. And that's the other thing that holds you, and you cannot just speak up and say "I want this, I want that." But if an American comes and says "I want this, I want that" you have to do it because they are fine, and your not like 100% with your rights. [. . .]

LISE: I know its hard to get a drivers license

AITANA: We don't' drive, we don't have a car, that's why I'm always walking and I get rides from my friends. But there's a lot of people that I know that drive, I don't know how they do it. I don't know if we're so afraid or we don't want to end up . . . because now if they get you, they take you back to immigration and from immigration back home. And [my husband and I] we're not ready to do that. We're going to buy the mobile home. My dad's social is going to be there, its going to look like he's going to by it, so where you can sign as the buyer [he will sign for us], and when you sell you don't need to provide any social or anything, you just sign that your selling the house. In a way it's good that we have him, if we need to get something he's here to help us. In that way he has helped, like he just got a cell phone from Verizon, you need a social, so he got [a phone] for himself and he got one for my brother, so we're good.

Aitana navigates illegality by not speaking up, remaining unable to "ask for what I want" in contrast to an American who has rights; by not driving and walking everywhere; and by feeling grateful to her father who has a Social Security number, making it easier for Aitana and her brothers to buy an iPhone or a mobile home. Aitana insists on filing taxes despite not being documented, as she seeks to be a good citizen and position herself for what she hopes is a legalization process in the future. Her social-civic precarity and poverty are part of the story why she accepted working seven days a week at the restaurant, and these are also part of the structural explanation for her time living in unhealthy, overcrowded conditions. Here we see how the feeling and material reality of illegality shapes her every movement through space.

An exchange during an interview with Alma, a 34-year-old Latina woman in Craig, Colorado, sheds light on the psychic cost of the deportation regime. Alma is a U.S.-born Latina whose parents were undocumented immigrants from Mexico who arrived in Colorado in the 1970s. She is married to an undocumented man from Guanajuato. She laughed when she said that she had promised herself that she would never marry an undocumented person, but she fell in love. Her husband works in construction in Steamboat. He commutes a long distance to work daily, placing him in a risky position every day:

ALMA: He got here when he was 14 and right now we're in the process of trying to help him get his green card, but it's hard. A lot of people got good points and a lot of people don't know what they're talking about. And there's one that just kills me everytime I hear it: the Spanish people, they're here illegally, and they're on welfare.

LISE: It is hard.

ALMA: It is, if he was to get deported right now . . . [pause, deep breath] [H]e is the breadmaker of the house. Right now, it's not just us, everybody is going through hard times and I was lucky enough, I'm a janitor in the evenings. I am struggling with two jobs, and I'm not used to working for other people.

Our town [mayor], when we start[ed] filling out our application for a green card, our town mayor, chief of police, they all wrote letters of recommendation hoping to speed things up and we're still just waiting. [. . .] The last letter we received was that they denied his application and that was it. So he called an attorney and we called two to three attorneys and they're like, you're lucky that they didn't tell him to leave and then give him a letter of denial, and then he couldn't come back. So right now,

> we're just kinda on hold, but we spen[t] like $15k to immigration and I think we lost it all. So we'll have to start over if the laws change, pay another whatever they decide that we need to pay. [. . .] We can't, he's got his driver's license in Washington, but its about to expire, so as soon as that expires we are stuck.

Alma, a U.S. citizen, lives in daily fear of her husband not returning home from work and thinking of how this will impact her children emotionally and economically. Like many others in our sample, she and her husband have worked hard to be good citizens and legalize his presence. His work in Steamboat is steady and secure, but his travel to and from work risks, on a daily basis, long-term family separation.

Many immigrants struggled with the effects of the deportation regime, which dramatically increased their stress. As Mateo, the restaurant owner in Rabun County, related to me:

> Everyone becomes desperate from feeling cornered, from not knowing if they should drive to work and if they would be stopped. Worry over not being able to arrive at my work, and because they put in places many road blocks (retenes). So they feel pressured because now they are going to get taken. Why are you here if you cannot drive or work? And you know there are all kinds, there are people who are bad, but there are people that come here to work, to support their family. They work hard and well, but there have been a number of families who have left in order to not feel so pressured. They move to other states.

These pressures existed for many years but were dramatically increased in 2011 when the Georgia legislature passed HB 87, a law modeled after Arizona's anti-immigrant law SB 1070, passed one year earlier. The law required employers with ten or more employees to use E-verify (to check the immigration status of people they were hiring), expanded the ability of the police to check suspects for their immigration status, made it a crime to intentionally transport an undocumented immigrant, and increased penalties for the use of fake identification.[13] In combination with the still-struggling economy only three years out from the Great Recession, many Latine families chose to leave Rabun County, according to a number of respondents. That was when people said Black Rock Apartments went from full to half empty. But for those that remained, many changed their movements and housing to reduce their risk—Elisa and her family moved from the trailer in the woods where I had interviewed her in 2010 to an apartment within walking distance to downtown Clayton (not Black Rock, but another small set of apartments also segregated, solely occupied by Latine immigrant families). When I spoke with Elisa again in 2011, she asked me nervously if the police could pick her up for just walking down the street as she brought her children to school.

Perhaps one of the most unexpected effects of HB 87, something I would not have predicted prior to interviewing immigrant workers and residents as the policy was implemented, was that the risks immigrants felt from this Georgia House Bill and other anxieties of "illegality" often drove them into a tighter relationship with their employers because it offered them a sense of protection. This made them *more* attractive and profitable to the employer, incentivizing further recruitment of "illegal" and racially marginalized workers. In Georgia employers scrambled on two levels when this measure passed: they reassured their workers that they would not be deported (e.g., told them that the e-verify was only for new hires or that their business was too small to qualify), or they attempted less conventional strategies to protect their workforce. For example, a number of immigrant labor brokers told me that their employers started loaning them commercially marked vehicles to drive around, even when they were not working. They drove the van home and used it all the time because they perceived (and so did their employers) that they would be less likely to be pulled over if they were in a commercially marked vehicle with the logo of the business on it.

Miguel, a construction worker and informal labor broker for a large construction firm in Rabun County, Georgia, described how his employer dealt with it when Miguel's driver's license expired. Miguel had obtained a license in Georgia before there were measures to prevent undocumented residents from receiving them, but he could not renew it, and he told his boss:

MIGUEL: I told him two–three months ago that my license expired because he asked me to take a company truck to get material to a site. I told him "you know that I do not have a license?" and he said "yes, I know, but the police do not know that. You drive well and you are my employee, if there is a problem I will help you."

LISE: Do you think the police do not fixate on you as much if the vehicle says [company name] on it? Do they leave you in peace more than if you were driving your own car?

MIGUEL: Exactly. There are even two people that work in the police department that we do work for. So all the trucks with [company name] on them, they do not bother us. My boss gets along well with everyone in the county. If you have power then they do not bother you if you have the logo of [business name]. Eventually I drove my own truck, but my boss let me put the logo on my door.

I happened to interview Miguel's boss Adam, quoted in chapter 3. Adam described to me another instance when he helped "his guys" get through a police checkpoint at the exit points to Burton Lake, where they were constructing a house. Adam described driving up to the checkpoint, recognizing the local police officers running it, and saying to them, "those are my guys in the van behind me," and nothing more. Despite the van carrying upward of seven undocumented employees of Adam, they did not get detained. I found several examples of immigrant workers remaining in Rabun County after HB 87 who sought to increase their security by developing a closer relationship to their employers on multiple levels (making themselves more indispensable to the employer, using company cars, or turning toward employer-provided housing). Employers were eager to extend measures to keep the workers safer from the deportation regime, particularly the labor brokers so critical to their business.

In Colorado these dynamics did not emerge in our interviews, I assume because there was less of a personalistic relationship between local elected leaders/police officials and business owners—it was a bigger place and did not have the long history of "local" locals who knew each other often over several generations. In Colorado undocumented immigrant residents responded differently to the risk of driving: if they lived in Craig they often moved to Steamboat if possible, allowing them to drive less. At the end of the day, although immigrant workers and residents in Colorado feared deportation and experienced negative interactions with the police, the fear was not as palpable as in Georgia. As Gloria (quoted in chapter 3, a restaurant worker living in Craig, Colorado) framed her feelings about the police: "In general I think they [the police] only focus on people who are getting into trouble (que andan en problemas). Thank God, they see that I am Hispanic, I have a dark color . . . but I am not doing anything bad and they do not stop me. But if Colorado becomes the same as Arizona, then it will be bad." House Bill 87 in Georgia was modeled after Arizona

Senate Bill 1070, and immigrants in Colorado were keenly aware of how Colorado was different from Arizona.

The risks of driving and the lack of access to get a driver's license was the most urgent and palpable effect of being "illegal" or racially marked as illegal in both Colorado and Georgia. We did not include direct questions about police interactions in our interview guide, given that our focus was labor markets and social reproduction more broadly, but it came up over and over. It shaped where people lived and how they moved through space on a daily basis, and it created a milieu of fear and insecurity above and beyond the precarity of low-wage employment and ever-changing demands for their labor.

ILLEGALITY IN EVERYDAY LIFE: LANGUAGE

Leo Chavez, in his groundbreaking book *The Latino Threat*, identifies language as a key dimension of the threat narrative aimed at Latine immigrants in U.S. society. This pervasive discourse constructs Latine immigrants as a reproductive threat, nominally "unwilling" to assimilate in ways framed as essential compared to other immigrant groups. Chavez points to the racialized assertion that "Latinos are unable or unwilling to learn English."[14] Among other dimensions of the threat narrative, Chavez shows how the idea that Latine immigrants are "unwilling" to learn English is linked to the construction of their *productivity* as workers (they are just here to work, not to assimilate).[15] While not all Latine immigrants struggle to speak English, low-wage workers and particularly undocumented ones are more likely to face challenges learning English while navigating life and work.

Language for our participants represented a fundamental and deeply embodied dimension of racialization and illegality—someone who reads phenotypically as Latine may assuage a police officer, and perhaps save themselves an immigration check, if they speak English without an accent. By the same token someone who is a U.S.-born citizen who only speaks English might nevertheless be assumed to be a foreigner and perhaps "illegal" due to their embodied racialization. Those who speak little English or struggle to understand and communicate face much higher challenges in terms of work (bilingual workers have more value) and navigating spaces of everyday life. Language use frequently becomes a code for expressing racist and xenophobic feelings, something along the lines of "I am not racist, they just need to learn English." But what is the context for immigrants to learn English as they labor to create and maintain landscapes of rural gentrification?

An important starting point is to consider what immigrant newcomers face in terms of their time and capacity to learn another language, challenges faced by both documented and undocumented residents, but particularly the latter. Crossing the border without authorization usually means going into debt, so the pressure to earn more income that might have inspired their decision to migrate is amplified by the political economy of crossing itself (produced by border militarization, explored in chapter 1). This situation structurally positions people to prioritize work over all else, as discussed in chapter 3, leaving little time to study English. As immigrant labor regimes consolidated in new destinations such as Routt and Rabun Counties and bilingual labor brokers began to manage monolingual speakers, people arriving without knowing English could get along. In fact that linguistic marginality increased their vulnerability and flexibility for employers—making them more attractive and profitable to recruit and manage through the labor broker regimes. Scholarship by Flores-Yeffal shows that the networks used to facilitate migration and job searching among undocumented immigrants can inhibit English language proficiency.[16] This is so not because people are unwilling to learn English, but because the circumstances of their lives make it exceedingly difficult, and many can achieve their goal of work and income without knowing much English—particularly once those labor regimes become consolidated.

Again and again when I asked immigrant participants the biggest challenges they faced after arriving in Rabun and Routt Counties, they usually started with language and the disorientation of navigating life and work when they could not understand English (many arrived before driver's licenses became much harder to obtain, so they were less likely to start the story there). Enrique, a 38-year-old Mexican who became documented through marriage with a Latina U.S. citizen from Texas, explained his arrival in Rabun County in 2003:

LISE: How did they treat you at the first job here?

ENRIQUE: They treated me okay, more or less. . . . [W]ell, my problem was that
I didn't speak English at that time, this created many problems.
Because I didn't speak it there were people [at work] that were
bothered (se molestaron) by me not understanding them. But others
treated me well. There are some people, it felt like they were making
fun of me when they would say something in English followed by
"comprende?" They laughed as they said it.

In this case White coworkers of Enrique felt empowered to make jokes
about his language skills as a socially acceptable way to reassert their superiority instead of treating him with compassion and respect. Despite
these challenges of language, Enrique was in a unique position compared
to most Latine immigrants in Rabun County at the time: not only was
he documented but he was well educated. In Guadalajara he worked as a
teacher of literature prior to marrying and moving to the United States.
He ended up in Rabun County because his Latina wife had a supervisory
job with a national clothing manufacturer in Rabun County. The company
asked her to transfer to the Rabun plant in the early 2000s from Texas.

Upon his arrival in Georgia Enrique had to get a job quickly—in another manufacturing company, not textiles—but he was legally authorized
to work. Within a few years he developed enough fluency that it began to
change his job prospects. This was rooted in the steadiness of his wife's job,
which made it possible for him to take evening English classes. Enrique,
unlike most of his fellow Latine immigrants, did not have to work multiple jobs. He described his second job at another manufacturing company
in Franklin, North Carolina (a twenty-five-minute drive from Clayton):

My work was temporary, but on one occasion they saw that I knew English
and Spanish. After one month I stopped doing much physical labor in order
to do administrative work. I would receive the trailers with wood, and
I would only unload them and make annotations for the paperwork, the documentation. They treated me much better at the new job. And then when
I was with the bosses and I spoke English with greater fluency I could communicate better and they treated me well. There were other workers that . . .
they didn't like Hispanos working there. They complained when the boss
closed an afternoon shift and I did not get laid off, which [the other workers]
expected because I was a temporary worker. The boss had to lay off three
Americans and they complained about why he was keeping me. The boss

said that they kept me because I speak two languages, and they don't. The bosses needed people like this because they had many Hispano employees.

What helped me the most over time in the work is that I had studied English in Mexico and when I began to listen and understand the pronunciation I began to get better and better. With the language I have many advantages compared to most Hispanos in this place. This was a very valuable tool to get better jobs and better positions.

For Enrique, his ability to learn English was fundamental to his job prospects, pay, and stability if he could put up with the derisive comments of some of his coworkers.

As mentioned in the previous chapter, immigrant workers moving into labor broker positions almost always had to show strong capabilities navigating English—whether to interface with customers or with employers. Raúl (58 years old), in Craig, Colorado, became highly fluent in English despite arriving without documents and having very little formal education, unlike Enrique. Raúl attributed his language skills to the demands of work. Although we conducted the interview in Spanish, his fluency in English was also apparent when I first contacted him for the interview, and I brought it up over the course of our conversation:

LISE: When and how did you learn English? Because you speak excellent English.

RAÚL: More or less. I still have a lot to learn but see, I understand it well. I do not write it perfectly, I write, I understand, I read well. I learned out of necessity, in order to work.

LISE: You have never taken English classes?

RAÚL: No. I didn't have the chance to go to school because I came here to work, if I go to school I don't work and that issue is neither here nor there. I came from Mexico because I did not have the opportunity to study there, because I am the oldest son of a family of nine, and with a family of nine and there are two parents, we were eleven. Eleven people put their hands in the tortilla basket and soon it is empty. So I decided to migrate to the United States (age of 15) and here we are.

Raúl had lived in Craig for thirty-two years at the time of our interview, owned his own house, and had two U.S.-born children attending college (he became documented through the IRCA program in the 1980s, discussed in chapter 1). While the level of Raúl's fluency was exceptional among interviewees who did not have access to educational resources in their sending communities or in the U.S. context, it was common for work to be cited as a primary motivator and context for learning English, even as respondents struggled against many barriers to achieve comfort in English as an adult and without language courses.

The second arena in which language figured prominently in immigrant family narratives was navigating raising children and interacting with school officials. Liliana, who cleans houses in Routt County, described her arrival in Colorado:

LILIANA: We had the two littlest ones when we got here, but when we arrived my children only spoke Spanish. It was hard for them, because for the bigger one, he cried a lot and didn't want to go to school. But he did learn.

LISE: Did the teachers at the school support them? How is the communication between the school and you as parents?

LILIANA: Not much communication. Because one doesn't speak English. For example I feel at times that I am not able to help my children with homework or this or that. . . . In other words, since one doesn't know the other language, it's difficult, it's hard, but that's where the poor come out in life.

Language created a barrier between Liliana and her children's teachers, preventing her from playing a central role in her children's education, but it was a situation that she could not change because "that's where the poor come out in life." Her sense of undeservingness permeated our conversation.

Liliana went on in the interview to describe how her son, then 18, wanted to attend college, but as an undocumented student he was under the impression he would not be able to use a diploma. She ended her story by saying, "For this reason I am sad. Because he wants to get ahead, and I want that for him too."

Other respondents echoed the feelings of Liliana as they described their struggle to engage the schools and support their children as they navigated them. Overall, Colorado had better ESL accommodations than Rabun County, which only had one full-time ESL teacher for the entire school district. What Liliana experienced over time, as her children grew and overcame the language hurdle that was so difficult at the beginning,

was a process by which the children became her and her husband's inter-
locutors with the wider society. This phenomenon, termed by sociologists
"language brokering" by children, often leads to new power dynamics between parents and children—a process that can be harmful as it places
children in a difficult position and level of responsibility, while at the same
time parents often feel disempowered and isolated in relation to their own
children.[17]

Ultimately the language question usually figured most prominently in
immigrant respondents' characterizations of their adjustment to life in the
United States, more so than documentation per se. I think that is because
language was something confronted daily and the effects were tangible,
while questions of documentation and possible deportation were very
stressful but more abstract. When I asked Pablo, a longtime documented
Mexican immigrant residing in Rabun County, how he felt in the community when he arrived in the mid-1990s (I did not ask about language, just
how he felt and how he was accepted by "locals"), he responded:

PABLO: Well, we have not had any problem. I think that it is normal [people
being wary] when someone strange arrives, and until you know them—
then you see what kind of person he is, how he will affect us. Someone
you do not know that you would want to see exactly what kind of person
it is. That happens to us a bit, but I have made many friends here in
Clayton [Rabun County, Georgia], I know many people. Many people
know me, and that is beautiful and why I like it here. To know people and
that people know you, because it is a small town, everyone knows everyone. That is why I like it here, and when we arrived it was small, but
there has never been an obstacle because she [my wife] speaks excellent
English, so whenever there was something that we needed to do, she did
it. . . . [F]or this reason there was never an obstacle for us in this respect.
Maybe for other people that [language] affected them more.

I share Pablo's narrative because he is one of our immigrant respondents
who felt most at home in Rabun County. The first factor he pointed to
when talking about the ease of his transition was the fact that his wife
speaks fluent English (she is Latina, born and raised in the borderland
region of the Southwest). Most immigrant respondents in either Routt
County, Colorado, or Rabun County, Georgia, did not have such a resource
as they settled into the community—most knew very little English upon

arrival, and most were not documented. This set them on a path for sub-ordinate integration into immigrant labor regimes (the path to more stability and money as a "labor broker" was not open without more fluency), which furthered their vulnerability in many ways and inhibited their opportunities to gain fluency.

To understand how language works as a mundane and embodied experience of belonging and exclusion, it is critical to consider how nonimmigrant residents in Rabun and Routt Counties respond to people speaking in Spanish at the workplace or in wider public spaces. These responses provide insight into what anthropologists Woolard and Schieffelin call "language ideology," or ideological beliefs about language use and behavior.[18] While this is a broad category that covers non-normative uses of slang, and so forth, a key component of how language ideology is constructed occurs via nationalism, by indicating membership among a people, an imagined community of the nation. Sarah, a local, White woman in Rabun County, described her frustration with the ubiquity of Spanish in some spaces, despite herself being fluent in Spanish and married to a Mexican immigrant. This followed a conversation in which she described helping Spanish-speaking friends fill out applications in English for work. She laughed at the thought, saying that in her own mind she found it contradictory that people who did not speak English would fill out employment applications for jobs for which they would need English:

[A]nd I'm thinking "don't these people at least need to speak some English to get work?" Cause it kind of infuriates me; to go to McDonald's and I can't even get through the drive through with what I want, I have to eventually speak Spanish to get through. And I'm like, at least have your English speakers doing anything that has to do with communication with customers, if you've got the kitchen running on Hispanic people, okay. As long as they know their job, and can read, whatever.

Sarah's perspective was a rather normalized one among White respondents, who regularly remarked on their frustration with working with Latine immigrants who struggled to speak English, even when those people were providing them services.

The challenges of language ideology and the narrative threat identified by Chavez manifests in daily life, sometimes in confrontational ways. In

2007 a young Mexican-born Latina who graduated from Rabun County High School in Georgia published an opinion piece in the local paper, the *Clayton Tribune*, decrying being confronted by a patron in Walmart because she was speaking Spanish to her mother:

> Since when is speaking Spanish in a public place not allowed? While shopping around Walmart with my Mom [...] a man said to us: "You should speak English, this is America." I had not even realized that I was speaking Spanish. Besides, I was speaking to my mother. She understood what I was saying, and I thought that was good enough. [...]
>
> A little irritated by this comment, I explained to him, in English, how I was speaking to my mother, who also spoke Spanish. He kept arguing that I should not speak Spanish because people could not understand me; and that in the United States one should only speak English.
>
> Where has he been? Has he not noticed the more than twelve million immigrants who live in this country? ... The United States is not, and has never been, a nation of only one race.[19]

I found this to be a remarkable story of resistance that not only echoed through the aisles of Walmart—of anyone was listening to her audible rejection of the man's comments—but because she had the courage to publicize the experience in the local paper. The mixed response to her editorial can be traced in the letters to the editor that followed, which included some people who agreed with her critique and others who proclaimed that "illegal immigrants" should go back to Mexico. In this story language use became the marker of "threat" and the embodied means for a White resident to defend a nominally homogeneous national community against racialized outsiders.

ILLEGALITY IN EVERYDAY LIFE: SOCCER

Finally, soccer and recreational spaces emerged in this research as a less recognized but important entry point into immigrant belonging and geographies of social exclusion.[20] The theme of soccer emerged during my interviews unexpectedly, leading me to start asking the question of other participants: Do you play soccer? Where? What does it mean to you? Over time stories of soccer and a space to play presented themselves as a critical

Figure 4. Parking lot in Rabun County on which nightly, informal immigrant soccer games were played. Photo by author.

site through which to understand how hierarchies of race and illegality—fundamental to the smooth functioning of the labor regimes underlying gentrification—rippled through broader spaces of everyday life.

A significant portion of our male immigrant respondents in both case study sites enjoyed playing soccer—to get exercise, to feel camaraderie with others, and as a respite from their often-punishing work schedules. In Rabun County we noticed Latino men playing soccer nearly every evening during our fieldwork in an abandoned parking lot (see figure 4). I found out *why* they were playing on concrete, which is very dangerous, during an interview with Alejandro, an interview that happened to take place near some grass soccer fields (he wanted to talk near a playground so his kids could play while we conducted the interview). When soccer came up in the interview, I pointed to the lighted, grass playing fields on the other side of the playground and asked if he played there. He responded, "Oh, they don't let Mexicans play on those fields." He said it in a matter-of-fact tone that was quite distinct from the surprise I felt upon hearing it. This was the beginning of my interest in soccer and spaces of recreation as a site for understanding race, illegality, and the geographies of social reproduction.

The focus of this section is to share the history of why Latine bodies could not play soccer on public soccer fields in Rabun County (at the time of our interviews), and the somewhat forgotten history of an immigrant soccer league that emerged in Rabun County for three years (~2000–2003) before the immigrant players were kicked off anything resembling a field in the community. I return at the close of this section to share some details of soccer and immigrant residents in our Colorado research, but the primary focus is on Rabun County, Georgia.

It is important to step back and consider how immigrant workers in Georgia often feel about soccer, and why some continued to play in a small, concrete parking area when their access to real fields was de facto eliminated. I share the story of Cayetano, a 34-year-old Central American immigrant who spoke about the moment he was able to join a soccer game after living in the U.S. for three years. He spoke about the moment in almost holy terms, relating the day that other immigrants on his job site (a construction site in Georgia) invited him to join them to play soccer on grass fields just over the state line in North Carolina, about a twenty-minute drive from his home: "It had been three years since I touched a soccer ball. That afternoon I was very excited (emocionado). I grabbed my money [on payday], I went to the store, and I got my soccer equipment. [. . .] Oh that night . . . all I wanted that night was for it to go quickly. I felt like when one falls in love, and as if I were about to see my novia." To understand his feelings, we have to put them in the context of his migrant journey and his long struggle to rise above severe economic precarity to have the time in his schedule to play soccer.

Cayetano had arrived five years before our conversation from Central America, crossing the border through the desert and ending up in California, where he had a cousin. While the cousin provided him a place to live, he also controlled Cayetano's labor and appropriated much of his earnings in the form of rent and utility bills—Cayetano described working twelve hours a day and being paid $60 at the end of the week, leaving very little to save while also making it impossible to find work outside of his cousin's networks and control. Cayetano remembers it as a miserable existence, but better then living under a bridge, which he said happens when new arrivals do not have *any* connections. He did not know how to escape until he could afford to buy a cell phone, after which he joined Facebook, and through Facebook created a friendship with someone in Georgia—someone whose parents came from the same rural town as Cayetano's father. This Facebook friend after a time invited him to come to Georgia, and so Cayetano spent months saving every penny to travel across the county (he said that due to his undocumented status he needed to pay someone privately to drive him; he did not feel safe purchasing a Greyhound ticket). The journey was a huge risk, as he might have found himself in a similar situation as in California, and he knew he needed to start working immediately because the good faith of this new friend would wear thin quickly.

He struggled to find jobs in Georgia, but eventually found work in painting, then construction, and finally masonry. For nearly a year he worked both in masonry and in exterior painting, seven days a week—no time for soccer. It was not until the painting job ended, and his coworkers at the masonry site asked him if he wanted to play, that he had the opportunity (the masonry job was Monday–Saturday and paid enough to make it possible to have Sundays free). After the pickup game, they saw he was good and invited him to join their formal team:

> They told me to come play with them on Sundays, in the league. I said "yes, but only if I have time and I am not working. If I am working, then no." Because for us to be able to play soccer on Sundays is a luxury. If I am not doing it, it is because of work. As I have told you, life is work and work. I have so many commitments, paying my car, paying my rent. This is all very difficult, but it is okay. So I told them "if I have time left over I will come to play." [. . .] For me, my passion is fútbol. It was a dream to me to play soccer here in the United States, it is a luxury because that was my passion in my country. I had gotten soccer out of my mind here, my mind was transformed by work commitments, by needing to send money to my family. Soccer was a dream, no more.

In the context of a life marked by profound economic precarity and the stress of the threat of deportation and the impacts of undocumented status on his life, soccer was a moment of respite, of joy and using one's body for something other than labor. It is in Cayetano's story that we see why

Latino immigrants in Rabun County who wanted to play soccer took to a concrete parking lot once regular fields became unavailable.

After the interview with Alejandro and his assertion that "they don't let Mexicans play on those fields," I began to ask all my respondents about soccer, in the context of our broader interview goals such as migration history, work, housing, and daily life in Rabun or Routt Counties. Over time these questions excavated the history of a Latino men's immigrant soccer league that thrived for a few years in Rabun County, until participants lost access to the one field where they were allowed to play—a field that from the outset was an abandoned field, not a sports field, which I discuss below. It should be noted that the robust and plentiful sports facilities in Rabun County— unusually plentiful for a rural and sparsely populated place—were tied to the level of property taxes brought into the county by gentrifiers, according to interviews with county officials and recreation department staff. This is not a story of there not being enough field space to host the soccer league's one game a week, it is a story about how race, illegality, and class shape daily spaces of belonging and recreational entitlement in Rabun County.

Pedro, a restaurant worker introduced in chapter 3, cofounded the Latino soccer league in 2000, with his friend José. I had the opportunity to interview them jointly at the side of a soccer field on Sunday in 2011. Pedro and José described being among the first Latino immigrants in the area, as they saw few others upon their arrival in the mid-1980s as farm- workers (recall from chapter 3 that Pedro described working on a farm for several seasons in a row and then being "lent" to a restaurant owner one weekend, which led over time to his working full time and year-round at the restaurant). They would play soccer now and then on a field behind the Civic Center in downtown Clayton—and by field, I mean a somewhat flat, open area with tall grass, not a formally maintained field with nets or lines (see first picture in figure 5).

It is a field quite hidden from view unless one is standing in the parking lot of the Civic Center, from where the picture in figure 5 was taken. It was in the context of these pickup games that Pedro met José, who described how they founded the league:

> In that time I met Pedro. We were younger then, and we both played soccer. We decided to begin a league here in Rabun County. . . . We were three to four teams. Oh, at first it was just two, Pedro is from Michoacán and I am

Figure 5. (*left*) Field behind the Civic Center in Clayton, Georgia. (*right*) Signs posted next to the same field in 2011. Photos by author.

from Guanajuato. The teams were always divided by place of origin. So we used to say "we are going to play a game on Sunday." There really wasn't anything else to do.

But finding a field to host league games proved difficult; when they approached the recreation department staff about starting a new league, they said that the staff responded "that there were leagues already, and that all the fields were occupied [by other sports] and besides only a minority play soccer." Unsuccessful in their efforts with the recreation department, they decided to talk to the sheriff:

I went to ask for permission to use that field behind the Civic Center. They told me that yes, they would let us use it. I spoke with the sheriff. I asked permission to see whether they would let us play, because there were people who wanted to play and instead of them doing something else [i.e., getting into trouble], it would be better if they came to play soccer. They said "yes, as long as there are no problems," but, he said "this field we are going to eventually destroy to make a parking lot. Until this happens, you can play." . . . Then a few years later we went again to renew our permission, and they said no. The explanation was that they were going to build the parking lot. But they have not done anything to that field.

Another respondent, Mariano, who was a cook in a restaurant (not the same one as Pedro and José), also spoke about the soccer league. I asked him about the field where they played, and he responded, "It was a field that nobody used, it was a desmonte, it was trashed. . . . [D]o you understand me? *We* cut the grass. I do not know how they got permission to play on that field." The Rabun-based teams would play to the south in Cornelia, and to the north in Franklin, North Carolina, and host visiting teams from those areas on the field behind the Civic Center.

Within about two years, however, the sheriff and city revoked the players' permission to play on the Civic Center field (I use that name not because the field has a formal name, but because it is the one proximate to the Civic Center). Because the players were not allowed to play on any regular soccer fields in the county, the teams based in Rabun County were compelled to drop out of the league; they had no field on which to host the games. It was at that time that the daily pickup games began in the parking lot space. Those players wanting formal teams and leagues were compelled to drive to Franklin, North Carolina, where an immigrant-based league survived and thrived. Given the risks of that drive and the increased time and expense to play, many felt unable to participate in a formal soccer league. Mariano said that while he had a driver's license, he simply did not have time to drive up to Franklin for league games, so could be found many weekday evenings playing in the parking lot space.

When I asked respondents why they thought the league's permission to play on the civic center "field" was revoked, there were many conflicting explanations, from "racism" to the idea that the players and spectators had brought it on themselves. As Mariano said when I asked him why they were kicked off the civic center field, "You know, the Hispanic people are always drinking, they spend time drinking. Problems start, they leave garbage. . . . [T]hat was why the county prohibited us from playing there. [. . .] Also, the organizers misspent the money they charged us to participate, $600 per team." A number of interviewees who played soccer agreed that the trash and the number of spectators got out of hand over time in a way that players could not keep up with or control. Another player interviewed for this project, Arturo, whom we quoted in the housing section above and who was involved in contractor/building services, said that over time the police would put checkpoints just outside of where people parked who played on the civic center field: "The players from Franklin who drove down here to play stopped wanting to come because there were many checkpoints put up (retenes) and the police became very difficult and hard. So we started to have to go to Franklin to play; now the league there is huge but there is no playing league games here in Rabun County."

Arturo felt that the police were motivated by money because they could ticket people for drinking and not having a license, which he calculated netted them about $1,200. (Many respondents characterized the Clayton police as interested more in money than in deporting people.) Whatever the motivation, Arturo described that more and more people got nervous and did not want to play, and eventually the police told the organizers that they could no longer use the unmaintained space filled with weeds for soccer games. According to José and Pedro the sheriff said that they could not play there because the city was going to turn the space into a parking lot; however, while I was conducting fieldwork nearly ten years later the field was still an unmaintained space with tall grass.

It is impossible to assess fully why the police ended the players' access to what was already a highly marginal space, but it begs the question of why the only space for this league to play was an *informal*, weed-filled space that the players themselves maintained and mowed before the games. It is not clear why the police, not the recreation department, were the authority on this matter. If there were problems with trash and people drinking when watching the game (not the players themselves), then perhaps it was a situation that could have been prevented or dealt with if they had been playing on a recreation department–controlled field. Formal sports fields are maintained, with regular mowing and trash collection, and they are governed by recreation department rules regarding alcohol and so forth. The problems that emerged were shaped by the marginality of the space itself (the "civic center field" was not a formal sports field, it was an abandoned, unused space) and the extent to which players themselves took on the role of governing the space.

It is easy to imagine that the regular Sunday league games, for a few years in the early 2000s, became a site of community congregation. Mariano's wife, for example, described attending the games with their children playing on the side. In a place where there were few public spaces of social interaction for immigrant residents, it is not a stretch to think that these regular games became a site for selling food and hanging out for Latine immigrants in the community. During fieldwork a decade later, I observed the league games that continued in Franklin, North Carolina, games at which many families and friends came together to cheer on the teams, chat with friends, and eat food (there were sellers making tacos and other Mexican and Latin American cuisine). This echoes the kind of spaces soccer games create among Latine immigrant communities across the United States, as sites for the production of social ties and belonging.[21]

It is also conceivable that as the games became a space for the immigrant community to gather, they became more visible to White residents and in a way that may have been surprising to them given that the field was being used with verbal permission, not as part of a formal recreation site. While from the perspective of immigrant residents these gatherings represented a normal cultural practice, White residents might have looked upon them with anxiety and started to ask authorities about these games and crowds. The only White participant in our pool who acknowledged the history/existence of this league (once I started asking about it with all respondents) was the sheriff himself, who refused to say much about it at all beyond that they needed to end the permission because things were getting out of hand. The police decision to end the league may have stemmed as much from actual complaints as from their anticipation of criticism as the visibility of these games increased. This is all speculation because the rise and demise of the Rabun County immigrant soccer league, playing on an unmaintained but city-owned property, was not covered in the local paper, nor does it appear in any formal records that I could locate. It is made visible only through the stories of the players themselves, who had multiple explanations for its ending.

The most problematic dimension of players' stories concerning why they were kicked off the civic center field after a few years is not their lack of unanimity about the cause, but the universal normalization of their exclusion from *formal* sports fields. None of our respondents, immigrant or nonimmigrant, questioned why Latino soccer players were compelled to use an unofficial space of play for which they bore the cost of maintenance and safety. Most players treated this exclusion from formal sports fields in the county as something that they simply had to adapt to, hence the courage shown by José and Pedro in approaching the sheriff about playing on a space they identified as workable (because they offered the labor to mow it, it was unused, and its was owned by the city). Once that permission was revoked, they shifted to pickup games in the parking lot near the day labor site (see figure 4) or drove to Franklin, North Carolina, for the league games that continued there.

A physical trace of this short-lived league, beyond the life stories of soccer players themselves, was still visible in the landscape during our time conducting fieldwork: behind the Civic Center, next to the field, stood a sign in Spanish (see figure 5, righthand image):

> Noticia: Este campo es para usarse por medio de reservación. Para reservar: Llamar 706-212-2149 o 706-982-9432. Uselo bajo su propio riesgo. *No bebidas alcoholicas; *Por favor no tire basura; *Remueva o levante toda la basura cuando se retire del campo; *No envasas de vidrio.

> [Notice: This field is only for use with prior reservation. To reserve, call: 706-212-2149 or 706-982-9432. Use at your own risk. *No alcoholic beverages; *Please do not leave garbage; *Remove all garbage when you leave the field; *No glass containers allowed.]

There was no English version of this sign, presumably because no White, presumably "legal" subject would wander into this field of knee-high switch grass, sandwiched between a parking lot and a gully, to play a sport. Instead, English speakers are assumed to be vested with the right to the ample sports fields and facilities maintained by the county. It is a marker produced to exclude immigrant soccer players, performing a meaningless bureaucratic gesture in its empty suggestion that one simply needed to call a number in order to use the space—when in fact it was not a field that was reservable. Ironically, it is this monument to their exclusion that represents the clearest material trace of the *presence* of Latino soccer players in this space beyond their own narratives of the league.

Soccer and a space to play also served as a window into the history of race, legality, and the politics of social reproduction in Colorado, albeit in a more fragmented and more deeply historical manner than in Rabun County. A number of male immigrants interviewed in Colorado also mentioned soccer when asked about what they did if they had free time, or in response to questions of when participants spent time with others outside of work or family. During my interview with Jorge, introduced in chapter 3, I asked him what he did to rest (descanso) or whether he attended social events despite his multiple jobs and long hours. He replied, "In the warmer season, people go play soccer or some go to the river and ride bicycles." As a fairly recent immigrant to Steamboat, Jorge played mostly pickup games when he could, in parks. He described these as usually including men and women players, White, Latine, and smaller groups from other minoritized communities, including refugees. Jorge said he felt welcome in these games, when he could carve out time to play. His comments reflected stories told by both immigrant and nonimmigrant participants who played soccer in Routt County; teams were often integrated and most felt welcome playing in public parks.

But a slightly more complicated history was suggested by Raúl, an immigrant from Mexico who had lived in Craig, Colorado, for over thirty years at the time of our interview and who was quoted in the section of this chapter devoted to language. Raúl shared his perspective on the history of accessing soccer space in Craig in the early 1990s, which was a struggle simply because few soccer fields were available. He and other Latine immigrant players initially got permission to play at a junior high school, but as word spread and the teams got bigger they were kicked off the middle school fields:

> From there we went to the high school, outside of the high school a little bit of space there [not a formal field] but they ran us out too. So we went to the space where the soccer fields are now, it was pure dirt and rock. We convinced the city to do something because we were bringing small kids there to play, because we believe in our blood the importance of soccer. [. . .] In this time I had friends who were county commissioners, and I told them that soccer fields were a necessity. The town was growing and we did not have a place to play, my children were not going to have a place to play, and my grandchildren were not going to have a place to play. What could we do?

Raúl described lining up over many years at the open comment period in county commissioner meetings and bringing this up over and over. He mentioned that the commissioners talked about putting in a dog park or an indoor roping arena (for roping cattle competitions, etc.), but eventually Raúl and others convinced them to put in three soccer fields—the only public spaces for soccer outside of school grounds. At the final meeting for this decision Raúl and others convinced many immigrant residents of Craig to attend the meeting—a show of unity that Raúl said was rare among Latine immigrant residents of the town.

The production and reproduction of hierarchies of race and illegality within spaces of recreation manifested differently in Georgia and Colorado, differences that reflect distinct regional racial formations and histories. While the significant and rapid growth of the Latine population in the hinterlands of Steamboat—including Craig—is linked strongly to the gentrification boom of the 1990s, it is a region that since the 1950s depended on Mexican immigrant labor on ranches and in sheep herding. This population was numerically small in comparison to what emerged decades later, but it was a legitimate presence woven into the fabric of the region. Raúl was part of this longer history (early on he worked on ranches), and due to the 1986 passage of IRCA he was able to become documented, which may have contributed (in addition to his fluency in English) to his willingness to stand and speak in front of the county commissioners in the early 1990s. Pedro and José were also "old timers" trying to create a soccer league in Georgia, but their position was much more precarious given their undocumented status, their limited English, and the fact they were navigating a context with more explicit refusal to accept the presence and equality of brown or black bodies, as reflected in the history of the area.

CONCLUSION

> Social reproduction encompasses the daily and long-term
> reproduction of the means of production, the labor power to
> make them work, and the social relations that hold them in
> place. . . . [S]ocial reproduction includes the production and
> reproduction of a differentiated labor force and the cultural
> forms and practices that at once maintain these differences
> and make them common sense.
> —Norton and Katz (2017, 1)

This chapter explored a range of spaces and practices that served to reproduce a low wage, "illegal" immigrant labor force critical to rural gentrification, examining in fine-grained detail the cultural forms and social
practices that held these relations of production in place. As discussed
in chapter 1, these local dynamics were constituted by national laws and
policies undergirding border militarization and the deportation regime,
processes that mark Latine bodies as criminal and undeserving and hold
within them the concrete possibility of deportation and its devasting impacts. These social relations were also and always held in place by racial
formations—both national and regional—that have normalized the erasure of indigenous peoples, the subordination of bodies of color, and the
seemingly permanent alien status of racialized immigrant newcomers.

Normalizing Latine bodies as other, as undeserving, as disposable lies
at the heart of the productivity and profitability of immigrant labor regimes discussed in chapter 3 and is fundamental to how spaces of social
reproduction are configured and experienced on the ground in Rabun
County, Georgia, and Routt County, Colorado. At work, legal status often
made only a marginal difference in terms of working conditions and
wages, given the racialized expectations about productivity, flexibility, and
loyalty applied to all Latine workers. The embodied effects of illegality
were more palpable in and through activities of social reproduction, as
one's actual legal status impacted people's housing choices, their movement through space, and simply the daily fear that the deportation regime
produced for most undocumented participants.

In terms of housing, the flexible labor regime was complemented by a
flexible tenant regime for landlords. Both counties saw property owners
with substandard housing overcrowd units, including renting by the room.
Landlords were willing to overcrowd their properties, motivated by profit
and perhaps racialized assumptions that immigrant tenants would or
should accept different standards of housing than White residents. Interviews with property managers suggested that in many cases immigrant
residents were seen as ideal tenants because they did not complain, paid
their rent on time, and could often be removed quickly without formal
eviction procedures.

Latine immigrant access to housing was shaped by cost and, for the
undocumented, an interest in avoiding deportation. Housing was often

racially segregated, particularly in Georgia, where entire apartment buildings were coded as a place where the "Mexicans" or "Whites" lived. We found no situation in Georgia in which both groups lived in the same complex. Employers in Rabun County frequently offered workers, particularly their labor brokers, housing on the owner's property, sometimes in their backyard. This housing strategy for employers increased their access and control over workers' labor, with many employers feeling entitled in this context to call on the workers twenty-four hours a day. Workers sometimes gravitated toward this relationship, as it was often less expensive and protected them somewhat from deportation dynamics—they were living in the back of the workshop and did not have to drive to work. In Routt County this employer-provided housing—as a permanent housing option—did not exist in our sample, but as the deportation regime deepened some Latine immigrant families who had lived in Craig, Colorado, because it was cheaper sought to relocate to Steamboat simply to reduce the chance of getting picked up while commuting fifty plus minutes each way.

Building a life within these constrained housing options, particularly if one had children, was further complicated by navigating daily life with the constant background stress of the deportation regime, which deepened through the 2000s as the 287G and Secure Communities programs were rolled out. Old timers who arrived before the crackdown on driver's licenses, and others who made long trips to New Mexico or other states that continue to not require proof of immigration status to receive a license, could drive with a valid license, but they nevertheless risked on a daily basis being caught up in the deportation process if they were pulled over by police for any reason. And due to the dispersed nature of these rural spaces, *not* driving was usually impossible; people simply endured the risk and made plans for their children in the event of the worst happening. These insecurities grew in tandem with the continued demand for their labor in gentrification-linked sectors.

Conclusion

> There were Mexicanos and Americanos working in the
> restaurant, and living in the rooms [behind the restaurant].
> As time passed he (the boss) needed more people, like
> during the '90s more people started to arrive, and he began
> to see that the Mexicano was more profitable than the
> Americano, because the Mexicano . . . well, he could
> manipulate him more than the Americano because the
> Americano is always going to demand his rights as the
> Americano that he is, as a resident. The Mexicano cannot
> claim his rights because he is afraid, because he doesn't
> know the language, or possibly because of ignorance. The
> boss continued needing more people, and it was easy.
>
> —Arturo, construction industry, Rabun County (June 27, 2011)

The takeoff of gentrification in Routt County, Colorado, and Rabun
County, Georgia, had slightly different timing—the early 2000s versus the
late 1990s—and in each place it emerged within distinct regional histories
and racial formations. Nevertheless, both places witnessed remarkably
similar outcomes in terms of labor regimes and in relation to the ways
spaces of social reproduction became structured by hierarchies of race,
illegality, and poverty. Both communities experienced a dynamic reflected
in Arturo's comments above: as gentrification took off, employers went
through a learning process regarding the profit and productivity available
to them if they recruited low-wage, racialized, and often undocumented
Latine workers. In a range of gentrification-linked sectors, employers
began to actively recruit Latine immigrant workers, transforming the
economies and social geographies of these high-amenity rural places.

This demographic and socioeconomic transformation was driven by the arrival of exurban domestic migrants, usually wealthy and overwhelmingly White, who sought to become part of (not just visit) the rural idyll, to rekindle a sense of connection to nature and community. A national phenomenon long ago described by Frey and Liaw as "large-scale white flight,"[1] wealthy newcomers in both places commonly described their decision in terms of escape from a dangerous city and a longing for traditional small town life, both racially coded descriptions. These urban newcomers could afford real estate in "their" rural paradise precisely because as a racialized class they benefited from capital accumulation in the context of globalizing urban economies of the 1980s and 1990s—patterns of accumulation that dispossessed many urban residents but led to impressive gains for the wealthiest in globally integrating cities including Atlanta, Miami, Denver, Los Angeles, and Chicago.[2]

In both cases studied here, wealthy newcomers quickly began to exercise political and economic power, usually holding distinct values that sometimes clashed with self-identified locals' sense of place and authenticity—authenticity reliant on the White colonial narratives that deny indigenous histories and presence. The locals felt a symbolic displacement if not a physical one as the demand for high-end housing rose, and new businesses were established catering largely to the tastes and needs of wealthier newcomers. New jobs and opportunities were created for working-class locals, but most of these jobs were low-wage and seasonally uneven. Their growth did not forestall a sense of declining fortunes for White working-class people, nor did they alleviate the often profound class differences between many locals and wealthy newcomers. These tensions have been well-documented and theorized as a process of "displacement" by a range of scholars studying rural gentrification and amenity migration. Yet insufficient attention has been paid to the processes of recruitment and *emplacement* explored in chapters 3 and 4 of this book.[3]

Illegality and the Production of Affluence excavates less visible processes and bodies "put into place" through rural gentrification, dynamics fundamentally constituted by race, illegality, and poverty. The situations of these workers and residents are nearly opposite those of wealthy, White newcomers driving these changes: real estate ads and local media continually circulated a commodified version of these landscapes as sites of wealth, relaxation, security, and (White) community. Yet to build and maintain the infrastructure of gentrification, to provide services to the growing number of residents with disposable income and urban tastes, these communities needed workers. Existing businesses in gentrification-linked sectors struggled to keep up with new opportunities offered by the arrival of amenity migrants. Interviews with business owners and local news stories published during the boom bemoaned the labor shortage. Construction contractors in particular reported hiring crews from larger cities to work in Rabun County, Georgia, or Routt County, Colorado, just to keep up, pressure that encompassed not only the number of houses under contract but new "city" expectations regarding the speed at which those residences would be built.

The employers who overcame the low-wage labor bottleneck in both Routt and Rabun Counties did so largely through the recruitment of low-wage, Latine immigrant workers, most of whom were undocumented. This was an unfamiliar labor force for these businesses. And while many of these employers envisioned using Latine immigrants as a stopgap measure to finish one or two jobs, over time this recruitment inspired them to transform their business models, allowing them to reach new levels of profit and reduce their stress. Construction businesses/contractors generally became exposed to Latine immigrant workers through subcontracted crews coming in from cities (Denver and Atlanta in particular), and in both Rabun and Routt Counties these employers reported hiring workers right off the subcontracted crew—offering higher wages and usually helping workers find housing to get them set up. Latine immigrants, at this stage overwhelmingly male, reported an interest in the higher wages offered by the prospective employer and a desire to move from the city to a small town. Many came from rural places in Mexico or other parts of Latin America and so felt small towns were more like home and easier to navigate, quieter.

It is important to remember that in these early years—late 1990s or early 2000s—the deportation regime as experienced post-2005 did not exist. Most undocumented immigrants could work without too many complications once across the border, if they used false papers (which employers readily accepted), and most could get driver's licenses once they had the documentation of living in a place (receipts for rent, utilities, etc.).

It was not until the federal Real ID Act of 2005 that state laws regarding driver's licenses began to be more stringent.[4] Equally important to understanding this early stage, border enforcement at the time took place largely at the border, local police officers were not connected to immigration enforcement, and workplace raids—while they did exist—were not common and generally targeted large-scale employers (factories, etc.).[5] Most employers interviewed for this project, who generally ran small or medium-sized businesses, did not seem to think twice about the immigration status of their Latine immigrant hires in the 1990s and early 2000s. They felt frustrated by the language barrier but did not seem interested in investigating the legal status of these new recruits, particularly once they saw the level of productivity and flexibility they offered.

As employers incorporated one or two Latine immigrant workers into their businesses, they and their workers—as in Arturo's account above—told a story of how employers developed a preference for undocumented immigrant labor, and hence the dynamic started to shift from a stopgap measure to a new labor regime. They found immigrant workers to be more productive, loyal, flexible, and compliant than the nonimmigrant labor they had relied upon before, because immigrant workers were disciplined by hierarchies of race and class, normalized by narratives of illegality, to become compliant workaholics.[6] Once the qualities of (undocumented) immigrant labor were fully understood by employers, they began to recruit immigrants more heavily and used informal labor brokers to recruit and manage more immigrant workers. These labor brokers were often those early recruits who demonstrated dedication to and understanding of the business, had sufficient language skills to communicate effectively with the employer, and had the networks to call up additional workers as needed.

To show how this worked concretely: employers who began to adopt this regime described telling "their guy" that five more workers were needed at a site on Monday. They felt confident that it would happen and that those workers would work hard and accept working only a few days if needed. The broker took care of hiring, firing, and often paying the workers. The employer did not have to learn their names, nor in most cases deal with paperwork regarding their employment. Labor brokers succeeded when they knew all the jobs in the company, were proactive at taking care of problems, and made sure "their guys" were productive and obedient. Brokers showing these qualities were paid more, and often they were given significant responsibility and oversight over large components of the business. They were frequently described by employers as a member of the family—with some employers purportedly spending significant sums trying to get their labor broker legalized (if they were undocumented). These efforts rarely worked, much to the surprise of the employer.

Employers who found a suitable labor broker—honest, responsible, hardworking, well networked, and conversant in English—and who cultivated a close relationship with that broker could outcompete any employer who did not find such a person or invest in such a relationship. The immigrant labor regime not only improved the efficiency and profitability of the business, it also usually made the employer's life easier than it had been previously, with the bonus of greater efficiency and profit. The proper functioning of this labor regime created a situation in which the employer often had fewer responsibilities—from the daily management of labor to overseeing entire job sites (this varied, but it was not uncommon for the employer to take long vacations and leave the whole business in the hands of their broker). Employers routinely commented that White workers rarely earned that level of trust because they simply did not have the same level of "commitment" to the job as most immigrant workers. This discourse essentialized White workers as unreliable and lazy and Latine workers as hardworking and loyal—both designations produced at the intersection of race, class, and illegality/legality.

Although the earliest stages of Latine immigrant recruitment and settlement in both Routt and Rabun Counties consisted primarily of men, within a few years Latina women began to join this migration stream. Latina immigrants generally were spouses or partners of men who had established themselves in these areas, and when they did work outside of the home they networked into female-coded employment, also linked to gentrification. They worked as housekeepers, hotel maids, and backroom restaurant labor, usually balancing those paid labor opportunities with childcare and other gendered responsibilities. Hierarchies of race, illegality, and gender made Latina women very attractive to employers, as they were paid less than men yet were also expected to be hardworking and always available. Employers hiring Latina women, like their construction industry counterparts, learned over time the benefits of immigrant networks for the recruitment and management of labor—asking women to bring in extra workers as needed.

The role of labor broker developed not only among formal businesses such as contractors and landscaping, but also among individual homeowners hiring help for cleaning, maintenance and other forms of social reproduction associated with the lifestyle of rural gentrifiers. Individual homeowners in both Rabun County, Georgia, and Routt County, Colorado, frequently developed personal relationships with immigrant workers who had the networks to broker labor for them. As happened with formal employers, this was not a dynamic homeowners planned from the outset, but in looking for help around the house and/or property they developed a relationship and trust with a Latine immigrant. They learned that this person was usually available on short notice to clean the house, fix a fence, build a deck, or repair a window. While "day labor" sites did exist in both Rabun and Routt Counties, wealthier homeowners tended to have a personal relationship with a Latino or Latina labor broker, sometimes both. The homeowner felt so confident about "their guy" or "their gal" that they would acquiesce if he or she sent a stranger to their door to get the job done. The labor broker hired, fired, and disciplined the worker for the homeowner. If that worker made a mistake or was unreliable, the labor broker had to put it right to maintain the relationship. These labor regimes became the cornerstone of economic changes associated with rural gentrification, produced at the intersection of neoliberal globalization, a militarized border, and the deportation regime.

The figure of the informal labor broker, and the way immigrant social networks were leveraged to produce and sustain a highly flexible and profitable labor regime, represents a different take on immigrant networks and labor markets than what has been offered by classic work on the topic by sociologists and political scientists. Classic contributions by Roger Waldinger and others portray immigrant hiring networks as taking power *from* employers and managers,[7] as acting "sui generis" in determining the settlement patterns of immigrant workers.[8] Yet this detailed portrait of the mundane practices that led to the emergence of an (undocumented) immigrant labor regime in sites of rural gentrification shows in contrast the fundamental role of employers in accelerating the recruitment of immigrant workers through the very networks that people had to use to successfully cross the border without documentation. The use of immigrant networks by employers to increase their profit is an effect of illegality that is not given enough attention by scholars, as it is distinct from the often-repeated assertion that "illegality" produces compliant workers based on fear of deportation.[9] While such fear *is* a fundamental component of low-wage immigrant labor regimes, it is also vital to explore how illegality produces networked subjects whose networks can be appropriated by the employer in the service of capital accumulation, to create a flexible and disciplined labor regime. These networks, produced and sustained by border militarization and deportation policies, allow employers to efficiently recruit and retain an undocumented workforce, extracting more profit form them as much because of workers' fear of deportation as of the way networks are used to discipline and manage a flexible workforce.[10]

Just as immigrant labor regimes operated through the overdetermined effects of race, illegality, and poverty, spaces of social production were remade in Routt and Rabun Counties along the same axes of social power. Most visibly, two overwhelmingly White rural communities in 1990 saw a rapid increase in Latine residents, most of them foreign born and undocumented or part of mixed-status families. By 2010, on the eve of our interviews, census data indicated that 8 percent of the population of Rabun County was Hispanic/Latino and 7 percent of Routt County's population, a 1230 percent and 180 percent increase since 1990, respectively. These numbers, however dramatic, likely underrepresent the true demographic impacts of gentrification, not only due to the difficulty of fully counting undocumented residents,[11] but also because the peak of labor demand under gentrification that decade happened in 2005–2007, followed by a decline in the wake of the housing bubble and before the 2010 Census had begun.

Beyond these core demographic shifts stimulated by gentrification, the research elaborated in chapter 4 unpacked how illegality, race, and class also reconfigured social reproduction at both case study sites. Although employers sometimes perceived that the workers they hired "disappeared" when they were not needed, immigrants did not disappear. Many had become an integral and sustained part of rural gentrifying economies; they lived in the community, shopped in the grocery stores, sent their children to school, and attended church, among other daily activities.

Shelter is a central space of social reproduction, and housing for immigrant newcomers varied considerably, with immigrants facing particular challenges in the context of gentrification, a process defined by rising housing costs. When Pete Nelson and I first laid the groundwork for our joint project, we hypothesized that Latine immigrants would be living outside of gentrifying areas and commuting in, for this reason. However, we did not find this to be the case, or at least not for most people. In Steamboat Springs, Colorado, immigrants often lived in the handful of trailer parks located inside the city limits but within the floodplain of the Yampa River, land that could not easily be redeveloped into high-end properties. Or they lived in other small pockets of low-end, rundown condos near town. Some chose to commute from Craig, Colorado, or other bedroom communities because of the lower-cost options, but living that far away felt riskier over time due to the deportation regime and the way it functioned largely through traffic stops.

In Rabun County, Georgia, employers showed a proclivity for housing workers on their own property—clearly a mechanism for assuring control over and access to their labor. For immigrants not living in employer-provided housing, one apartment complex within walking distance of downtown Clayton, close to a laundromat that served as a day labor site, was known and racially coded as the apartments where "the Mexicans" lived. In reality, immigrants lived throughout the county (outside of the lakeshores themselves) given the highly uneven geography of housing stock and prices. Immigrants with children usually stayed away from these overcrowded apartment buildings housing mostly single men, sometimes living in very isolated areas to be less visible in relation to their perception of the deportation regime.

Despite the unique geographies of housing across the two cases, one commonality was a tendency for immigrant residents, particularly those without families settling locally, to live in overcrowded and indecent housing conditions. That is not to suggest that immigrants "chose" those living conditions, as these choices were bound up in their economic precarity and the impacts of race and illegality, which allowed landlords to normalize these conditions. The precarious labor system explored in chapter 3 produces workers who orient their lives around work, to become compliant workaholics, which is also about maximizing earnings. Choosing very low-cost housing options and the suffering that entails allows one to maximize support for the family (or paying off debts, etc.). At the end of the day immigrant-based labor regimes in areas of gentrification were intimately bound up with marginal housing, often hidden from public view and certainly not appearing in brochures recruiting wealthy homebuyers.

Despite the importance of considering housing and social reproduction, the first thing most Latine immigrants brought up when asked about the challenges of everyday life was language. The language barrier was its own kind of vulnerability, intersecting with race and illegality to solidify immigrants' subordinate position in the labor market and in navigating everyday life. The long journey across the border, the debts owed, and the intense work schedules left little opportunity to learn English. Not speaking English well made folks more dependent on existing immigrant networks to survive and navigate life in the United States, which in turn kept the labor regimes operating "efficiently."

Most Latine immigrants arriving in these communities were driven to leave their homes due to poverty and to seek a way to help their families, a situation that frequently signaled having had less access to education in their youth. Those who could muster the space and resources to learn English—some on the job, some through classes, and some through romantic relationships with English speakers—usually saw an immediate increase in their social and economic power. It was the first step in becoming a labor broker or at least moving up the ladder, whether they were documented or not. Becoming conversant or significantly fluent in English had a range of benefits beyond work: they could help their children navigate school more easily and could avoid relying on children as translators. But for most immigrant workers whose presence in the economy was predicated on low wages and long hours, the time and resources were simply not available. For many discussing their daily lives, it was clear that being a monolingual Spanish speaker was a primary embodiment of not belonging and being an undeserving social subject.

Finally, our understanding of new spaces of social reproduction produced in the context of amenity migration must consider the impact of the deportation regime, particularly the devolution of deportation processes from the U.S.-Mexico borderlands to interior communities starting in the early 2000s and gaining steam over time. If exclusions based on race, nationality, and language profoundly shaped the experiences of low-wage immigrants from Latin America for decades before, being undocumented took on new dimensions when the 287G program and then Secure Communities opened the door for local police departments to act as mechanisms for border enforcement and federal deportation processes.

The increased and more palpable fear of deportation toward the end of the decade made daily life a space of fear and insecurity—with parents feeling a need to plan what would happen to their children (some U.S. citizens) if they did not come home from work one evening. Some people responded by moving their residences (in Colorado some moved from Craig to Steamboat in order to avoid the commute, but it meant living in more overcrowded conditions and spending more on rent) or changing jobs. Particularly in Georgia, one common response to feel more protected from deportation was to make themselves *more* indispensable to their employers, many perceiving that an employer could intervene and protect them from deportation. While this perception may have exaggerated the power of the employer, employers did undertake various strategies to protect workers, particularly labor brokers, from deportation—ranging from moving them into housing on the owner's property to letting them drive commercially marked vehicles.

In these ways, despite the critical function of immigrant workers in rural gentrifying economies, settling down and developing a sense of place with dignity proved elusive to many immigrant newcomers. The labor regime and the associated geographies of social reproduction constituted by race and illegality functioned to efficiently incorporate the labor and productivity of Latine immigrant workers, while profoundly limiting their social and civic inclusion. Daily life for Latine immigrants in communities commodified as sites of luxury and relaxation is often marked by devoting oneself to work, keeping one's head down, and navigating a palpable sense of fear moving through daily life.

It is vital for scholars of rural gentrification/amenity migration/exurbanization and related areas to avoid reproducing the invisibility of Latine populations in their scholarship, a problem that is empirical, conceptual, and ethical in nature. What this means in practice is looking actively for their presence and potential role in rural gentrifying landscapes, because by definition low-wage and often undocumented immigrants can be quite invisible to outsiders. It is important to push beyond the surface of luxury and whiteness that characterizes rural amenity landscapes. And if one finds a significant immigrant workforce and population, it is important to do more than add immigrants to the analysis and stir.

The presence and role of Latine immigrants in areas of rural gentrification demand four changes that are conceptual and methodological in nature. First, scholars cannot avoid connecting processes of rural gentrification to multiscale political economic changes in immigrant-sending regions/nations. Many scholars of rural gentrification recognize globalization as the driver of wealth accumulation among amenity migrants, but we need to push this further to consider globalization-driven processes of displacement that push a low-wage labor force toward employers in these communities. From this perspective, the history and political economy of globalization in Mexico and Central America have become part of the story of Routt County, Colorado, as they have of Rabun County, Georgia.

Second, if Latine or other minoritized immigrants are present as a workforce and as residents in high-amenity rural spaces, scholars of rural gentrification must explicitly engage the histories of racialized nationalism, immigration policies, and border politics. If a significant portion of these workers lacks documentation, then questions of illegality and the impacts of the deportation regime should also be an important concern. Too often the undocumented status of workers is mentioned but does not receive sustained interrogation as a factor structuring the economy and social life in a high-amenity landscapes of luxury.[12]

Third, questions of race and racialization must also be foregrounded as factors structuring the economy, social relationships, ecological transformations, and politics in the context of rural gentrification. Attention to "race" in the rural gentrification literature is not only about the need for scholars to pay more attention to the growing presence of racialized workers critical to the gentrification process and the lifestyle of wealthy new residents. It is about recognizing gentrification as an already and always racialized process even without the physical presence of racialized others. White longtime residents and gentrifying newcomers (also overwhelmingly White) are racialized subjects positioned in the long durée of White settler colonial imaginaries. Moreover, White exurban residents often accumulated wealth to purchase a home in "their" rural paradise, in relation to their privileged position vis-à-vis the political economies of globalization. This is not a coincidence or a "nonracial" process simply because longtime locals also often identify as White.[13]

Fourth, it is important to use methods and ethical frames appropriate for engaging vulnerable groups across class, race, legal status, and language difference. Engaging and interviewing immigrant residents, many of whom are undocumented and struggling under poverty, needs to be done by researchers with appropriate linguistic, historical, and cultural expertise. Research with vulnerable communities also demands extended periods of engagement and ongoing reflexivity attentive to power relations and dynamics within the research process.[14] None of this absolves a researcher from ongoing power relations between researchers and participants in this context, but it strengthens the research in terms of ethics and rigor. I call on scholars of rural gentrification to consider closely whether and how low-wage immigrant workers should be at the center, not the margins, of their inquiries.

THIS IS NOT THE END

This book provides a detailed empirical exploration of the emergence of immigrant-based labor regimes and new geographies of social reproduction in two gentrifying rural communities at an important point in the history of this phenomenon in the United States. It is a story that remains relevant today because it fills ongoing conceptual and methodological gaps in the rural gentrification literature, which has not grappled fully with the presence and role of low-wage immigrant workers in rural gentrification. It is also relevant because it provides novel insights into how employers leverage the networked subjects produced by illegality to build flexible and profitable labor regimes, insights that might be relevant to a range of urban and rural contexts. Finally, it is a story worthy of telling because the production and expansion of immigrant-based labor regimes is likely to continue as urban to rural amenity flows intensify in our postpandemic world.

The core fieldwork period of the project (in 2010–2012) happened when both case study communities were reeling from the effects of the Great Recession, which dramatically *slowed* rural gentrification processes as wealth contracted and construction languished. Despite the effects of the recession, it was anticipated at the time that the flow of domestic amenity migrants would rebound, due in part to the demographic drivers of this process—specifically the aging of the baby boom—and in part to the enduring tendency of neoliberal globalization to disproportionately benefit a racialized class that desired to own a piece of the rural idyll. This expectation proved correct; within a few years amenity flows rebounded, as documented in an Alaska Airlines in-flight magazine article in 2013:

> When Kay Constantine and her husband, George, finally began looking for a vacation home, they had a list of "must-haves" in mind, including a place close to a golf course, a mountain view, a swimming pool, and most of all, warm weather. . . . In 2010, they purchased a home in the Coachella Valley (California) and discovered it was a fine way to spend time with friends and family. "We have found that a second home is a great gathering space," says Kay Constantine. "It is a place where we can mentally relax, and where we can do as much or as little as we want." The best part is having a getaway without needing to pack a thing.[15]

The movement of amenity migrants, and wealthy White urbanites' dream of their rural paradise, rebounded as the nation began to recover from the Great Recession.

What few could anticipate at the time, however, was the effects of the COVID pandemic in 2020 and its acceleration of urban to rural amenity migration. In short, the technology facilitating location-neutral professional work expanded during and after the pandemic, as did corporate willingness to permit high-wage professionals to work remotely.[16] This has allowed a much larger number of (middle- and upper-class) people to transfer their professional lives to any location, inspiring many to exit high-cost global cities. A 2022 National Public Radio story suggests the importance of this phenomenon: "In small towns all across the country, there's a shift underway, and it's rattling the status quo. As remote workers from big cities continue to move in, they buy up old houses, chasing up property values and housing costs. . . . With the option to work from just about anywhere, increasing numbers of remote workers are leaving big cities behind. They're instead opting for homes in small towns near outdoor attractions, like ski slopes or river canyons, where housing is often much cheaper."[17]

Census data show clearly that during and after the pandemic a growing number of professionals were leaving high-cost real estate in cities and heading to more affordable and smaller cities such as Missoula and Boise.[18] But truly rural amenity locations are also feeling the impact, as reflected in the NPR story quoted above. In the wake of the pandemic, high-amenity rural places will likely continue to see the in-migration of wealthier and mostly White domestic migrants, those often not seeking local job opportunities but a suite of amenities in combination with more affordable housing prices compared to large cities.

The story of rural gentrification presented over the course of this book captures a specific historical moment that allows us to understand the interplay between amenity migration and the geographic dispersal of low-wage, often undocumented Latine immigrant workers to new destinations. It shows how the movement of wealthy, White amenity-seekers to beautiful, "safer" rural communities emplaced networks of recruitment and regimes of labor constituted by race and illegality. In the early phases of gentrification the presence of immigrant workers was new. Employers had not yet figured out how to restructure their businesses entirely around this new productive and flexible labor regime. Today, however, they are not new. These regimes continue and are available to quickly mobilize productive and flexible labor as demand for it increases as a result of continuing urban to rural amenity migrants.

Ultimately, however, it is important not to see these political economic transformations in the wake of the pandemic as inevitable or to see immigrant labor regimes in high-amenity areas as an assumed, "natural" corollary to the production of these gentrifying landscapes. It is vital to remember that these landscapes are a result of choices, and as a society we can make different choices more in line with democratic and human rights ideals. Perhaps first and foremost, we need to recognize that our economy needs Latine and other immigrant groups' labor in a range of sectors, a recognition that is quite the opposite of narratives that frame cross-border labor migration as an "invasion." Creating legal mechanisms for low-wage, transnational workers to work in the United States, paths that include the possibility of permanent residency and citizenship, would erode the profound distortion of the job market created by the forces of illegalization. While substantive immigration reform would not solve the ways race and racism also constitute these labor regimes, nor would it solve the structural poverty of low-wage work in the United States, comprehensive and ethical immigration reform could reduce the pressures for Latine immigrants to organize their lives around work, providing for a decent family life and more just communities.

APPENDIX More on Methodology

Much of the qualitative data collected in Colorado and Georgia analyzed in this book draws on interviews I conducted as part of a research project developed jointly with Peter Nelson, a geographer from Middlebury College. Despite our shared surname we are not related; we did attend graduate school at the same time in the 1990s, at the University of Washington. While talking informally at the Association of American Geographers conference in Denver in 2005, we reflected on the extent to which scholars of rural gentrification/amenity migration (at the time) generally made no mention of the presence of low-wage immigrant workers in many gentrifying rural U.S. communities. This struck us as odd, because both of us had observed over the years a growing presence of immigrant workers in high-amenity areas of Colorado and other western states. We also discussed the fact that the "new immigrant destinations" literature (explored in chapter 1) generally assumed the emergence of new rural destinations for Latine immigrants in the United States was a process driven by rural industrial restructuring (e.g., meatpacking), not the kind of dispersed service-oriented work typically found in the context of gentrification.

Our observations suggested to us that both the literature on new immigrant destinations and the scholarship on rural gentrification in the United States were missing something: the arrival of Latine immigrants in high-amenity rural areas as part and parcel of the economic change wrought by gentrification.[1] Our collaboration was born, and we worked on designing quantitative and qualitative strategies to test this hypothesis, among other questions. The project drew on our distinct strengths: on my field research experiences in rural Mexico and work in U.S. new immigrant destinations, both of which required expertise in cross-cultural interviewing and fluency in Spanish;[2] and on Pete's established research examining quantitatively and qualitatively domestic amenity migration and rural gentrification.[3]

We started by exploring quantitative evidence for linked migration in the context of rural gentrification, that is, the spatial and temporal overlap of domestic amenity migration and the arrival of Latine immigrants in high-amenity rural areas. Such correlation does not prove causation, but it was an important first step. We used census data to map quantitatively, across nonmetropolitan counties nationwide, the spatial overlap between the in-migration of White baby boomers (the leading demographic edge of domestic amenity migration at the time) and "Latino/Hispanic" newcomers between 1990 and 2000 ("Latino/Hispanic" is the census category). In a publication stemming from that analysis we found that at the county scale, recreation and retirement counties that attracted relatively high inflows of ageing baby boomers also had higher levels of growth of their "Hispanic/Latino" population.[4] Moreover, we found that in 2000 the "Hispanic/Latino" population in those counties tended to be employed in construction, accommodation/food services, and managerial services (which includes landscaping and waste management). These sectors are exactly the kinds associated with rural gentrification, in contrast to rural industries such as meatpacking that had been assumed to be the primary pull factor for low-wage Latine immigrants into rural America.

With this preliminary quantitative confirmation of our initial hypothesis, we developed a three-year, mixed-method research project that after a few attempts was funded by the National Science Foundation. We sought to harness the power of a mixed-method approach to the question of whether and how domestic amenity migration and rural gentrification processes might be linked to transnational low-wage labor migration and the effects of those linkages on economic and social geographies of gentrifying rural communities. The first stage of our research used quantitative analysis of census data from nonmetropolitan counties to identify and map broad geographic patterns of rural gentrification and Latine population change between 1990 and 2000, an analysis which, unlike the previous one, included more complex proxies to identify gentrifying nonmetro counties (I detail those below).[5] The second stage selected two of the gentrifying rural counties indicated in the quantitative results for in-depth qualitative research. This second stage of research funded by NSF spanned two summers and comprised interviews, participant observation, and document analysis to explore if the correlation (shown in the quantitative findings) between indicators of gentrification and growing Latine population was causally related. Beyond establishing this causal connection, we wanted to collect data on *how* employers in gentrification-stimulated sectors recruited Latine immigrant workers during the gentrification boom and how immigrants found these isolated, nontraditional destinations. We sought to assess the role Latine immigrants had in the gentrification process and to consider the extent to which these shifting economic and demographic processes reshaped social landscapes.

For stage I, Pete Nelson and Middlebury College undergraduate assistant Alex Oberg used census data to identify nonmetropolitan counties in the United States (classified as nonmetro in 2000) that between 1990 and 2000 showed signs of gentrification, through a cluster analysis of changing home values, percentage of new housing stock, changing Gini coefficients, share of housing over $500K, and change in percentage of personal income coming from dividends, interests, and rent—variables that serve as proxies for the in-migration and settlement of high-income amenity migrants.[6] That cluster analysis identified eighty-six nonmetro counties showing signs of gentrification over that decade, a crucial decade in the history of rural gentrification processes across the United States. As importantly, Pete and Alex then examined the changing Latine population in these places compared to other nonmetro counties, showing that gentrifying counties (as indicated in the cluster analysis) saw their Latine population double during that decade, and that Latine residents comprised "close to 10% of the population in gentrifying counties, a considerably larger relative share compared to other nonmetropolitan counties" by 2000.[7]

The quantitative analysis provided evidence that as rural gentrification accelerated in the 1990s, the arrival of gentrifiers in many rural amenity communities across the United States coincided with a growing Latine population in those areas. We chose two counties highlighted in the quantitative results for in-depth qualitative research: Routt County, Colorado, and Rabun County, Georgia. We thought it important to choose one case in the already highly studied U.S. West (highly studied in terms of amenity migration/rural gentrification) and one case in a region that has not received much attention in the gentrification literature, the U.S. South.

While it is critical to use the power of quantitative analysis, which can identify broad demographic and economic patterns associated with rural gentrification, we identified a range of questions for our joint project that could only be answered through qualitative fieldwork. In choosing Rabun County and Routt County as our two field sites, we sought to investigate if the quantitative correlation between wealthy domestic amenity migrants and a growing Latine population highlighted by our maps was a causal, structural relationship: Were Latine newcomers recruited into the sectors most transformed by the arrival of amenity migrants? (It is plausible that gentrification was happening in one part of the county, and our maps were picking up the arrival of Latine populations working in unrelated sectors.) Equally important, if this correlation showed signs of causality, we were interested in how employers found and recruited this unfamiliar workforce; how migrants themselves chose these destinations; and how the integration of immigrant workers transformed business practices, labor practices, and social life in gentrifying locales. Although less of a focus within the original research design, I brought an abiding interest in whether and how the racial and legal hierarchies found in the spaces of work and production rippled out within broader spaces of social reproduction and community life.

We used a comparative qualitative approach to explore differences and similarities across these places during the gentrification process, providing robust insight into dynamics that might be emerging in high-amenity rural communities across the U.S., and perhaps in other postindustrial contexts. The connections between the quantitative and qualitative stages of our project increased the explanatory power of our qualitative work—the cases were chosen to shed insight on broader patterns of linked migration shown in the quantitative analysis. Nevertheless, this is not the same as claiming processes explored in Rabun and Routt Counties are generalizable in a classic positivist sense. There may be rural areas experiencing gentrification that do not recruit Latine workers into gentrification-linked sectors, and certainly there may be different immigrant groups or refugees that are part of the story in different places.

We scheduled two summers of fieldwork in Colorado and Georgia. In the summer of 2010 (then) University of Oregon graduate research assistant Laurie Trautman and I spent four weeks at each field site, conducting interviews in Spanish and English with immigrant and nonimmigrant workers, employers, gentrifiers, city leaders, and educators as well as a range of longtime residents. We also conducted participant observation in a range of social spaces, from the streets of downtown to recreational and religious events. Pete Nelson joined us for two weeks in each community, with his interview schedule focused on employers in gentrification-linked sectors and elected leaders, as well as participant observation with the entire team. I then returned for two weeks' fieldwork in 2011 in each site, this time accompanied by a new research assistant from University of Oregon, Graciela "Meche" Lu—during which we reconnected with previous interviewees and recruited new participants from the same groups studied in 2010. Meche and I also sought opportunities to continue participant observation and collect documents only available in the field—from local real estate magazines to archival searches in the local newspaper archives, which at the time were available only through the local public library.

Pete Nelson and I spent significantly different lengths of time in the field because I was recruiting and working with a more vulnerable population in both sites: Latine residents, the vast majority foreign born and Spanish speaking, and many of whom were undocumented. The rationale was that I needed more time to develop rapport and trust with this population, but it also led to each of us collecting different amounts and kinds of qualitative data. Over time this led us to conceptualize our findings in distinct ways, with my own emphasis being on race and illegality as well as social reproduction—topics that emerged from my interviews with immigrant participants.

Pete and I coauthored a series of articles from the NSF project, publications that made important contributions to scholarly understandings of linked migration and rural gentrification.[8] Yet the format of articles could not fully engage the rich data that I and my research assistants collected during the NSF-supported project, leading me to consider a book-length writing project. I returned to the field in the summers of 2012 and 2015 (four weeks total), the latter funded by my home institution at that time, Penn State. During those field visits I continued participant observation and interviews with immigrant and nonimmigrant workers, gentrifiers, local officials, and employers in gentrification-linked sectors. I explored further the emergence and consolidation of immigrant-based labor regimes across and through hierarchies of race and illegality, as well as how these were linked to the social geography of everyday life. I deepened my interest in pursuing a book-length exploration of questions that lay beyond those articulated in our original NSF-funded project. I was grateful that Pete was supportive of this single-authored book project, as by that time he had moved on to other collaborations and research endeavors.

List of Quoted Interviewees

This list is alphabetical by pseudonym.

Adam: contractor, Rabun County, White (July 1, 2011)

Aitana: restaurant worker, Routt County, Latina (August 11, 2011)

Alan: contractor, Steamboat Springs, White (August 17, 2011)

Alejandro: construction worker, Rabun County, Latino (July 2, 2010).

Alma: janitor, Craig, Colorado, Latina (August 10, 2010)

Amanda: unemployed, Rabun County, White (June 22, 2010).

Arnold: owner, landscaping company, Routt County, White (July 27, 2010, interviewed by Pete Nelson)

Arturo: contracting/construction industry–related work, Rabun County, Latino (June 27, 2011)

Ben: retail business owner, Routt County (August 13, 2010)

Betty: professional and self-identified local, Rabun County, White (June 29, 2010)

Brian: contractor, Rabun County, White (June 22, 2010)

Carlos: landscaping worker, Rabun County (July 1, 2010)

Cayetano: masonry, Rabun County, Latino (July 8, 2015)

Charlie: midlevel administrator, Routt County, White (August 27, 2011)

Diana: housekeeper, Routt County, Latina (August 12, 2011)

Delia: retail worker, self-identified local, Rabun County, White (June 14, 2010)

Diego: roofing and property maintenance worker, Rabun County, Latino (July 2, 2010)

Elisa: housekeeper, Rabun County, Latina (June 26, 2010)

Enrique: supervisor of manufacturing, Rabun County, Latino (May 30, 2010)

Eric: nonprofit manager, professional Routt County, White (August 23, 2011)

Gabriel: H2B visa worker in landscaping, Routt County, Latino (August 18, 2010)

Gloria: restaurant worker, Routt County, Latina (August 18, 2010)

Jack: owner of landscaping business, Rabun County, White (July 15, 2012)

John: construction worker, Rabun County, White (July 28, 2011)

Jorge: commercial cleaning crew and other seasonal jobs, Routt County, Latino (August 9, 2011)

José: restaurant worker, Rabun County, Latino (July 26, 2011)

Leopoldo: home maintenance worker, Routt County, Latino (June 24, 2010)

Liliana: house cleaner, Routt County, Latina (August 16, 2010)

Logan: working-class property maintenance, Routt County, White (August 23, 2011)

Lola: restaurant worker, Craig, Colorado, Latina (August 19, 2010)

Luis: agro-food processing, Rabun County, Latino (June 22, 2010)

Maggie: trailer park manager and resident, Routt County, White (August 24, 2010)

Mariano: restaurant worker, Rabun County, Latino (June 12, 2011)

Mark: contractor, Rabun County, White (June 30,2010)

Marilyn: real estate, Rabun County, White (June 28, 2012)

Mateo: restaurant industry, Rabun County, Latino (July 15, 2015)

Max: home inspector, Rabun County, White (June 23, 2015)

Miguel: construction worker, Rabun County, Latino (June 25, 2011)

Nelly: cook, Rabun County, Latina (June 20, 2011)

Pablo: cook, Rabun County, Latino (June 24, 2010)

Pedro: restaurant worker, Rabun County, Latino (June 26, 2011)

Rachel: contractor, Routt County, White (August 17, 2011)

Raúl: ranching and mining worker, Craig, Colorado, Latino (August 19, 2010)

Richard: retired, amenity migrant, Rabun County, Georgia, White (June 8, 2010)

Rick: landscaper, Rabun County (June 10, 2010).

Roberto: construction worker, Rabun County, Georgia, Latino (July 25, 2011)

Roger: business owner of concierge property management, Routt County, White (August 22, 2011).

Rosa: restaurant worker and housekeeper, Rabun County, Latina (June 10, 2010)

Rose: small business owner, Rabun County, Georgia, White (June 17, 2010)

Sarah: business owner and self-identified local, Rabun County, White (June 17, 2010)

Sergio: roofing and construction worker, Rabun County, Latino (June 18, 2011)

Sonia: grew up in Rabun County, Latina (May 13, 2010)

Tom: contractor, Routt County, White. Unrecorded interview (August 18, 2010).

Virginia: administrative assistant, self-identified local, Rabun County, White (July 14, 2010)

Notes

1. Bentancur (2023); see also Slemp (2020).

INTRODUCTION

1. *Steamboat Magazine* (2010).

2. The category of "local" is slippery and laden—a self-identification that is at the core of authenticity politics in both Rabun and Routt Counties (similar to other sites of rural gentrification; see Osbaldiston 2011; Sherman 2023). It also produces a politics of authenticity constituted by White settler colonial imaginaries, as it disavows the violent erasure of indigenous peoples and territories in both places. I return to explore the identity of "being a local" in chapter 3.

3. On urban gentrification, see Glass (1964); Rose (1984); Zukin (1987). On rural gentrification definitions, see Phillips (1993) and Phillips and Smith (2022).

4. *Newcomers Guide to Rabun County* (2010, 3).

5. Similar experiences with land and housing costs, as well as battles over development, have emergedin other boomtowns of the U.S. West. See Walker and Fortmann (2003); Ghose (2004); Winkler et al. (2007); Sherman (2018); Phillips et al. (2021). It is important to note that newer waves of gentrifiers often came to

identify themselves quickly as "locals," and many sought to slow down development and conserve open space.

6. See *Merriam-Webster* (2021).

7. On approaches exploring capitalist transformation that center displacement , see Strauss (2023); Pull et al. (2020).

8. U.S. Census Bureau (2020); note that the census counts this population using the terms "Hispanic/Latino."

9. These numbers draw from the 1990 Census of Population, "General Population Characteristics Colorado," https://www2.census.gov/library/publications /decennial/1990/cp-1/cp-1-7.pdf; and CensusViewer, "Population of Routt County Colorado," http://censusviewer.com/county/CO/Routt, comparing 2010 and 2000 data.

10. These numbers draw from the 1990 Census of Population, "General Population Characteristics Georgia," https://www2.census.gov/library/publications /decennial/1990/cp-1/cp-1-12.pdf.

11. On the rise of deportation and "interior" border enforcement, see Coleman and Kocher (2011); Golash-Boza (2015); Martínez, Slack, and Martínez-Schuldt (2018). The history and implications of deportation policy and interior border policing are explored in detail in chapter 1.

12. See Martínez and Slack (2013).

13. De Genova (2002, 2005).

14. De Genova (2002, 2005); Herrera (2016); Gómez (2021).

15. A core assertion developed over the course of this book is the relational production of affluence and illegality, building from existing work in relational poverty studies; see Elwood, Lawson, and Sheppard (2017); Duncan and Duncan (2004).

16. Half of all immigrants entering the United States in the 1980s settled in one of eight cities: Los Angeles, New York, Miami, Anaheim, Chicago, Washington, D.C., Houston, and San Francisco (Fix and Passel 1994; see also Sassen 1994).

17. A Pew Research Center report, drawing on data through 2022, estimated that the undocumented population in the United States peaked in 2007 at approximately 12.2 million, a number that declined steadily through 2019 (10.2 million), after which there was an increase to approximately 11 million by 2022 (Passel and Krogstad 2024).

18. On the growing inequality associated with neoliberal globalization, see Hytrek and Zentgraf (2008); Navarro (1998).

19. On these global patterns, see Sassen (1990); Castles (1998).

20. Farmers in Rabun County began hiring Latine farmworkers on a seasonal basisi in the mid-1980s, according to interviews with farmers. They were short term and housed on the farm. Also, Mexican ranch hands were commonly hired on cattle ranches outside of Steamboat, a practice reaching into the 1950s.

However, the presence of each group of immigrants was not year-round nor close to the scale and permanence of gentrification-linked recruitment and settlement in the late 1990s and beyond.

21. See Bakker (2007).

22. Katz (2013, 111).

23. See Mitchell, Marston, and Katz (2004); Bakker (2007); and Meehan and Strauss (2015).

24. For both study areas I characterize gentrification-driven immigrant labor regimes as "new," although Latine immigrant farmworkers had begun to arrive seasonally in Rabun County starting in the 1980s, and Mexican cowboys and Peruvians had worked on ranches outside of Steamboat for several decades prior to that time. Further explanation of this position can be found in chapter 3.

25. On the emergence of new immigrant destinations, see Massey (2008); Zúñiga and Hernández-León (2005); Gozdziak and Martin (2005). For more recent scholarship on the ongoing challenges and dynamics in new immigrant destinations, see McAreavey (2017); Lanesskog (2018).

26. Marrow (2011); Winders (2013); Schmalzbauer (2014). See also Licona and Maldonado (2014).

27. One scholar who does engage closely questions of the political economy of low-wage labor migration in the context of rural gentrification is Schmalzbauer (2014).

28. Scholars who identify and analyze the presence of Latine immigrants in landscapes of rural gentrification in the United States include Nelson and Nelson (2010); Park and Pellow (2011); Schmalzbauer (2014); Nelson et al. (2015); Stuber (2021); Farrell (2021). Only Schmalzbauer (2014) and my publications coauthored with Peter Nelson (also discussed in chapter 1) consider processes of recruitment and evolving labor regimes in these contexts.

29. See Menjívar (2016); Gomberg-Muñoz (2012).

30. Rodríguez (2004); De Genova (2005); Gomberg-Muñoz (2012).

31. See Chavez (2013).

32. Details about interviewees are included in a list in the backmatter.

33. Dimke, Lee, and Bayham (2021); Kolko, Badger, and Bui (2021); Nelson and Frost (2023); Weeden, Hardy, and Foster (2022).

1. GENTRIFICATION, MIGRATION, AND RACE

1. Glass (1964); Smith (1979, 1982); Bondi (1991); Dubin (1992).

2. Regarding the direct quotations from transcribed interviews found here and throughout the book, to indicate a pause or hesitation by the speaker I use a plain ellipsis, and to indicate when I have left out words spoken by the interviewee I use an ellipsis in square brackets.

3. Founding texts include Smith (1979); Rose (1984); Lyons (1996). For more contemporary overviews of urban gentrification, see Hamnett (2021); Lees, Slater, and Wyly (2023).

4. For a Marxist "capital-driven" approach, see Smith (1979); on demand-side explanations, see Ley (1986); on social movements and resistance, see Robinson (1995); Betancur (2002); Levy, Comey, and Padilla (2007); and on planning strategies to prevent gentrification, see Howell (2016); Cassola (2018).

5. Smith (2002).

6. Hamnett (1991, 174).

7. Harvey (2001).

8. Smith (1982).

9. Molina (2015); Prince (2016).

10. On housing policy and urban planning, see Dubin (1992); Wyly and Hammel (2001); Lees and Ley (2008); Goetz (2011); on mortgage lending practices, see Wyley and Hammel (1999); Wyly, Atia, and Hammel (2004). On gentrification and the dynamics of gender and urban change, see Pratt (1990); Bondi (1991); Kern (2007); on the intersection of race and gentrification, see Freeman (2011); Goetz (2011); on the role of art and artists in gentrification, see Deutsche and Ryan (1984); Mathews (2010).

11. Urban social movements and gentrification are explored in Kling and Posner (1991); Robinson (1995); and Pearsall (2013). On less formal modes and manners of resistance, see Slater (2008); Anguelovski (2015).

12. Parsons (1980); Little (1987); Phillips (1993).

13. Smith and Phillips (2001); Phillips (2004).

14. Aledo (2008); Abrams et. al. (2012); Benson and O'Reilly (2018); Botterill (2017); Emard and Nelson (2021).

15. P. Nelson (2008); Cromartie and Nelson (2009).

16. Nelson and Nelson (2011); Nelson and Hines (2018).

17. Robinson (1995); Betancur (2002).

18. Cloke (1993); Phillips (1993); McCarthy (2008).

19. Walker and Fortmann (2003); Stedman (2006); Solana-Solana (2010); Larsen and Hutton (2012); Ulrich-Schad (2018).

20. Shumway and Otterstrom (2001); see also Smith and Krannich (2000).

21. Walker and Fortmann (2003).

22. Ghose (2004).

23. Pilgeram (2021).

24. Sherman (2021).

25. Ulrich-Schad (2018); Winkler (2013).

26. Larsen et al. (2011).

27. May (2019).

28. A sample of additional scholarship on rural gentrification/amenity migration/lifestyle migration in the U.S. and UK includes Smith et al. (2021);

Hjerpe, Armatas, and Haefele (2022); Phillips and Smith (2022); Song, Robinson, and Bardsley (2022); Fritzsche (2023); Frolich and Schmidt (2023); Walrath et al. (2024). On global geographies of rural gentrification see Emard and Nelson (2021); Herrero-Jáuregui and Concepción (2023).

29. Census data shared here represent a rough proxy for demographic changes in or near sites of rural gentrification studied by these scholars—rough not only because we cannot tell specifically from these simple stats what is drawing in this population (the nature of employment), but also because the high cost of housing in areas of rural gentrification may compel low-wage workers to live far from the gentrifying locale and commute to work—thus complicating how we can read simple population data in a particular locale as indicating a role of Latine workers or not. There could be significant employment of Latine workers in a place, but if they commute a long distance to work, they might not be captured in the census data for that particular locale. Finally, in rural places census data are organized around race/ethnicity but not immigrant status of the Latine population, so any numbers shown here are labeled "Latine population" in recognition that for the time period under study the decadal census did not indicate foreign-born status. Nevertheless, we expect most of the growing Latine population in these places to be Latine immigrants, given that U.S.-born Latinos do not represent a large group migrating to rural places for low-wage work.

30. The literature on amenity migration, rural gentrification, lifestyle migration, and exurbanization in the U.S. context indicates that wealthier newcomers in areas of rural gentrification are overwhelmingly White; see Loeffler and Steinicke (2007); Nelson, Oberg, and Nelson (2010); Gosnell and Abrams (2011). Most of the literature on rural gentrification continues to not explicitly frame these inflows of amenity migrants as overwhelmingly White. However, most of these scholars imply that they are White because they do not name them as racialized flows—suggesting whiteness as an unmarked category of analysis in rural gentrification scholarship. See for example Stoker et al. (2021) and Sherman (2021).

31. Ulrich-Schad (2018, 44).

32. Breen, Hurley, and Taylor (2016).

33. Frey and Liaw (1998).

34. On White settler imaginaries and their dependence on the construction of "empty" landscapes devoid of indigenous presence, see Verancini (2010) and Hore (2022).

35. These racialized codes emerge in the U.S. and in a range of global contexts impacted by rural gentrification and lifestyle migration (see Benson 2014; Emard and Nelson 2021; McGarrigle 2022).

36. Nelson, Lee, and Nelson (2009). On how this impacted debates around rural gentrification/amenity migration and new immigrant destinations, see Nelson and Nelson (2011).

37. Park and Pellow (2013)

38. Schmalzbauer (2014).

39. Farrell (2021); Stuber (2021).

40. Stuber (2021, 250).

41. Stuber (2021, 223).

42. This instruction to the bilingual research assistants was motivated by ethical considerations. It does take significant finesse and intercultural understanding to not ask anyone about legal status but to nevertheless allow those stories to emerge and be explored further if the participant raises the issues themselves. By keeping it completely off the table, Stuber misses an opportunity to explore how illegality affects work and life in Aspen.

43. Farrell (2021, 9).

44. See Farrell (2021, 20–21).

45. Farrell (2021, 243–44) (emphasis added).

46. Coleman (2007); Fussell (2011); Golash-Boza (2015, 2019).

47. The quantitative empirical evidence for this is shown in Nelson, Lee, and Nelson (2009) as well as Nelson, Oberg, and Nelson (2010).

48. Sassen (1990, 1994).

49. This was also explored quantitatively for Jackson Hole in Nelson, Lee, and Nelson (2009).

50. Cornelius (1986); Bustamante, Reynolds, and Ojeda (1992); Delgado Wise and Covarrubias (2007).

51. See Harvey (2007); on the case of Mexico specifically, see Pastor and Wise (1997).

52. Otero (2011); Delgado Wise and Covarrubias (2008).

53. Not all undocumented immigrants in the United States are Mexican, and as of 2016 more non-Mexicans (largely from Central America) cross the U.S.-Mexico border without authorization; see Passel and Cohn (2019). Nevertheless, the history of U.S.-Mexico labor migration represents a paradigmatic case of how globalization shapes cross-border migration flows and is the history most relevant to the cases explored in this book.

54. Passel (2015).

55. See American Immigration Council (2021).

56. The model of production labeled "Fordist" is the industrial model first developed by Henry Ford in the production of the Model T—and it characteristically is based on mass production using an assembly line within a large, spatially centralized production system. It has many fixed costs, including high-wage workers, often unionized, as well as sunk costs in terms of inventory and equipment. Fordist production systems had difficulty meeting shifts in demand or to innovate in the face of flexible competition. Fordist production (U.S. based) confronted post-Fordist or flexible production systems emerging in Japan and Germany in the 1970s and 1980s, spelling the rapid decline in the Fordist model. For more discussion, see Dicken (1998); Esser and Hirsch (2009).

57. Harvey (2007).

58. Schmitt (2000); Sassen (2002); Park (2013).

59. MacLeavy (2016).

60. Sassen (1990, 1998); Castles (1998); Pamuk (2004).

61. Hondagneu-Sotelo (2007).

62. Otero (2011); see also Delgado-Wise (2004).

63. The story of how Mexico became deeply indebted is complex, even though the rapid rise in global interest rates between 1978 and 1982 was perhaps the single most important factor shifting that debt from manageable to unmanageable. Most of the loans in this period were taken out with private banks under variable interest-rate contracts. During the 1970s U.S. and European banks eagerly marketed loans to countries throughout the Global South, in part because they assumed governments could not declare bankruptcy. Mexico and other countries took on these loans for a range of purposes: to forestall structural problems in their economies, to pay off political allies, or to expand military operations against "internal enemies" in the context of the Cold War. The bottom line is that little of this spending supported equitable and sustained economic development, leaving countries in a very precarious economic position when interest rates went up. For more on the debt crisis, see Thorp and Whitehead (1987); Pastor (1989).

64. On the role of the International Monetary Fund in restructuring debtor nations' economies during the 1980s and 1990s, see George (1988); Pastor (1989); Bello, Cunningham, and Rau (1994).

65. Gates (1993).

66. Massey (1986); Mize and Swords (2010).

67. Passel and Cohn (2018).

68. Passel and Cohn (2019)

69. Durand, Massey, and Charvet (2000); Kandel and Cromartie (2004).

70. Massey (1990); Massey et al. (1990).

71. Kandel and Parrado (2005); Zúñiga and Hernández-León (2005); Massey (2008); Flippen and Farrell-Bryan (2021).

72. Light (2006).

73. Hernández-León and Zúñiga (2000); Durand, Massey, and Capoferro (2005); Barcus (2006).

74. Scholars emphasizing labor recruitment and economic change in new destination sites include Stull, Broadway, and Griffith (1995); Krissman (2000); Johnson-Webb (2002); Kochhar, Suro, and Tafoya (2005); Griffith (2005); Kandel and Parrado (2005).

75. Parrado and Kandel (2011); Torres et al. (2013).

76. Donato et al. (2007); Buckley (2014).

77. See Stiffler (2005); Champlin and Hake (2006); Broadway and Stull (2008).

78. De Genova (2002); Harrison and Lloyd (2012); Miraftab (2016); Gomberg-Muñoz (2019).

79. Kandel and Parrado (2005); Rich and Miranda (2005); Barcus (2006); Sarathy (2012).

80. Hernández-León and Zúñiga (2000).

81. Gozdziak and Bump (2004); Zúñiga and Hernández-León (2005); Jensen and Yang (2016).

82. Henderson (2011); Hing (2010).

83. Light (2006).

84. Melamed (2015).

85. In accordance with human subjects protocols, the names of research participants used in this book are pseudonyms, unless otherwise indicated. A list of interviewees quoted in this book can be found in the appendix, which lists participants alphabetically by pseudonym and includes accurate descriptions of interview date, study site, and rough approximation of role in gentrification (employer, worker, gentrifer), gender, and race/ethnicity. The only time such information is changed is if including it would compromise the anonymity of participants.

86. On the intensification of "illegal alien" narratives, see Nevins (2001); Chavez (2013); Ngai (2014). On the deportation policies and politics in the 2000s, see Coleman and Kocher (2011); De Genova (2010); Golash-Boza and Hondagneu-Sotelo (2013).

87. Dunbar-Ortiz (2014).

88. On settler colonialism see Wolfe (2006); Veracini (2014); Morgensen (2011).

89. Weitzer (1990, 26). Weitzer goes on to summarize what distinguishes settler colonialism from traditional colonial systems. Colonial systems such as many found in Africa "were organized around imperial economic and geopolitical objectives, such as acquiring territory from other European competitors, establishing military outposts, monopolizing trade, opening markets and exploiting natural resources," often maintaining a "skeletal coercive structure and small contingents of colonial administrators—a 'thin White line' throughout Africa" (25).

90. Stasiulis and Yuval-Davis (1999, 7).

91. Gilmore (2002).

92. Kanstroom (2007).

93. Here "racialization" refers to any effort to essentialize or biologize difference, whether framed explicitly through the language of phenotypic racial difference or other metaphors, such as religion or cultural difference. On race in the construction of national political community in U.S. history, see Gotanda (1997); Hing (2012).

94. On nineteenth-century labor markets and immigration, see Rosenbloom (2002).

95. Chan (1989); Cloud and Galenson (1987).

96. Kibler (2015). On the gendered dimensions of the racialized representations, see Urban (2009).

97. Miller (1969); Saxton (1975).

98. Cloud and Galenson (1987).

99. On history and the nation see Duara (1996).

100. Higham (2002).

101. Ngai (2014).

102. Ngai (2014, 26).

103. Ignatiev (1995).

104. Smithsonian Museum (2024).

105. Del Castillo (1992).

106. Carrigan and Webb (2013).

107. It is the paradox of formal citizenship and racialized exclusion and violence that inspired Mae Ngai (2014, 8) to coin the concept of "alien citizen" to discuss the position of Mexican Americans, Filipino, and other racialized descendants of immigrants in U.S. history.

108. Garcilazo (2012); Gutiérrez (1995).

109. Piore (1979).

110. Nevins (2001).

111. Nevins (2001); Ngai (2014).

112. During the 1930s "repatriation" campaigns targeting Mexicans led to over one million forced deportations. A significant percentage of those deported were U.S. citizens who were targeted on the basis of race and forcibly put on trains heading south; see Balderrama and Rodríguez (2006).

113. Cohen (2011).

114. Gamboa (2000).

115. Massey and Liang (1989); Heisler (2008).

116. Tichenor (2009).

117. Ngai (2014).

118. Ngai (2014, 261) notes that in the early 1960s legal Mexican migration included two hundred thousand Braceros and thirty-five thousand regular admissions. The quota set in 1968 as the Hart-Celler Act was implemented allowed 120,000 migrants for the entire Western Hemisphere, a number that declined to twenty thousand by 1976.

119. Nevins (2001).

120. Cornelius (1986); Hondagneu-Sotelo (1994); Goldring (1992).

121. Bean, Edmonston, and Passel (1990). See also Hagan (1998). I should note that IRCA included a special provision for agricultural workers, the Special Agricultural Worker (SAW) program, which created more lenient residency requirements for people who could demonstrate employment in farmwork. This represented a gesture to the critical role of undocumented workers in the agriculture industry; see Chishti and Kamasaki (2014).

122. Chiswick (1988).

123. Baker (1997).

124. Massey, Durand, and Pren (2015).

125. U.S. Border Patrol (2018).

126. Passel and Cohn (2016).

127. Martinez et al. (2013).

128. Golash-Boza (2015).

129. Crossing the border without documents is not a violation of the criminal code, so it is not a criminal violation. Thus protections accorded criminals, including legal representation for the accused, are not applied to undocumented border crossers; see Golash-Boza (2015).

130. Coleman (2007, 56).

131. Varsanyi (2010).

132. Nelson (2019, 51).

133. De Genova (2005); Harrison and Lloyd (2012); Herrera (2016); Gomberg-Muñoz (2019).

134. De Genova (2005, 8).

135. Shapiro and Sharma (2018).

2. METHODS AND CASE STUDIES

1. Hernández et al. (2013); Doucet and Mauthner (2008).

2. These epistemological positions and their methodological implications are discussed in Wolf (1993); Hesse-Biber (2011). On questions of intersectionality and feminist methods, see Lykke (2010); Faria and Mollett (2016); Raghuram (2019).

3. A more detailed discussion of this joint project can be found in the appendix. I should note that despite our shared surname, Peter Nelson and I are not related.

4. See Nelson, Lee, and Nelson (2009); Nelson, Oberg, and Nelson (2010).

5. For discussion and critique see Gosnell and Abrams (2011).

6. Moss, Al-Hindi and Kawabata (2002); Simandan (2019).

7. This is a decision distinct from Farrell's approach in *Billionaire Wilderness*, where he thought it was methodologically innovative to interview a White billionaire alongside their Latina nanny or Latino groundskeeper (see Farrell 2020, 14). It is hard for me to imagine a more ethically questionable or data-compromising approach than to interview a worker alongside their employer—particularly in the context of Jackson Hole and the profound differences of wealth and racial positioning between those two groups. For an excellent exploration of the ethics of recruiting and interviewing employers and workers in the same research project, see Mullings (1999).

8. *Yampa Valley Quarterly* (2009).

9. Real estate prices began to climb in Steamboat as amenity migration deepened in the 1990s. It should be noted that the ability of amenity migrants to purchase real estate in places such as Steamboat was also tied to rising real estate values in the larger cities where they were coming from. Particularly for folks

who moved to Steamboat as part of retirement, many were able to use the equity in their urban homes to afford the increasingly pricey real estate in Steamboat. On the linkages between urban real estate markets and the economics of rural gentrification in the United States, see Nelson, Oberg, and Nelson (2010); Gosnell and Abrams (2011).

10. Clifford (1995).

11. *Georgia Mountain Laurel* (2010, 4–5).

12. Russell (2021, ch. 11).

13. Russell (2021, ch. 10).

14. U.S. Forest Service (2022).

15. Rabun County (2006).

16. On Atlanta's 1990s growth machine, see Rutheiser (1996).

17. Rabun County (2006, 2–5).

18. On the spatial reorganization of the textile industry in the U.S. South, see Anderson, Schulman, and Wood (2001).

19. Atlanta Business Chronicle (2006).

20. On positional goods driving rural gentrification, see Phillips (1993, 126).

21. Coppola (2001, 72–73).

22. Frey and Liaw (1998).

23. Ritchie (1959, 23).

24. Ritchie (1959, 15–16).

25. The removal of the Cherokee and other native communities in the Southeast and their deadly forced march to so-called Indian Territory west of the Mississippi was one of the most violent and genocidal acts undertaken by the U.S. government against Native cultures and peoples (see Perdue and Green 2007; Smithers 2015). It is a violence made invisible by triumphalist White settler colonial narratives of pioneers building civilization. Ritchie's account is largely a series of biographies of early White male settlers. For example, he discusses in detail John Dillard (after whom the town of Dillard is named), who served in the American Revolution and settled in the northeast corner of Georgia after receiving 250 acres of land for his service with "General Andrew Pickens in his expeditions against the Cherokee Indians" (Ritchie 1959, 26). The land occupied by White settlers who founded Rabun County was available because of the violent removal of Cherokee communities.

26. Ritchie (1959, 279).

27. Fraser (2006).

28. See Walker and Fortmann (2003); Abrams and Bliss (2013).

3. IMMIGRANT LABOR REGIMES

1. Massey and España (1987); Gurak and Caces (1992).

2. Waldinger (1997); Munshi (2003); Bashi (2007).

3. U.S. Census Bureau (2021).

4. Passel and Cohn (2009).

5. Harrison and Lloyd (2012).

6. Krissman (2000); Kissam, Intili, and Garcia (2001); Striffler (2005); Alves Peña (2012); Horton (2016); Stuesse (2016).

7. Salinas (2018).

8. Sarah Bronwen Horton (2016) provides a fine-grained portrait of how the formal labor contracting system not only shields agribusiness from the repercussions of hiring undocumented labor but creates a situation for the evasion of health and safety standards for farmworkers. She explores how California passed new rules to protect farmworkers, ones that have little impact due to the structure of the system that allows contractors to punish workers who ask for breaks or slow down the crew. As temperatures rise, the rate of illness and death among farmworkers is growing and is a process abetted by a system based on labor contracting.

9. Among scholars studying industrial agriculture, the use of labor contractors as a means to sidestep consequences for hiring undocumented farmworkers is well known (see Kissam 2000; Horton 2016). An interesting article by Ambrosini (2017) discusses the role of various intermediaries in the functioning of undocumented migration and the search for employment for undocumented workers. However, Ambrosini does not delve into how these intermediaries are cultivated by employers and make it possible for employers to manage undocumented labor.

10. Benson (2008); Hollander (2006); Nelson (2006).

11. Congressional Research Service (2020). "H-2A and H-2B Temporary Worker Visas: Policy and Related Issues" (R44849), Prepared for Members and Committees of Congress, by Andorra Bruno, https://crsreports.congress.gov /product/pdf/R/R44849/5.

12. Hackman (2022).

13. I can speculate as to why it was not uncommon for landscapers in Colorado to use short-term guestworkers, which was rare among landscape businesses in northern Georgia (or any of the employers interviewed in other gentrification-linked sectors). Perhaps most importantly, the process of hiring H2B guestworkers is complicated and highly bureaucratic, with an annual risk that the national cap would be reached before one's request had been processed, leaving employers having invested in paperwork without any results. Generally it was larger-scale employers who could navigate those uncertainties, and there were larger-scale landscaping businesses in Colorado compared to Georgia, tied to the fact that Steamboat is/was a destination not only for amenity migrants, but also for short-term tourists. There are more hotels and condos in Steamboat, scaling up the demand for landscapers. The ski resort industry in Steamboat regularly uses H2B visas for winter-time employees (lift operators from

Jamaica, ski instructors from Australia, etc.), creating more local knowledge and familiarity with applying for and using H2B workers

14. Day labor sites are places where immigrants looking for work congregate and prospective employers drive up to hire someone, usually for a day or two. In many cities these sites are associated with the parking lots of Home Depot or similar large home building box stores. This is one of the most precarious forms of labor for mostly undocumented immigrants. See Valenzuela (2003).

15. Beauregard (2013).

16. County Business Patterns Datasets for 1990, 2000, and 2010. See https://www.census.gov/programs-surveys/cbp/data/datasets.html.

17. These dynamics echo those found in other amenity studies: P. Nelson (2001); Abrams and Gosnell (2012) ; Pilgeram (2021).

18. Harrison and Lloyd (2012).

19. De Genova (2005).

4. SOCIAL REPRODUCTION, RACE, AND "ILLEGALITY"

1. Laslett and Brenner (1989); Meehan and Stauss (2015); Federici (2019).

2. Metz (2004).

3. Lawrence (2010).

4. De Genova (2005, 2014).

5. Coleman and Kocher (2011); Golash-Boza (2015); Armenta (2017).

6. Nguyen and Gill (2016).

7. Waslin (2011).

8. Secure Communities was passed in 2008 by George W. Bush but rolled out in a geographically uneven manner, reaching Rabun County and Routt County by 2012 (Miles and Cox 2014). An important point to make, however, is that immigrant residents in both areas often lived in other areas in the United States before coming to Routt or Rabun Counties—meaning that people's encounters and perceptions about the risk of police could have been formed in other places with active 287G enforcement and deportation mechanisms.

9. Martínez, Slack, and Martínez-Schuldt (2018).

10. Dreby (2013); Brabeck, Brinton Lykes, and Hunter (2014); Gonzalez and Patler (2021).

11. See Berger Cardoso et al. (2018).

12. Gonzalez-Barrera and Lopez (2016); Moinester (2019).

13. Redmond (2011). The impacts of E-verify legislation on labor relations are explored in Gomberg-Muñoz and Nussbaum-Barbarena (2011). Gomberg-Muñoz and Nussbaum-Barbarena examine how employers use E-verify as well as Social Security Administration "No-Match" letters (signaling a false social security

number) to control workers and retaliate against union organizing. The employers in our sample were eager to retain undocumented workers despite this Georgia legislation and sought to reassure their workers it would not apply to them.

14. Chavez (2013).

15. Chavez (2013, 59).

16. Flores-Yeffal (2019).

17. Alvarez (2017); Morales and Hanson (2005).

18. Woolard and Schieffelin (1994).

19. Guevara (2007).

20. Messeri (2008); Santos-Gómez (2014); on a right to play see Mullen (2014).

21. Messeri (2008); Trouille (2021).

CONCLUSION

1. Frey and Liaw (1998).

2. Robinson (2004).

3. For examples of emphasis on class-based displacement see Phillips et al. (2021); Lorenzen (2021).

4. Cheong (2021).

5. Coleman (2007).

6. Harrison and Lloyd (2012).

7. Waldinger (1997); Waldinger and Lichter (2003).

8. Light (2006).

9. De Genova (2002, 2010); Harrison and Lloyd (2012); Menjívar and Kanstroom (2013).

10. An important article by Laura López-Sanders (2014) examines the role of "embedded" labor brokers in the production of workplace hierarchies within larger-scale industrial enterprises drawing on an undocumented labor pool. There are many shared insights between what I am calling informal labor brokers and López-Sanders's theorization of "embedded brokers." However, we start and end in a different place, rooted in the fact that employers in Routt and Rabun Counties were not motivated to develop a labor broker in order to shield themselves from the legal consequences of hiring undocumented workers—the starting point of López-Sanders's analysis due to its focused on large-scale urban industries. Instead, employers in the context of rural gentrification were motivated to develop internal and informal labor brokers when they learned that cultivating this relationship increased their profits, allowing them full access to the flexibility and productivity of a racialized and "illegal" workforce.

11. On the undercount of Latino immigrants, see O'Hare (2019).

12. Both Farrell (2021) and Stuber (2021) for example note that many of the workers in Jackson Hole, Wyoming and Aspen, Colorado are undocumented, but

they do not closely consider how immigrant legal status and perceptions of "illegality" shape work and daily life for immigrants in their research.

13. On racial capitalism see Melamed (2015); Pulido (2017).

14. For a discussion of feminist and other critical methodologies, see Twine (2000); Valentine (2007); Gunaratnam and Jones (2020); Zaragocin and Caretta (2021).

15. Economou (2013).

16. Cook (2020); Ozimek (2020).

17. NPR (2022).

18. Dimke, Lee, and Bayham (2021); Kolko, Badger, and Bui (2021); Nelson and Frost (2023).

APPENDIX: MORE ON METHODOLOGY

1. We explore this in detail in Nelson and Nelson (2011).

2. L. Nelson (2004, 2006, 2008); Nelson and Hiemstra (2008).

3. Beyers and Nelson (2000); Nelson et al. (2004).

4. Nelson, Lee, and Nelson (2009).

5. Nelson, Oberg, and Nelson (2010).

6. See Nelson, Oberg, and Nelson (2010). For that stage of the project, Peter Nelson and Alex Oberg developed quantitative indicators of rural gentrification, including "rates of change" measures of new housing stock growing faster than population, the expansion of high-end housing in particular, and GINI indexes of inequality, among other factors theorized as being associated with gentrification. For a complete methodological discussion of this quantitative analysis, see Nelson, Oberg, and Nelson (2010).

7. Nelson, Oberg, and Nelson (2010, 349).

8. Nelson, Lee, and Nelson (2009); Nelson and Nelson (2011); Nelson, Oberg, and Nelson (2011); Nelson, Trautman, and Nelson (2015).

References

Abrams, Jesse B., and Hannah Gosnell. 2012. "The Politics of Marginality in Wallowa County, Oregon: Contesting the Production of Landscapes of Consumption." *Journal of Rural Studies* 28 (1): 30–37.

Abrams, Jesse, and John C. Bliss. 2013. "Amenity Landownership, Land Use Change, and the Re-creation of 'Working Landscapes.'" *Society & Natural Resources* 26 (7): 845–59.

Abrams, Jesse B., Hannah Gosnell, Nicholas J. Gill, and Peter J. Klepeis. 2012. "Re-creating the Rural, Reconstructing Nature: An International Literature Review of the Environmental Implications of Amenity Migration." *Conservation and Society* 10 (3): 270–84.

Aledo, A. 2008. "De la tierra al suelo: La transformación del paisaje y el nuevo turismo residencial" [From land to soil: Landscape transformation and new residential tourism]. *Arbor: Ciencia, Pensamiento y Cultura* 729: 99–113.

Alvarez, Steven. 2017. "Brokering Literacies: Child Language Brokering in Mexican Immigrant Families." *Community Literacy Journal* 11 (2): 1–15.

Alves Peña, Anita. 2012. "Undocumented Immigration and the Business of Farm Labor Contracting in the USA." *American Journal of Business* 27 (1): 10–26.

Ambrosini, Maurizio. 2017. "Why Irregular Migrants Arrive and Remain: The Role of Intermediaries." *Journal of Ethnic and Migration Studies* 43 (11): 1813–30.

American Immigration Council. 2021. "Take a Look: How Immigrants Drive the Economy in the United States of America." https://map

.americanimmigrationcouncil.org/locations/national/. Accessed November 1, 2023.

Anderson, Cynthia D., Michael D. Schulman, and Phillip J. Wood. 2001. "Globalization and Uncertainty: The Restructuring of Southern Textiles." *Social Problems* 48 (4): 478–98.

Anguelovski, Isabelle. 2015. "Healthy Food Stores, Greenlining and Food Gentrification: Contesting New Forms of Privilege, Displacement and Locally Unwanted Land Uses in Racially Mixed Neighborhoods." *International Journal of Urban and Regional Research* 39 (6): 1209–30.

Armenta, Amada. 2017. *Protect, Serve, and Deport: The Rise of Policing as Immigration Enforcement*. University of California Press.

Atlanta Business Chronicle. 2006. "Fruit of the Loom, Springs Global to Trim Georgia Jobs." March 23. https://www.bizjournals.com/atlanta/stories/2006 /03/20/daily34.html. Accessed October 3, 2018.

Baker, Susan Gonzalez. 1997. "The 'Amnesty' Aftermath: Current Policy Issues Stemming from the Legalization Programs of the 1986 Immigration Reform and Control Act." *International Migration Review* 31 (1): 5–27.

Bakker, Isabella. 2007. "Social Reproduction and the Constitution of a Gendered Political Economy." *New Political Economy* 12 (4): 541–56.

Balderrama, Francisco E., and Raymond Rodríguez. 2006. *Decade of Betrayal: Mexican Repatriation in the 1930s*. University of New Mexico Press.

Barcus, Holly. 2006. "New Destinations for Hispanic Migrants: An Analysis of Rural Kentucky." In *Latinos in the New South: Transformations of Place*, edited by Heather A. Smith and Owen J. Furuseth, 89–110. Ashgate Publishing.

Bashi, Vilna Francine. 2007. *Survival of the Knitted: Immigrant Social Networks in a Stratified World*. Stanford University Press.

Bean, Frank D., Barry Edmonston, and Jeffrey S. Passel, eds. 1990. *Undocumented Migration to the United States: IRCA and the Experience of the 1980s*. Vol. 7. The Urban Institute. https://webarchive.urban.org/publications /203864.html.

Beauregard, Robert A. 2013. "The Chaos and Complexity of Gentrification." In *Gentrification of the City*, edited by Neil Smith and Peter Williams, 51–71. Routledge.

Bello, Walden F., Shea Cunningham, and Bill Rau. 1994. *Dark Victory: The United States, Structural Adjustment, and Global Poverty*. Pluto Press.

Benson, Michaela. 2014. "Negotiating Privilege in and through Lifestyle Migration." In *Understanding Lifestyle Migration: Theoretical Approaches to Migration and the Quest for a Better Way of Life*, edited by Michaela Benson and Nick Obaldiston, 47–68. Palgrave Macmillan.

Benson, Micheala, and Karen O'Reilly. 2018. *Lifestyle Migration and Colonial Traces in Malaysia and Panama*. Palgrave Macmillan.

Bentancur, Bryan. 2023. "Why I Hate the Term 'Latinx.'" *Inside Higher Education* (January 25). https://www.insidehighered.com/views/2023/01/26/why-i -hate-term-Latine-opinion.

Benson, Peter. 2008. "El Campo: Faciality and Structural Violence in Farm Labor Camps." *Cultural Anthropology* 23 (4): 589–629.

Berger Cardoso, Jodi, Jennifer L. Scott, Monica Faulkner, and Liza Barros Lane. 2018. "Parenting in the Context of Deportation Risk." *Journal of Marriage and Family* 80 (2): 301–16.

Betancur, John J. 2002. "The Politics of Gentrification: The Case of West Town in Chicago." *Urban Affairs Review* 37 (6): 780–814.

Beyers, William B., and Peter B. Nelson. 2000. "Contemporary Development Forces in the Nonmetropolitan West: New Insights from Rapidly Growing Communities." *Journal of Rural Studies* 16 (4): 459–74.

Bondi, Liz. 1991. "Gender Divisions and Gentrification: A Critique." *Transactions of the Institute of British Geographers* 16 (2): 190–98.

Botterill, Kate. 2017. "Discordant Lifestyle Mobilities in East Asia: Privilege and Precarity of British Retirement in Thailand." *Population, Space and Place* 23 (5): 1–11.

Brabeck, Kalina M., M. Brinton Lykes, and Cristina Hunter. 2014. "The Psychosocial Impact of Detention and Deportation on US Migrant Children and Families." *American Journal of Orthopsychiatry* 84 (5): 496–505.

Breen, Jessica McCallum, Patrick T. Hurley, and Laura E. Taylor. 2016. "No (Back)Sliding: Amenity Migration, Viewsheds, and Contesting Steep Slope Ordinances in Western North Carolina." In *A Comparative Political Ecology of Exurbia: Planning, Environmental Management, and Landscape Change*, edited by Laura E. Taylor and Patrick T. Hurley, 197–219. Springer.

Broadway, Michael J., and Donald D. Stull. 2008. "'I'll Do Whatever You Want, But It Hurts': Worker Safety and Community Health in Modern Meatpacking." *Labor: Studies in Working-Class History of the Americas* 5 (2): 27–37.

Buckley, Michelle. 2014. "On the Work of Urbanization: Migration, Construction Labor, and the Commodity Moment." *Annals of the Association of American Geographers* 104 (2): 338–47.

Budiman, Abby, Christine Tamir, Lauren Mora, and Luis Noe-Bustamante. 2008. "Facts on U.S. Immigrants." Pew Research Center, August 20. https:// www.pewresearch.org/hispanic/ 2020/08/20/facts-on-u-s-immigrants.

Bustamante, Jorge, Clark W. Reynolds, and Raúl A. H. Ojeda, eds. 1992. *US-Mexico Relations: Labor Market Interdependence*. Stanford University Press.

Carrigan, William D., and Clive Webb. 2013. *Forgotten Dead: Mob Violence against Mexicans in the United States, 1848–1928*. Oxford University Press.

Cassola, Marie-Adele. 2018. "Planning for Equitable Neighborhood Change: A Mixed-Methods Analysis of 80 Cities' Displacement Mitigation Approaches." PhD dissertation, Columbia University.

Castles, Stephen. 1998. *The Age of Migration: International Population Movements in the Modern World*. Macmillan International Higher Education.

Champlin, Dell, and Eric Hake. 2006. "Immigration as Industrial Strategy in American Meatpacking." *Review of Political Economy* 18 (1): 49–70.

Chan, Sucheng. 1989. *This Bittersweet Soil: The Chinese in California Agriculture, 1860–1910*. University of California Press.

Chan, Sucheng. 1991. "The Exclusion of Chinese women." In *Entry Denied: Exclusion and the Chinese Community in America, 1882–1943*, edited by Sucheng Chan, 94–146. Temple University Press.

Chavez, Leo. 2013. *The Latino Threat: Constructing Immigrants, Citizens, and the Nation*. 2nd ed. Stanford University Press.

Cheong, Amanda R. 2021. "How Driver's Licenses Matter for Undocumented Immigrants." *Contexts* 20 (3): 22–27.

Chishti, Muzaffar, and Charles Kamasaki. 2014. "IRCA in Retrospect." *Migration Policy Institute-Issue Brief* (9). https://www.migrationpolicy.org/research/irca-retrospect-guideposts-today-s-immigration-reform.

Chiswick, Barry R. 1988. "Illegal Immigration and Immigration Control." *Journal of Economic Perspectives* 2 (3): 101–15.

Clifford, Hal. 1995. "Ski Resort Flops in midst of Land Boom." *High Country News*, June 26. https://www.hcn.org/issues/38/1130.

Cloke, Paul. 1993. "The Countryside as Commodity: New Rural Spaces for Leisure." In *Leisure and the Environment: Essays in Honour of Professor J. A. Patmore*, edited by Sue Glyptis, 53–67. Belhaven.

Cloke, Paul. 2006. "Rurality and Racialized Others: Out of Place in the Countryside?" In *Handbook of Rural Studies*, edited by Paul Cloke, Terry Marsden, and Patrick H. Mooney, 379–87. Sage Publications.

Cloke, Paul, and Nigel Thrift. 1987. "Intra-Class Conflict in Rural Areas." *Journal of Rural Studies* 3 (4): 321–33.

Cloud, Patricia, and David W. Galenson. 1987. "Chinese Immigration and Contract Labor in the Late Nineteenth Century." *Explorations in Economic History* 24 (1): 22–42.

Cohen, Deborah. 2011. *Braceros: Migrant Citizens and Transnational Subjects in the Postwar United States and Mexico*. University of North Carolina Press.

Coleman, Mathew. 2007. "Immigration Geopolitics beyond the Mexico-US Border." *Antipode* 39 (1): 54–76.

Coleman, Mathew, and Austin Kocher. 2011. "Detention, Deportation, Devolution and Immigrant Incapacitation in the US, Post 9/11." *Geographical Journal* 177 (3): 228–37.

Congressional Research Service. 2020. "H-2A and H-2B Temporary Worker Visas: Policy and Related Issues" (R44849). Prepared for Members and Committees of Congress, by Andorra Bruno. https://crsreports.congress.gov/product/pdf/R/R44849/5.

Cook, Dave. 2020. "The Global Remote Work Revolution and the Future of Work." In *The Business of Pandemics: The COVID-19 Story*, edited by Jay Liebowitz, 143–66. CRC Press, Taylor & Francis Group.

Coppola, Victor. 2001. "You Can Buy Your Way onto Rabun, Burton or Seed, but You Can't Buy Your Way In." *Atlanta Magazine*, August, 72–73.

Cornelius, Wayne A. 1986. *From Sojourners to Settlers: The Changing Profile of Mexican Migration to the United States* (No. 86). Americas Program, Stanford University.

CPWR (Center for Construction and Research Training). 2022. "Labor Force Characteristics—Hispanic Workers in Construction and Other Industries." https://www.cpwr.com/research/data-center/the-construction-chart-book /chart-book-6th-edition-labor-force-characteristics-hispanic-workers-in -construction-and-other-industries/.

Cromartie, John B., and Peter B. Nelson. 2009. "Baby Boom Migration Tilts toward Rural America." *Economic Research Service USDA* 7 (3): 16–21.

Cromartie, John B., and John M. Wardwell. 1999. "Migrants Settling Far and Wide in the Rural West." *Rural Development Perspectives* 14 (2): 2–8.

Davidson, Hugh R. 2005. "Bent to Nature: Bend, Oregon as a Case Study in Twentieth-Century Property Development." PhD dissertation, University of Oregon.

De Genova, Nicholas. 2002. "Migrant 'Illegality' and Deportability in Everyday Life." *Annual Review of Anthropology* 31 (1): 419–47.

De Genova, Nicholas. 2005. *Working the Boundaries: Race, Space, and "Illegality" in Mexican Chicago*. Duke University Press.

De Genova, Nicholas. 2010. *The Deportation Regime: Sovereignty, Space, and the Freedom of Movement*. Duke University Press.

De Genova, Nicholas. 2014. "Immigration Reform and the Production of Migrant Illegality." In *Constructing Immigrant "Illegality": Critiques, Experiences, and Responses*, edited by Cecilia Menjívar and Daniel Kanstroom, 37–62. Cambridge University Press.

Del Castillo, Richard G. 1992. *The Treaty of Guadalupe Hidalgo: A Legacy of Conflict*. University of Oklahoma Press.

Delgado Wise, Raúl. 2004. "Critical Dimensions of Mexico-US Migration under the Aegis of Neoliberalism and NAFTA." *Canadian Journal of Development Studies/Revue canadienne d'études du développement* 25 (4): 591–605.

Delgado Wise, Raúl, and Humberto M. Covarrubias. 2007. "Para entender la migración a Estados Unidos: El papel de la fuerza de trabajo barata mexicana en el mercado laboral transnacional" [In order to understand migration to the United States: The role of cheap Mexican labor force in the transnational labor market]. *Problemas del Desarrollo* 38 (149): 11–34.

Delgado Wise, Raúl, and Humberto M. Covarrubias. 2008. "Capitalist Restructuring, Development and Labour Migration: The Mexico-US Case." *Third
World Quarterly* 29 (7): 1359–74.

Deutsche, Rosalyn, and Cara G. Ryan. 1984. "The Fine Art of Gentrification."
October 31: 91–111.

Dicken, Peter. 1998. *Global Shift: Transforming the World Economy.* Paul
Chapman Publishing.

Dimke, Christine, Marissa Lee, and Jude Bayham. 2021. "COVID-19 and the
Renewed Migration to the Rural West." *Western Economics Forum* 19 (1):
89–102.

Donato, Katherine M., Nicole Trujillo-Pagán, Carl L. Bankston III, and Audrey
Singer. 2007. "Reconstructing New Orleans after Katrina: The Emergence of
an Immigrant Labor Market." In *The Sociology of Katrina: Perspectives on a
Modern Catastrophe*, edited by David Brunsma, David Overfelt, and
J. Steven Picou, 231–53. Rowman & Littlefield.

Doucet, Andrea, and Natasha Mauthner. 2008. "Qualitative Interviewing and
Feminist Research." In *The SAGE Handbook of Social Research Methods*,
edited by Pertti Alasuutari, Julia Brannen, and Leonard Bickman, 328–43.
Sage Publications.

Dreby, Joanna. 2013. "The Modern Deportation Regime and Mexican Families:
The Indirect Consequences for Children in New Destination Communities."
In *Constructing Immigrant "Illegality": Critiques, Experiences, and
Responses*, edited by Cecilia Menjívar and Daniel Kanstroom, 181–202.
Cambridge University Press.

Duara, Prasenjit. 1996. *Rescuing History from the Nation: Questioning Narratives of Modern China.* University of Chicago Press.

Dubin, J. C. 1992. "From Junkyards to Gentrification: Explicating a Right to
Protective Zoning in Low-Income Communities of Color." *Minnesota Law
Review* 77: 739.

Dunbar-Ortiz, Roxanne. 2014. *An Indigenous People's History of the United
States.* Beacon Press.

Duncan, James S., and Nancy Duncan. 2004. *Landscapes of Privilege: The
Politics of the Aesthetic in an American Suburb.* Routledge.

Durand, Jorge, Douglas S. Massey, and Chiara Capoferro. 2005. "The New
Geography of Mexican Immigration." In *New Destinations: Mexican
Immigration in the United States*, edited by Víctor Zúñiga and Rubén
Hernández-León, 1–20. Russell Sage Foundation.

Durand, Jorge, Douglas S. Massey, and Fernando Charvet. 2000. "The Changing Geography of Mexican Immigration to the United States: 1910–1996."
Social Science Quarterly 81 (1): 1–15.

Economou, Elizabeth. 2013. "Homes Improvement: The Demand for Second
Homes Is Rebounding." *Alaska Airlines In-flight Magazine*, March.

Elliott-Cooper, Adam, Phil Hubbard, and Loretta Lees. 2020 "Moving beyond Marcuse: Gentrification, Displacement and the Violence of Un-homing." *Progress in Human Geography* 44 (3): 492–509.

Elwood, Sarah, Vicky Lawson, and Eric Sheppard. 2017. "Geographical Relational Poverty Studies." *Progress in Human Geography* 4 (6): 745–65.

Emard, Kelsey, and Lise Nelson. 2021. "Geographies of Global Lifestyle Migration: Towards an Anticolonial Approach." *Progress in Human Geography* 45 (5): 1040–60.

Epstein, Kathleen, Julia H. Haggerty, and Hannah Gosnell. 2019. "Super-Rich Landowners in Social-Ecological Systems: Opportunities in Affective Political Ecology and Life Course Perspectives." *Geoforum* 105: 206–9.

Esser, Josef, and Joachim Hirsch. 2009. "The Crisis of Fordism and the Dimensions of a 'Post-Fordist' Regional and Urban Structure." *International Journal of Urban and Regional Research* 13 (3): 417–37.

Fallon, K. F. 2021. "Reproducing Race in the Gentrifying City: A Critical Analysis of Race in Gentrification Scholarship." *Journal of Race, Ethnicity and the City* 2 (1): 1–28.

Faria, Caroline, and Mollett, Sharlene. 2016. "Critical Feminist Reflexivity and the Politics of Whiteness in the 'Field.'" *Gender, Place & Culture* 23 (1): 79–93.

Farrell, Justin. 2020. *Billionaire Wilderness: The Ultra-wealthy and the Remaking of the American West*. Princeton University Press.

Federici, Silvia. 2019. "Social Reproduction Theory." *Radical Philosophy* 2 (4): 55–57.

Fix, Michael, and Jeffry S. Passel. 1994. "Immigration and Immigrants: Setting the Record Straight." The Urban Institute, Washington D.C.

Flippen, Chenoa A., and Dylan Farrell-Bryan. 2021. "New Destinations and the Changing Geography of Immigrant Incorporation." *Annual Review of Sociology* 47: 479–500.

Flores-Yeffal, Nadia Y. 2019. "English Proficiency and Trust Networks among Undocumented Mexican Migrants." *Annals of the American Academy of Political and Social Science* 684 (1): 105–19.

Fraser, Donald. 2006. "County: New Look, Goals." *Clayton Tribune*, November 21, 6.

Freeman, Lance. 2011. *There Goes the Hood: Views of Gentrification from the Ground Up*. Temple University Press.

Frey, William H., and Kao-Lee Liaw. 1998. "Immigrant Concentration and Domestic Migrant Dispersal: Is Movement to Nonometropolitan Areas 'White Flight'?" *Professional Geographer* 50 (2): 215–32.

Fritzsche, Lauren. 2023. "Precarious Refuge: Housing Affordability, Amenity Migration, and the Embodied Experience of Refugee Resettlement in Missoula, MT." *GeoJournal* 88 (5): 5627–42.

Frolich, Larry M., and Matthias Schmidt. 2023. "Population Movements, Colonization Trends, and Amenity Migrants in Mountainscapes." In *Montology Palimpsest: A Primer of Mountain Geographies*, 357–74. Springer International Publishing.

Fulton, John A., Glenn V. Fuguitt, and Richard M. Gibson. 1997. "Recent Changes in Metropolitan-Nonmetropolitan Migration Streams." *Rural Sociology* 62 (3): 363–84.

Fussell, Elizabeth. 2011. "The Deportation Threat Dynamic and Victimization of Latino Migrants: Wage Theft and Robbery." *Sociological Quarterly* 52 (4): 593–615.

Gamboa, Erasmo. 2000. *Mexican Labor & World War II: Braceros in the Pacific Northwest, 1942–1947*. University of Washington Press.

Garcílazo, Jeffrey M. 2012. *Traqueros: Mexican Railroad Workers in the United States, 1870 to 1930*. University of North Texas Press.

Gates, Marilyn. 1993. *In Default: Peasants, the Debt Crisis, and the Agricultural Challenge in Mexico*. Westview Press.

Genovese, Eugene D., and Elizabeth Fox-Genovese. 2011. *Fatal Self-Deception: Slaveholding Paternalism in the Old South*. Cambridge University Press.

George, Susan. 1988. *Fate Worse than Debt*. Grove Press.

Georgia Mountain Laurel. 2010. "Harry Norman Real Estate Listing." 4–5. Clayton, Georgia.

Ghose, Rina. 2004. "Big Sky or Big Sprawl? Rural Gentrification and the Changing Cultural Landscape of Missoula, Montana." *Urban Geography* 25 (6): 528–49.

Gilmore, Ruth Wilson. 2002. "Fatal Couplings of Power and Difference: Notes on Racism and Geography." *Professional Geographer* 54 (1): 15–24.

Glass, R. 1964. "Aspects of Change." In *London: Aspects of Change*, edited by Centre for Urban Studies, xii–xlii. MacGibbon & Kee.

Goetz, Edward. 2011. "Gentrification in Black and White: The Racial Impact of Public Housing Demolition in American Cities." *Urban Studies* 48 (8): 1581–604.

Golash-Boza, Tanya M. 2015. *Immigration Nation: Raids, Detentions, and Deportations in Post-9/11 America*. Routledge.

Golash-Boza, Tanya. 2019. "Punishment beyond the Deportee: The Collateral Consequences of Deportation." *American Behavioral Scientist* 63 (9): 1331–49.

Golash-Boza, Tanya, and Pierrette Hondagneu-Sotelo. 2013. "Latino Immigrant Men and the Deportation Crisis: A Gendered Racial Removal Program." *Latino Studies* 11 (3): 271–92.

Goldring, Luin P. 1992. "La migración Mexico-EUA y la transnacionalización del espacio político y social: Perspectivas desde el Mexico rural." [Mexico-U.S. migration and the transnationalization of political and social space: Perspectives from rural Mexico.] *Estudios Sociológicos* 10 (29): 315–40.

Gomberg-Muñoz, Ruth. 2012. "Inequality in a 'Postracial' Era: Race, Immigration, and Criminalization of Low-Wage Labor. *Du Bois Review: Social Science Research on Race* 9 (2): 339–53.

Gomberg-Muñoz, Ruth. 2019. *Labor and Legality: An Ethnography of a Mexican Immigrant Network*. Oxford University Press.

Gomberg-Munoz, Ruth, and Laura Nussbaum-Barberena. 2011. "Is Immigration Policy Labor Policy? Immigration Enforcement, Undocumented Workers, and the State." *Human Organization* 70 (4): 366–75.

Gómez Cervantes, Andrea. 2021. "'Looking Mexican': Indigenous and Nonindigenous Latina/o Immigrants and the Racialization of Illegality in the Midwest." *Social Problems* 68 (1): 100–117.

Gonzalez, Gabriela, and Caitlin Patler. 2021. "The Educational Consequences of Parental Immigration Detention." *Sociological Perspectives* 64 (2): 301–20.

Gonzalez-Barrera, Ana, and Mark H. Lopez. 2016. "US Immigrant Deportations Fall to Lowest Level Since 2007." Pew Research Center, December 16. https://www.pewresearch.org/short-reads/2016/12/16/u-s-immigrant-deportations-fall-to-lowest-level-since-2007/.

Gosnell, Hannah, and Jesse Abrams. 2011. "Amenity Migration: Diverse Conceptualizations of Drivers, Socioeconomic Dimensions, and Emerging Challenges." *GeoJournal* 76 (4): 303–22.

Gotanda, Neil. 1997. "Race, Citizenship, and the Search for Political Community among We the People." *Immigration and Nationality Law Review* 18: 607.

Gozdziak, Elzbieta M., and Mica N. Bump. 2004. "Poultry, Apples, and New Immigrants in the Rural Communities of the Shenandoah Valley: An Ethnographic Case Study." *International Migration* 42 (1): 149–64.

Gozdziak, Elzbieta M., and Susan F. Martin, eds. 2005. *Beyond the Gateway: Immigrants in a Changing America*. Lexington Books.

Gramlich, John, and Alissa Scheller. 2019. "Non-Mexicans Now Outnumber Mexicans in Southwest Border Apprehensions in 2019." Pew Research Center, November 11. https://www.pewresearch.org/fact-tank/2019/11/01/whats-happening-at-the-u-s-mexico-border-in-5-charts/.

Griffith, David. 2005. "Rural Industry and Mexican Immigration and Settlement in North Carolina." In *New Destinations: Mexican Immigration in the United States*, edited by Víctor Zúñiga and Rubén Hernández-León, 50–75. Russell Sage Foundation.

Guevara, Daniela. 2007. "Learning English Necessary, but Don't Forget One's Roots." *Clayton Tribune*, August 23, Opinion section, A-5.

Gunaratnam, Yasmin, and Hannah Jones. 2020. "Same Difference? Researching Racism and Immigration." In *Routledge International Handbook of Contemporary Racisms*, edited by John Solomos, 391–405. Routledge.

Gurak, Douglas, and Fee Caces. 1992. "Migration Networks and the Shaping of Migration Systems." In *International Migration Systems: A Global*

Approach, edited by Mary M. Kritz, Lin Lean Lim, and Hania Zlotnik, 150–76. Oxford University Press.

Gutiérrez, David G. 1995. *Walls and Mirrors: Mexican Americans, Mexican Immigrants, and the Politics of Ethnicity*. University of California Press.

Gyory, Andrew. 1998. *Closing the Gate: Race, Politics, and the Chinese Exclusion Act*. University of North Carolina Press.

Hackman, Michelle. 2022. "U.S. to Make 35,000 more H-2B Visas Available for Seasonal Workers." *Wall Street Journal*, March 31, Politics section.

Hagan, Jacqueline M. 1998. "Social Networks, Gender, and Immigrant Incorporation: Resources and Constraints." *American Sociological Review* 63 (1): 55–67.

Halfacree, Keith. 1993. "Locality and Social Representation: Space, Discourse and Alternative Definitions of the Rural." *Journal of Rural Studies* 9 (1): 23–37.

Hamnett, Chris. 1991. "The Blind Men and the Elephant: Towards a Theory of Gentrification." *Transactions of the Institute of British Geographers* 16 (2): 173–89.

Hamnett, Chris. 2021. *Advanced Introduction to Gentrification*. Edward Elgar Publishing.

Haraway, Donna J. 1991. *Simians, Cyborgs and Women: The Reinvention of Nature*. Routledge.

Harding, Sandra. 1987. "Is There a Feminist Method." *Social Research Methods: A Reader* 1 (45): 456–64.

Harrison, Jill L., and Sarah E. Lloyd. 2012. "Illegality at Work: Deportability and the Productive New Era of Immigration Enforcement." *Antipode* 44 (2): 365–85.

Harvey, David. 2001. "Globalization and the 'Spatial Fix.'" *Geographische Revue: Zeitschrif für Literatur und Diskussion* 3 (2): 22–30.

Harvey, David. 2003. "The Right to the City." *International Journal of Urban and Regional Research* 27 (4): 939–41.

Harvey, David. 2007. *A Brief History of Neoliberalism*. Oxford University Press.

Heisler, Barbara S. 2008. "The Bracero Program and Mexican Migration to the United States." *Journal of the West* 47 (3): 65–72.

Henderson, Timothy J. 2011. *Beyond Borders: A History of Mexican Migration to the United States*. Wiley.

Hernández, María G., Jacqueline Nguyen, Saskias Casanova, Carola Suárez-Orozco, and Carrie L. Saetermoe. 2013. "Doing No Harm and Getting It Right: Guidelines for Ethical Research with Immigrant Communities." *New Directions for Child and Adolescent Development* (141): 43–60.

Hernández-León, Rubén, and Víctor Zúñiga. 2000. "'Making Carpet by the Mile': The Emergence of a Mexican Immigrant Community in an Industrial Region of the US Historic South." *Social Science Quarterly* 81 (1): 49–66.

Herrera, Juan. 2016. "Racialized Illegality: The Regulation of Informal Labor and Space." *Latino Studies* 14 (3): 320–43.

Herrero-Jáuregui, Cristina, and E. D. Concepción. 2023. "Effects of Counter-Urbanization on Mediterranean Rural Landscapes." *Landscape Ecology* 38 (12): 3695–711.

Hesse-Biber, Sharlene, ed. 2011. *Handbook of Feminist Research: Theory and Praxis*. Sage Publications.

Hewitt de Alcántara, Cynthia. 1994. "Economic Restructuring and Rural Subsistence in Mexico: Corn and the Crisis of the 1980s." UC San Diego Discussion Paper, Transformation of Rural Mexico, no. 2.

Higham, John. 2002. *Strangers in the Land: Patterns of American Nativism, 1860–1925*. Rutgers University Press.

Hing, Bill O. 2010. *Ethical Borders: NAFTA, Globalization, and Mexican Migration*. Temple University Press.

Hing, Bill O. 2012. *Defining America through Immigration Policy*. Temple University Press.

Hjerpe, Evan, Christopher A. Armatas, and Michelle Haefele. 2022. "Amenity-Based Development and Protected Areas in the American West." *Land Use Policy* 116: 106064.

Hollander, Gail M. 2006. "'Subject to Control': Shifting Geographies of Race and Labour in US Sugar Agroindustry, 1930–1950." *Cultural Geographies* 13 (2): 266–92.

Hondagneu-Sotelo, Pierrette. 1994. *Gendered Transitions: Mexican Experiences of Immigration*. University of California Press.

Hondagneu-Sotelo, Pierrette. 2007. *Doméstica: Immigrant Workers Cleaning and Caring in the Shadows of Affluence*. University of California Press.

Hore, Jarrod. 2022. *Visions of Nature: How Landscape Photography Shaped Settler Colonialism*. University of California Press.

Horton, Sarah Bronwen. 2016. *They Leave Their Kidneys in the Fields: Illness, Injury, and Illegality among US Farmworkers*. University of California Press.

Howell, Kathryn. L. 2016. "Planning for Empowerment: Upending the Traditional Approach to Planning for Affordable Housing in the Face of Gentrification." *Planning Theory and Practice* 17 (2): 210–26.

Hytrek, Gary, and Kristine M. Zentgraf. 2008. *America Transformed: Globalization, Inequality, and Power*. Oxford University Press.

Ignatiev, Noel. 1995. *How the Irish Became White*. Routledge.

Iskander, Natasha, and Nichola Lowe. 2013. "Building Job Quality from the Inside-Out: Mexican Immigrants, Skills, and Jobs in the Construction Industry." *Industrial & Labor Relations Review* 66 (7): 785–807.

Jensen, Leif, and Tse-Chuan Yang. 2016. "Taken by Surprise: New Immigrants in the Rural United States." In *International Migration and Rural Areas*, edited by Birgit Jentsch and Myriam Simard, 33–58. Routledge.

Johnson-Webb, Karen D. 2002. "Employer Recruitment and Hispanic Labor Migration: North Carolina Urban Areas at the End of the Millennium." *Professional Geographer* 54 (3): 406–21.

Kandel, William, and Emilio A. Parrado. 2005. "Restructuring of the US Meat Processing Industry and New Hispanic Migrant Destinations." *Population and Development Review* 3 (3): 447–71.

Kandel, William E., and John Cromartie. 2004. "New Patterns of Hispanic Settlement in Rural America." U.S. Department of Agriculture, Economic Research Service, no. 99.

Kanstroom, Daniel. 2007. *Deportation Nation: Outsiders in American History.* Harvard University Press.

Katz, Cindi. 2013. "Power, Space, and Terror: Social Reproduction and the Public Environment." In *The Politics of Public Space*, edited by Setha Low and Neil Smith, 105–21. Routledge.

Kent-Stoll, Peter. 2020. "The Racial and Colonial Dimensions of Gentrification." *Sociology Compass* 14 (12): 1–17.

Kern, Leslie. 2007. "Reshaping the Boundaries of Public and Private Life: Gender, Condominium Development, and the Neoliberalization of Urban Living." *Urban Geography* 28 (7): 657–81.

Kibler, M. Alison. 2015. *Censoring Racial Ridicule: Irish, Jewish, and African American Struggles over Race and Representation, 1890–1930.* University of North Carolina Press.

Kirkland, Elizabeth. 2008. "What's Race Got to Do with it? Looking for the Racial Dimensions of Gentrification." *Western Journal of Black Studies* 32 (2): 18–30.

Kissam, Edward, Jo Ann Intili, and Anna García. 2001. "The Emergence of a Binational Mexico-US Workforce: Implications for Farm Labor Workforce Security." U.S. Department of Labor.

Kling, Joseph, and Prudence Posner. 1991. *Dilemmas of Activism: Class, Community, and the Politics of Local Mobilization.* Temple University Press.

Kochhar, Rakesh, Roberto Suro, and Sonya Tafoya. 2005. "The New Latino South: The Context and Consequences of Rapid Population Growth." Pew Research Center, July 26. https://www.pewresearch.org/hispanic/2005/07/26/the-new-latino-south/.

Kolko, Jed, Emily Badger, and Quoctrung Bui. 2021. "How the Pandemic Did, and Didn't, Change Where Americans Move." *New York Times*, April 26.

Krannich, Richard S., and Michael D. Smith. 1998. "Local Perceptions of Public Lands Natural Resource Management in the Rural West: Toward Improved Understanding of the 'Revolt in the West.'" *Society & Natural Resources: An International Journal* 11 (7): 677–95.

Krissman, Fred. 2000. "Immigrant Labor Recruitment: U.S. Agribusiness and Undocumented Migration from Mexico." In *Immigration Research for a New*

Century: Multidisciplinary Perspectives, edited by Nancy Foner, Rubén Rumbaut, and Steven Gold, 277–300. Russell Sage Foundation.

Lanesskog, Deirdre. 2018. "'The Only Thing We Can Do Is Treat Them Well Here': Public Health with Latinos in a New Immigrant Destination." *Social Work and Public Health* 33 (6): 382–95.

Larsen, Soren, Matt Foulkes, Curtis J. Sorenson, and Amy Thompson. 2011. "Environmental Learning and the Social Construction of an Exurban Landscape in Fremont County, Colorado." *Geoforum* 42 (1): 83–93.

Larsen, Soren, and Craig Hutton. 2012. "Community Discourse and the Emerging Amenity Landscapes of the Rural American West." *GeoJournal* 77 (5): 651–65.

Laslett, Barbara, and Johanna Brenner. 1989. "Gender and Social Reproduction: Historical Perspectives." *Annual Review of Sociology* 15 (1): 381–404.

Lawrence, Mike. 2010. "Steamboat Tenants See Help after Duplex Fire." *Steamboat Pilot,* August 16. https://www.steamboatpilot.com/news/steamboat-tenants-see-help-after-duplex-fire/.

Lees, Loretta, and David Ley. 2008. "Introduction to Special Issue on Gentrification and Public Policy." *Urban Studies* 45 (12): 2379–84.

Lees, Loretta, Tom Slater, and Elvin K. Wyly, eds. 2010. *The Gentrification Reader.* Routledge.

Lees, Loretta, Tom Slater, and Elvin K. Wyly, eds. 2023. *The Planetary Gentrification Reader.* Routledge.

Lekies, Kristi, David Matarrita-Cascante, Rebecca Schewe, and Richelle Winkler. 2015. "Amenity Migration in the New Global Economy: Current Issues and Research Priorities." *Society and Natural Resources* 28 (10): 1144–51.

Levy, Diane K., Jennifer Comey, and Sandra Padilla. 2007. "In the Face of Gentrification: Case Studies of Local Efforts to Mitigate Displacement." *Journal of Affordable Housing & Community Development Law* 16: 238–315.

Ley, David. 1986. "Alternative Explanations for Inner-City Gentrification: A Canadian Assessment." *Annals of the Association of American Geographers* 76 (4): 521–35.

Licona, Adela C., and Marta Maria Maldonado. 2014. "The Social Production of Latin@ Visibilities and Invisibilities: Geographies of Power in Small Town America." *Antipode* 46 (2): 517–36.

Light, Ivan. 2006. *Deflecting Immigration: Networks, Markets, and Regulation in Los Angeles.* Russell Sage Foundation.

Little, Jo. 1987. "Gentrification and the Influence of Local Level Planning." In *Rural Planning: Policy into Action?,* edited by Paul Cloke, 185–99. Harper and Row.

Loeffler, Roland, and Ernst Steinicke. 2007. "Amenity Migration in the US Sierra Nevada." *Geographical Review* 97 (1): 67–88.

López-Sanders, Laura. 2014. "Embedded and External Brokers: The Distinct Roles of Intermediaries in Workplace Inequality." *American Behavioral Scientist* 58 (2): 331–46.

Lorenzen, Matthew. 2021. "Rural Gentrification, Touristification, and Displacement: Analyzing Evidence from Mexico." *Journal of Rural Studies* 86: 62–75.

Lowe, Philip, Jonathan Murdoch, Terry Marsden, Richard Munton, and Andrew Flynn. 1993. "Regulating the New Rural Spaces: The Uneven Development of Land." *Journal of Rural Studies* 9 (2): 205–22.

Lykke, Nina. 2010. *Feminist Studies: A Guide to Intersectional Theory, Methodology and Writing*. Routledge.

Lyons, Michal. 1996. "Gentrification, Socioeconomic Change, and the Geography of Displacement." *Journal of Urban Affairs* 18 (1): 39–62.

MacLeavy, Julie. 2016. "Neoliberalism and Welfare." In *The Handbook of Neoliberalism*, edited by Simon Springer, Kean Birch, and Julie MacLeavy, 252–61. Routledge.

Marrow, Helen. 2011. *New Destination Dreaming: Immigration, Race, and Legal Status in the Rural American South*. Stanford University Press.

Martinez, Daniel, and Jeremy Slack. 2013. "What Part of 'Illegal' Don't You Understand? The Social Consequences of Criminalizing Unauthorized Mexican Migrants in the United States." *Social & Legal Studies* 22 (4): 535–51.

Martínez, Daniel E., Jeremy Slack, and Ricardo Martínez-Schuldt. 2018. "The Rise of Mass Deportation in the United States." In *The Handbook of Race, Ethnicity, Crime, and Justice*, edited by Ramiro Martinez, Meghan E. Hollis, and Jacob Stowell, 173–201. John Wiley & Sons.

Martinez, Daniel, Robin Reineke, Raquel Rubio-Goldsmith, Bruce Anderson, Gregory Hess, and Bruce Parks. 2013. "A Continued Humanitarian Crisis at the Border: Undocumented Border Crosser Deaths Recorded by the Pima County Office of the Medical Examiner, 1990–2012." Binational Migration Institute, University of Arizona. https://bmi.arizona.edu/sites/bmi.arizona .edu/files/ BMI-Continued-Humanitarian-Crisis-at-the-Border-2013.pdf.

Martínez-Matsuda, Verónica. 2020. *Migrant Citizenship: Race, Rights, and Reform in the U.S. Farm Labor Camp Program*. University of Pennsylvania Press.

Massey, Douglas. 1990. "Social Structure, Household Strategies, and the Cumulative Causation of Migration." *Population Index* 56 (1): 3–26.

Massey, Douglas, ed. 2008. *New Faces in New Places: The Changing Geography of American Immigration*. Russell Sage Foundation.

Massey, Douglas S. 1986. "The Social Organization of Mexican Migration to the United States." *Annals of the American Academy of Political and Social Science* 487 (1): 102–13.

Massey, Douglas S., and Felipe G. España. 1987. "The Social Process of International Migration." *Science* 237 (4816): 733–38.

Massey, Douglas S., Rafael Alarcón, Jorge Durand, and Humberto González. 1990. *Return to Aztlan: The Social Process of International Migration from Western Mexico*. University of California Press.

Massey, Douglas S., Jorge Durand, and Karen A. Pren. 2015. "Border Enforcement and Return Migration by Documented and Undocumented Mexicans." *Journal of Ethnic and Migration Studies* 41 (7): 1015–40.

Massey, Douglas S., and Zai Liang. 1989. "The Long-Term Consequences of a Temporary Worker Program: The US Bracero Experience." *Population Research and Policy Review* 8: 199–226.

Mathews, Vanessa. 2010. "Aestheticizing Space: Art, Gentrification and the City." *Geography Compass* 4 (6): 660–75.

May, Candace K. 2019 "Political Ecology of Culture Clash: Amenity-Led Development, Vulnerability, and Risk in Coastal North Carolina." *Journal of Rural and Community Development* 14 (3): 23–47.

McAreavey, Ruth. 2017. *New Immigration Destinations: Migrating to Rural and Peripheral Areas*. Taylor & Francis.

McCarthy, James. 2008. "Rural Geography: Globalizing the Countryside." *Progress in Human Geography* 32 (1): 129–37.

McGarrigle, Jennifer. 2022. "Lifestyle Migration." In *Introduction to Migration Studies: An Interactive Guide to the Literatures on Migration and Diversity*, edited by Peter Scholten, 169–78. Springer.

Meehan, Katie, and Kendra Stauss, eds. 2015. *Precarious Worlds: Contested Geographies of Social Reproduction*. University of Georgia Press.

Melamed, Jodi. 2015. "Racial Capitalism." *Critical Ethnic Studies* 1 (1): 76–85.

Menjívar, Cecilia. 2016. "Immigrant Criminalization in Law and the Media: Effects on Latino Immigrant Workers' Identities in Arizona." *American Behavioral Scientist* 60 (5–6): 597–616.

Menjívar, Cecilia, Andrea Gómez Cervantes, and Daniel Alvord. 2018. "The Expansion of 'Crimmigration,' Mass Detention, and Deportation." *Sociology Compass* 12 (4): 1–15.

Menjívar, Cecilia, and Daniel Kanstroom. 2013. *Constructing Immigrant "Illegality": Critiques, Experiences, and Responses*. Cambridge University Press.

Metz, Christine. 2004. "Second Homes' Effects Studied." *Steamboat Pilot*, September 18.

Merriam-Webster. 2021. "Emplacement."https://www.merriam.webster.com/dictionary/emplacement.

Messeri, Ilann S. 2008. "Vamos, Vamos Aceirteros: Soccer and the Latino Community in Richmond, California." *Soccer & Society* 9 (3): 416–27.

Migration Policy Institute. 2020. "Profile of the Unauthorized Population: United States." https://www.migrationpolicy.org/data/unauthorized-immigrant-population/state/US.

Miles, Thomas J., and Adam B. Cox. 2014. "Does Immigration Enforcement Reduce Crime? Evidence from Secure Communities." *Journal of Law and Economics* 57 (4): 937–73.

Miller, Stuart C. 1969. *The Unwelcome Immigrant: The American Image of the Chinese, 1785–1882*. University of California Press.

Miraftab, Faranak. 2016. *Global Heartland: Displaced Labor, Transnational Lives, and Local Placemaking*. Indiana University Press.

Mitchell, Katharyne, Sallie A. Marston, and Cindi Katz, eds. 2004. *Life's Work: Geographies of Social Reproduction*. Blackwell.

Mize, Ronald L., and Alicia C. S. Swords. 2010. *Consuming Mexican Labor: From the Bracero Program to NAFTA*. University of Toronto Press.

Moinester, Margot. 2019. "A Look to the Interior: Trends in US Immigration Removals by Criminal Conviction Type, Gender, and Region of Origin, Fiscal Years 2003–2015." *American Behavioral Scientist* 63 (9): 1276–98.

Molina, Natalia. 2015. "The Importance of Place and Place-Makers in the Life of a Los Angeles Community: What Gentrification Erases from Echo Park." *Southern California Quarterly* 97 (1): 69–111.

Morales, Alejandro, and William E. Hanson. 2005. "Language Brokering: An Integrative Review of the Literature." *Hispanic Journal of Behavioral Sciences* 27 (4): 471–503.

Morgensen, Scott L. 2011. "The Biopolitics of Settler Colonialism: Right Here, Right Now." *Settler Colonial Studies* 1 (1): 52–76.

Moss, Pamela, Karen Falconer Al-Hindi, and Hope Kawabata. 2002. *Feminist Geography in Practice: Research and Methods*. Wiley-Blackwell.

Mullen, Matthew. 2014. "Getting Serious about the Human Right to Play." *Asia Pacific Journal of Sport and Social Science* 3 (2): 130–42.

Mullings, Beverley. 1999. "Insider or Outsider, Both or Neither: Some Dilemmas of Interviewing in a Cross-Cultural Setting." *Geoforum* 30 (4): 337–50.

Munshi, Kaivan. 2003. "Networks in the Modern Economy: Mexican Migrants in the US Labor Market." *Quarterly Journal of Economics* 118 (2): 549–99.

Navarro, Vicente. 1998. " Neoliberalism, 'Globalization,' Unemployment, Inequalities, and the Welfare State." *International Journal of Health Services* 28 (4): 607–82.

Nelson, Lise. 2004. "Topographies of Citizenship: Purhépechan Mexican Women Claiming Political Subjectivities." *Gender, Place and Culture* 11 (2): 163–87.

Nelson, Lise. 2006. "Geographies of State Power, Protest, and Women's Political Identity Formation in Michoacán, Mexico." *Annals of the Association of American Geographers* 96 (2): 365–88.

Nelson, Lise. 2008. "Racialized Landscapes: Whiteness and the Struggle over Farmworker Housing in Woodburn, Oregon." *Cultural Geographies* 15 (1): 41–62.

Nelson, Lise. 2019. "Illegality." In *Keywords in Radical Geography: Antipode at 50*, edited by Antipode Editorial Collective, 151–54. Wiley-Blackwell.

Nelson, Lise, and Nancy Hiemstra. 2008. "Latino Immigrants and the Renego-
tiation of Place and Belonging in Small Town America." *Social and Cultural
Geography* 9 (3): 319–42.

Nelson, Lise, and Peter B. Nelson. 2011. "The Global Rural: Gentrification and
Linked Migration in the Rural USA." *Progress in Human Geography* 35 (4):
441–59.

Nelson, Lise, Laurie Trautman, and Peter B. Nelson. 2015. "Latino Immigrants
and Rural Gentrification: Race, 'Illegality,' and Precarious Labor Regimes
in the United States." *Annals of the Association of American Geographers*
105 (4): 841–58.

Nelson, Peter B. 2001. "Rural Restructuring in the American West: Land Use,
Family and Class Discourses." *Journal of Rural Studies* 17 (4): 395–407.

Nelson, Peter B. 2008. "Life-Course Influences on Nonearnings Income
Migration in the United States." *Environment and Planning A* 40 (9):
2149–68.

Nelson, Peter B., and Wright Frost. 2023. "Migration Responses to the
COVID-19 Pandemic: Case Study of New England Showing Movements
down the Urban Hierarchy and Ensuing Impacts on Real Estate Markets."
Professional Geographer 75 (3): 415–29.

Nelson, Peter B., and Dwight Hines. 2018. "Rural Gentrification and Networks
of Capital Accumulation: A Case Study of Jackson, Wyoming." *Environment
and Planning A: Economy and Space* 50 (7): 1473–95.

Nelson, Peter B., Ahn Wei Lee, and Lise Nelson. 2009. "Linking Baby Boomer
and Hispanic Migration Streams into Rural America—A Multi-scaled
Approach." *Population, Space and Place* 15 (3): 277–93.

Nelson, Peter B., James P. Nicholson, and E. Hope Stege. 2004. "The Baby Boom
and Nonmetropolitan Population Change, 1975–1990." *Growth and Change*
24 (4): 526–44.

Nelson, Peter B., Alexander Oberg, and Lise Nelson. 2010. "Rural Gentrification
and Linked Migration in the United States." *Journal of Rural Studies* 26 (4):
343–52.

Nevins, Joseph. 2001. *Operation Gatekeeper: The Rise of the "Illegal Alien" and
the Remaking of the US-Mexico Boundary.* Routledge.

Newcomers Guide to Rabun County. 2010. Lunar Cow (Akron, Ohio).

Ngai, Mae M. 2014. *Impossible Subjects: Illegal Aliens and the Making of
Modern America.* Princeton University Press.

Nguyen, Mai Thi, and Hannah Gill. 2016. "Interior Immigration Enforcement:
The Impacts of Expanding Local Law Enforcement Authority." *Urban
Studies* 53 (2): 302–23.

Norton, Jack, and Cindi Katz. 2017. "Social Reproduction." In *The International
Encyclopedia of Geography*, edited by Douglas Richardson et al., 1–11. John
Wiley & Sons.

NPR (National Public Radio). 2022. "The Ramifications of Exploding Interests in Small-Town Living during the Pandemic." *Morning Edition*, January 21.

O'Hare, William. P. 2019. *Differential Undercounts in the US Census: Who Is Missed?* Springer Nature.

Osbaldiston, Nick. 2011. "The Authentic Place in the Amenity Migration Discourse." *Space and Culture* 14 (2): 214–26.

Otero, Gerardo. 2011. "Neoliberal Globalization, NAFTA, and Migration: Mexico's Loss of Food and Labor Sovereignty." *Journal of Poverty* 15 (4): 384–402.

Ozimek, Adam. 2020. "The Future of Remote Work." May 27. http://dx.doi.org/10.2139/ssrn.3638597.

Pamuk, Ayse. 2004. "Geography of Immigrant Clusters in Global Cities: A Case Study of San Francisco." *International Journal of Urban and Regional Research* 28 (2): 287–307.

Park, Hong. 2013. "Economic Globalization and Income Inequality in the United States." *International Research Journal of Applied Finance* 4 (1): 15–34.

Park, Lisa Sun-Hee, and David Pellow. 2013. *The Slums of Aspen: Immigrants vs. the Environment in America's Eden*. New York University Press.

Parrado, Emilio A., and William Kandel. 2011. "Industrial Change, Hispanic Immigration, and the Internal Migration of Low-Skilled Native Male Workers in the United States, 1995–2000." *Social Science Research* 40 (2): 626–40.

Parsons, David. J. 1980. "Rural Gentrification: The Influence of Rural Settlement Policies." Research Papers in Geography. University of Sussex.

Passel, Jeffrey S. 2015. "Unauthorized Immigrant Population: National and State Trends, Industries and Occupations." Testimony Submitted to U.S. Senate Committee on Homeland Security and Governmental Affairs, March 26.

Passel, Jeffrey S., and D'Vera Cohn. 2009. "A Portrait of Unauthorized Immigrants in the United States." Pew Hispanic Center Report, April 14. https://www.pewresearch.org/race-and-ethnicity/2009/04/14/a-portrait-of-unauthorized-immigrants-in-the-united-states/.

Passel, Jeffrey S. and D'vera Cohn. 2016. "Unauthorized Immigration Population Stable for Half a Decade." Pew Research Center, September 16. http://www.pewresearch.org/fact-tank/2016/09/21/unauthorized-immigrant-population-stable-for-half-a-decade/.

Passel, Jeffrey S., and D'Vera Cohn. 2018. "U.S. Unauthorized Immigration Total Lowest in a Decade." Pew Research Center, November 27. https://www.pewresearch.org/hispanic/2018/11/27/u-s-unauthorized-immigrant-total-dips-to-lowest-level-in-a-decade/.

Passel, Jeffrey S., and D'Vera Cohn. 2019. "Mexicans Decline to Less than Half the U.S. Unauthorized Immigrant Population for the First Time." Pew

Research Center, June 12. https://www.pewresearch.org/short-reads/2019/06/12/us-unauthorized-immigrant-population-2017/.

Passel, Jeffrey S., and Jens M. Krogstad. 2024. "What We Know about Unauthorized Immigrants Living in the U.S." Pew Research Center, July 22. https://www.pewresearch.org/short-reads/2024/07/22/what-we-know-about-unauthorized-immigrants-living-in-the-us/.

Pastor, Manuel. 1989. "Latin America, the Debt Crisis, and the International Monetary Fund." *Latin American Perspectives* 16 (1): 79–110.

Pastor, Manuel, and Carol Wise. 1997. "State Policy, Distribution and Neoliberal Reform in Mexico." *Journal of Latin American Studies* 29 (2): 419–56.

Pearsall, Hamil. 2013. "Superfund Me: A Study of Resistance to Gentrification in New York City." *Urban Studies* 5 (11): 2293–310.

Perdue, Theda, and Michael D. Green. 2007. *The Cherokee Nation and the Trail of Tears*. Penguin.

Phillips, Martin. 1993. "Rural Gentrification and the Processes of Class Colonization." *Journal of Rural Studies* 9 (2): 123–40.

Phillips, Martin. 2002. "The Production, Symbolization and Socialization of Gentrification: Impressions from Two Berkshire Villages." *Transactions of the Institute of British Geographers* 27 (2): 282–308.

Phillips, Martin. 2004. "Other Geographies of Gentrification." *Progress in Human Geography* 28 (1): 5–30.

Phillips, Martin, Darren Smith, Hannah Brooking, and Mara Duer. 2021. "Re-placing Displacement in Gentrification Studies: Temporality and Multidimensionality in Rural Gentrification Displacement." *Geoforum* 118: 66–82.

Phillips, Martin, and Darren P. Smith. 2022. "Comparative Approaches to Gentrification: Lessons from the Rural." In *The Planetary Gentrification Reader*, edited by Loretta Lees, Tom Slater and Elvin K. Wyly, 147–73. Routledge.

Pilgeram, Ryanne. 2021. *Pushed Out: Contested Development and Rural Gentrification in the US West*. University of Washington Press.

Piore, Michael J. 1979. *Birds of Passage: Migrant Labor and Industrial Societies*. Cambridge University Press.

Pratt, Geraldine. 1990. "Feminist Analyses of the Restructuring of Urban Life." *Urban Geography* 11 (6): 594–605.

Prince, Sabiyha. 2016. *African Americans and Gentrification in Washington, DC: Race, Class and Social Justice in the Nation's Capital*. Ashgate Publishing.

Pulido, Laura. 2017. "Geographies of Race and Ethnicity II: Environmental Racism, Racial Capitalism and State-Sanctioned Violence." *Progress in Human Geography* 41 (4): 524–33.

Pull, Emil, Jacob Lind, Ioanna Wagner Tsoni, and Guy Baeten. 2020. "Introduction to the Themed Issue 'Narratives of Displacements.'" *ACME: An International Journal for Critical Geographies* 19 (1): 330–38.

Rabun County. 2006. "Comprehensive Plan 2005–2025." Georgia Mountains Regional Development Center.

Rabun County Chamber of Commerce. 2010. *Newcomers Guide*.

Raghuram, Parvati. 2019. "Race and Feminist Care Ethics: Intersectionality as Method." *Gender, Place & Culture* 26 (5): 613–37.

Rasmussen, Patty. 2007. "Rabun County: Looking Ahead, Perfecting Plans for Land Use and Development." *Georgia Trend*, April 1. https://www.georgia trend.com/2007/04/01/rabun-county-looking-ahead/.

Redmond, Jeremy. 2011. "Georgia Lawmakers Pass Illegal Immigration Crackdown." *Atlanta Journal-Constitution*, April 15. https://www.ajc.com /news/local/georgia-lawmakers-pass-illegal-immigration-crackdown /dvEcDeIuAOvpGvoHzCVodN/.

Rich, Brian L., and Marta Miranda. 2005. "The Sociopolitical Dynamics of Mexican Immigration in Lexington, Kentucky, 1997 to 2002: An Ambivalent Community Responds." In *New Destinations: Mexican Immigration in the United States*, edited by Víctor Zúñiga and Rubén Hernández-León, 187–219. Russell Sage Foundation.

Ritchie, Andrew J. 1959. *Sketches of Rabun County History, 1819–1948*. Foote & Davies.

Robinson, Tony. 1995. "Gentrification and Grassroots Resistance in San Francisco's Tenderloin." *Urban Affairs Quarterly* 30 (4): 483–513.

Robinson, Willliam I. 2004. *A Theory of Global Capitalism: Production, Class, and State in a Transnational World*. Johns Hopkins University Press.

Rodriguez, Nestor. 2004. "'Workers Wanted': Employer Recruitment of Immigrant Labor." *Work and Occupations* 31 (4): 453–73.

Rose, Damaris. 1984. "Rethinking Gentrification: Beyond the Uneven Development of Marxist Urban Theory." *Environment and Planning D: Society and Space* 2 (1): 47–74.

Rosenbloom, Joshua L. 2002. *Looking for Work, Searching for Workers: American Labor Markets during Industrialization*. Cambridge University Press.

Rudzitis, Gundars. 1999. "Amenities Increasingly Draw People to the Rural West." *Rural Development Perspectives* 14 (2): 9–13.

Russell, Lisa. M. 2021. *Underwater Ghost Towns of North Georgia*. Arcadia Publishing.

Rutheiser, Charles. 1996. *Imagineering Atlanta: The Politics of Place in the City of Dreams*. Verso.

Salinas, Cristina. 2018. *Managed Migrations: Growers, Farmworkers, and Border Enforcement in the Twentieth Century*. University of Texas Press.

Santos-Gomez, Hugo. 2014. *Immigrant Farmworkers and Citizenship in Rural California: Playing Soccer in the San Joaquin Valley*. LFB Scholarly Publishing.

Sarathy, Brinda. 2012. *Pineros: Latino Labour and the Changing Face of Forestry in the Pacific Northwest*. University of British Columbia Press.

Sassen, Saskia. 1990. *The Mobility of Labor and Capital: A Study in International Investment and Labor Flow*. Cambridge University Press.

Sassen, Saskia. 1994. *Cities in a World Economy*. Pine Forge.

Sassen, Saskia. 1998. *Globalization and Its Discontents: Essays on the New Mobility of People and Money*. The New Press.

Sassen, Saskia. 2002. "Deconstructing Labor Demand in Today's Advanced Economies: Implications for Low-Wage Employment." In *Laboring Below the Line: The New Ethnography of Poverty, Low-Wage Work, and Survival in the Global Economy*, edited by Frank Munger, 73–94. Russell Sage Foundation.

Saxton, Alexander. 1975. *The Indispensable Enemy: Labor and the Anti-Chinese Movement in California*. University of California Press.

Schmalzbauer, Leah. 2014. *The Last Best Place? Gender, Family, and Migration in the New West*. Stanford University Press.

Schmitt, John. 2000. "Inequality and Globalization: Some Evidence from the United States." In *The Ends of Globalization*, edited by Don Kalb et al., 157–68. Rowman and Littlefield.

Shapiro, Leslie, and Manas Sharma. 2018. "How Many Migrant Children Are Still Separated from Their Families?" *Washington Post*, August 30. https://www.washingtonpost.com/graphics/2018/local/tracking-migrant -family-separation.

Sherman, Jennifer. 2018. "'Not Allowed to Inherit My Kingdom': Amenity Development and Social Inequality in the Rural West." *Rural Sociology* 83 (1): 174–207.

Sherman, Jennifer. 2021. *Dividing Paradise: Rural Inequality and the Diminishing American Dream*. University of California Press.

Sherman, Jennifer. 2023. "'Please Don't Take This': Rural Gentrification, Symbolic Capital, and Housing Insecurity." *Social Problems* 70 (2): 491–510.

Shumway, J. Matthew, and Samuel M. Otterstrom. 2001. "Spatial Patterns of Migration and Income Change in the Mountain West: The Dominance of Service-Based, Amenity-Rich Counties." *Professional Geographer* 53 (4): 492–502.

Simandan, Dragos. 2019. "Revisiting Positionality and the Thesis of Situated Knowledge." *Dialogues in Human Geography* 9 (2): 129–49.

Slater, Tom. 2008. "'A Literal Necessity to Be Re-placed': A Rejoinder to the Gentrification Debate." *International Journal of Urban and Regional Research* 32 (1): 212–23.

Slemp, Katie. 2020. "Latino, Latina, Latin@, Latine, and Latine: Gender Inclusive Oral Expression in Spanish." PhD dissertation, University of Western Ontario, Canada.

Smith, Darren P., and Debbie A. Phillips. 2001. "Socio-cultural Representations of Greentrified Pennine Rurality." *Journal of Rural Studies* 17 (4): 457–69.

Smith, Darren P., Martin Phillips, Andreas Culora, and Chloe Kinton. 2021. "The Mobilities and Immobilities of Rural Gentrification: Staying Put or Moving on?" *Population, Space and Place* 27 (7): e2496.

Smith, Michael. D., and Richard S. Krannich. 2000. "'Culture Clash' Revisited: Newcomer and Longer-Term Residents' Attitudes toward Land Use, Development, and Environmental Issues in Rural Communities in the Rocky Mountain West." *Rural Sociology* 65 (4): 396–421.

Smith, Neil. 1979. "Toward a Theory of Gentrification: A Back to the City Movement by Capital, Not People." *Journal of the American Planning Association* 45 (4): 538–48.

Smith, Neil. 1982. "Gentrification and Uneven Development." *Economic Geography* 58 (2): 139–55.

Smith, Neil. 2002. "New Globalism, New Urbanism: Gentrification as Global Urban Strategy." *Antipode* 34 (3): 427–50.

Smithers, Gregory D. 2015. *The Cherokee Diaspora: An Indigenous History of Migration, Resettlement, and Identity.* Yale University Press.

Smithsonian Museum. 2024. "Wars of Expansion Exhibit Case (7 of 13)." National Museum of the American Latino. https://latino.si.edu/exhibitions/presente/wars-expansion-exhibit-case-7-13.

Solana-Solana, Miguel. 2010. "Rural Gentrification in Catalonia, Spain: A Case Study of Migration, Social Change and Conflicts in the Empordanet Area." *Geoforum* 41 (3): 508–17.

Song, Bingjie, Guy M. Robinson, and Douglas K. Bardsley. 2022. "Hobby and Part-Time Farmers in a Multifunctional Landscape: Environmentalism, Lifestyles, and Amenity." *Geographical Research* 60 (3): 480–97.

Stasiulis, Daiva, and Nira Yuval-Davis. 1999. "Introduction: Beyond Dichotomies; Gender, Race, Ethnicity and Class in Settler Societies." In *Unsettling Settler Societies: Articulations of Gender, Race, Ethnicity and Class*, edited by Daiva K. Stasiulis and Nira Yuval-Davis, 1–38. Sage Publishers.

Steamboat Magazine. 2010. July/August.

Stedman, Richard C. 2006. "Understanding Place Attachment among Second Home Owners." *American Behavioral Scientist* 50: 187–205.

Stoker, Philip, Danya Rumore, Lindsey Romaniello, and Zacharia Levine. 2021. "Planning and Development Challenges in Western Gateway Communities." *Journal of the American Planning Association* 87 (1): 21–33.

Strauss, Kendra, ed. 2023. *Geographies of Displacement/s.* Taylor & Francis.

Striffler, Steve. 2005. *Chicken: The Dangerous Transformation of America's Favorite Food.* Yale University Press.

Stuber, Jenny. 2021. *Aspen and the American Dream: How One Town Manages Inequality in the Era of Supergentrification.* University of California Press.

Stuesse, Angela. 2016. *Scratching Out a Living: Latinos, Race, and Work in the Deep South.* University of California Press.

Stull, Donald D., Michael J. Broadway, and David Griffith, eds. 1995. *Any Way You Cut It: Meat Processing and Small-Town America.* University of Kansas Press.

Thorp, Rosemary, and Laurence Whitehead. 1987. *Latin American Debt and the Adjustment Crisis.* Springer.

Tichenor, Daniel. J. 2009. *Dividing Lines: The Politics of Immigration Control in America.* Princeton University Press.

Torres, Rebecca, Rich Heyman, Solange Munoz, Lauren Apgar, Emily Timm, Cristina Tzintzun, Charles R. Hale, John Mckiernan-Gonzalez, Shannon Speed, and Eric Tang. 2013. "Building Austin, Building Justice: Immigrant Construction Workers, Precarious Labor Regimes and Social Citizenship." *Geoforum* 45: 145–55.

Trouille, David. 2021. *Fútbol in the Park: Immigrants, Soccer, and the Creation of Social Ties.* University of Chicago Press.

Twine, Francis. W. 2000. Racial Ideologies and Racial Methodologies. In *Racing Research, Researching Race: Methodological Dilemmas in Critical Race Studies,* edited by Francis W. Twine and Jonathan W. Warren, 1–34. New York University Press.

Ulrich-Schad, Jessica D. 2018. "'We Didn't Move Here to Move to Aspen': Community Making and Community Development in an Emerging Rural Amenity Destination." *Journal of Rural and Community Development,* 13 (4): 43–65.

Ulrich-Schad, Jessica D., and Hua Qin. 2018. "Culture Clash? Predictors of Views on Amenity-Led Development and Community Involvement in Rural Recreation Counties." *Rural Sociology* 83 (1): 81–108.

Urban, Andrew. 2009. "Irish Domestic Servants, 'Biddy' and the Rebellion in the American Home 1850–1900." *Gender and History* 21 (2): 263–82.

U.S. Border Patrol. 2018. "US Border Patrol Fiscal Year Budget Statistics (FY1990–FY2017). https://www.cbp.gov/document/stats/us-border-patrol -fiscal-year-budget-statistics-fy-1990-fy-2017. Accessed October 8, 2018.

U.S. Census Bureau. 2020. "Quick Facts: Rabun County, Georgia." https://www .census.gov/quickfacts/fact/table/rabuncountygeorgia/PST040223. Accessed November 3, 2022.

U.S. Census Bureau. 2021. "Building Permits Survey, 1959–2021." https://www .census.gov/construction/bps/data_visualizations/. Accessed October 11, 2021.

U.S. Forest Service. 2022. "Chattahoochee-Oconee National Forest History." https://www.fs.usda.gov/detail/conf/learning/history-culture/. Accessed October 18, 2022.

Valentine, Gill. 2007. "Theorizing and Researching Intersectionality: A Challenge for Feminist Geography." *Professional Geographer* 59 (1): 10–21.

Valenzuela, Abel, Jr. 2003. "Day Labor Work." *Annual Review of Sociology* 29 (1): 307–33.

Varsanyi, Monica. 2010. *Taking Local Control: Immigration Policy Activism in US Cities and States.* Stanford University Press.

Veracini, Lorenzo. 2010. "The Imagined Geographies of Settler Colonialism." In *Making Settler Colonial Space: Perspectives on Race, Place and Identity,* edited by Tracey Banivanua Mar and Penelope Edmonds, 179–97. Palgrave Macmillan.

Veracini, Lorenzo. 2014. "Understanding Colonialism and Settler Colonialism as Distinct Formations." *Interventions* 16 (5): 615–33.

Vias, Alexander C., and John I. Carruthers. 2005. "Regional Development and Land Use Change in the Rocky Mountain West, 1982–1997." *Growth and Change* 36 (2): 244–72.

Vukomanovic, Jelena, and Barron J. Orr. 2014. "Landscape Aesthetics and the Scenic Drivers of Amenity Migration in the New West: Naturalness, Visual Scale, and Complexity." *Land* 3 (2): 390–413.

Waldinger, Roger D. 1997. "Social Capital or Social Closure? Immigrant Networks in the Labor Market." UCLA Working Paper Series, Lewis Center for Regional Policy Studies.

Waldinger, Roger, and Michael I. Lichter. 2003. *How the Other Half Works: Immigration and the Social Organization of Labor.* University of California Press.

Walker, Peter, and Louise Fortmann. 2003. "Whose Landscape? A Political Ecology of the 'Exurban' Sierra." *Cultural Geographies* 10 (4): 469–91.

Walrath, Margaret C., Anita T. Morzillo, Kathleen P. Bell, Chris R. Colocousis, Mindy S. Crandall, Michaela I. Poppick, and Darla K. Munroe. 2024. "Rural Forested Community Shocks as Perceived by In-Migrants versus Long-Term Residents." *Journal of Rural Studies* 105: 103188.

Warren, Robert, and John Robert Warren. 2013. "Unauthorized Immigration to the United States: Annual Estimates and Components of Change, by State, 1990 to 2010." *International Migration Review* 47 (2): 296–329.

Waslin, Michele. 2011. "The Secure Communities Program: Unanswered Questions and Continuing Concerns." Immigration Policy Center Special Report. https://www.americanimmigrationcouncil.org/research/secure -communities-fact-sheet.

Weeden, S. Ashleigh, Jean Hardy, and Karen Foster. 2022 "Urban Flight and Rural Rights in a Pandemic: Exploring Narratives of Place, Displacement, and 'The Right to Be Rural' in the Context of COVID-19." *Annals of the American Association of Geographers* 112 (3): 732–41.

Weitzer, Ronald. 1990. *Transforming Settler States: Communal Conflict and Internal Security in Northern Ireland and Zimbabwe.* University of California Press.

Wilson, Franklin D. 1988. "Components of Change in Migration and Destination-Propensity Rates for Metropolitan and Nonmetropolitan Areas: 1935–1980." *Demography* 25 (1): 129–39.

Winders, Jamie. 2013. *Nashville in the New Millennium: Immigrant Settlement, Urban Transformation, and Social Belonging.* Russell Sage Foundation.

Winkler, Richelle. 2013. "Living on the Lakes: Segregated Communities and Inequality in a Natural Amenity Destination." *Sociological Quarterly* 54: 105–29.

Winkler, Richelle, Donald R. Field, A. E. Luloff, Richard S. Krannich, and Tracy Williams. 2007. "Social Landscapes of the Inter-mountain West: A Comparison of 'Old West' and 'New West' Communities." *Rural Sociology* 72 (3): 478–501.

Wolf, Diane. 1993. "Introduction: Feminist Dilemmas in Fieldwork." *Frontiers: A Journal of Women Studies* 13 (3): 1–8.

Wolfe, Patrick. 2006. "Settler Colonialism and the Elimination of the Native." *Journal of Genocide Research* 8 (4): 387–409.

Woolard, Kathryn A., and Bambi B. Schieffelin. 1994. "Language Ideology." *Annual Review of Anthropology* 23 (1): 55–82.

Wyly, Elvin, and Daniel J. Hammel. 1999. "Islands of Decay in Seas of Renewal: Housing Policy and the Resurgence of Gentrification." *Housing Policy Debate* 10 (4): 711–71.

Wyly, Elvin K., Mona Atia, and Daniel Hammel. 2004. "Has Mortgage Capital Found an Inner-City Spatial Fix?" *Housing Policy Debate* 15 (3): 623–85.

Wyly, Elvin K., and Daniel Hammel. 2001. "Gentrification, Housing Policy, and the New Context of Urban Redevelopment." In *Critical Perspectives on Urban Redevelopment*, edited by Fox Gotham, 211–76. Emerald Group Publishing.

Yampa Valley Quarterly. 2009. "Living Green" (Summer/Fall).

Zaragocin, Sofia, and Martina Angela Caretta. 2021. "Cuerpo-Territorio: A Decolonial Feminist Geographical Method for the Study of Embodiment." *Annals of the American Association of Geographers* 111 (5): 1503–18.

Zukin, Sharon. 1987. "Gentrification: Culture and Capital in the Urban Core." *Annual Review of Sociology* 13 (1): 129–47.

Zúñiga, Victor, and Rúben Hernández-León, eds. 2005. *New Destinations: Mexican Immigration in the United States.* Russell Sage Foundation.

Index

Founded in 1893,
UNIVERSITY OF CALIFORNIA PRESS
publishes bold, progressive books and journals
on topics in the arts, humanities, social sciences,
and natural sciences—with a focus on social
justice issues—that inspire thought and action
among readers worldwide.

The UC PRESS FOUNDATION
raises funds to uphold the press's vital role
as an independent, nonprofit publisher, and
receives philanthropic support from a wide
range of individuals and institutions—and from
committed readers like you. To learn more, visit
ucpress.edu/supportus.